Reading Fiona Sampson

Reading Fiona Sampson

A Study in Contemporary Poetry and Poetics

Omar Sabbagh

ANTHEM PRESS

Anthem Press
An imprint of Wimbledon Publishing Company
www.anthempress.com

This edition first published in UK and USA 2022
by ANTHEM PRESS
75–76 Blackfriars Road, London SE1 8HA, UK
or PO Box 9779, London SW19 7ZG, UK
and
244 Madison Ave #116, New York, NY 10016, USA

First published in the UK and USA by Anthem Press in 2020

Copyright © Omar Sabbagh 2022

The author asserts the moral right to be identified as the author of this work.

All rights reserved. Without limiting the rights under copyright reserved above,
no part of this publication may be reproduced, stored or introduced into
a retrieval system, or transmitted, in any form or by any means
(electronic, mechanical, photocopying, recording or otherwise),
without the prior written permission of both the copyright
owner and the above publisher of this book.

British Library Cataloguing-in-Publication Data
A catalogue record for this book is available from the British Library.

Library of Congress Control Number: 2020936290

ISBN-13: 978-1-83998-453-2 (Pbk)
ISBN-10: 1-83998-453-8 (Pbk)

This title is also available as an e-book.

Fort-da

CONTENTS

About the Author ix
Preface xi
Acknowledgements xiii

Introduction 1
What This Book Is Not; What This Book Is 1
Fiona Sampson: A Brief Biographical Reconnaissance 6

1. Hearthsides and Hospices 9
   An Editor's Poetics: On Fiona Sampson as Editor and Curator 9
   Hospitable Words, Or, Care for Idiosyncrasy 19

2. From the Looking Glass to the Lamp 27
   Into the Looking Glass: Fiona Sampson as Poet and Critic from 2005–2007 27
   Homely Duplicities: Reading Fiona Sampson's Rough Music 45
   Haunting Ambivalence: Reading Fiona Sampson's Coleshill 59
   Ways of Empathy: Reading Fiona Sampson's The Catch 71
   Falling into Hope: Reading Fiona Sampson's Come Down 87

3. Prose Animations 105
   Animating Places: Reading Fiona Sampson's Limestone Country *beneath a Durrellian lens* 105
   Animating Instruments, Or, the Creative Artist as Biographer: On Fiona Sampson's In Search of Mary Shelley 119

4. For the Love of Music 135
   Literary Friendship(s), Or, 'trying, to get closer […]': On Fiona Sampson's Beyond the Lyric 135
   Expanding the Formal Project: On Fiona Sampson's Lyric Cousins 148

   Conclusion: Democracy and Excellence 159

Appendix: Inaugural Wellcome Trust Annual Public Mike
   White Memorial Lecture, June 14, 2016   163
   *Seminal Publication of Professor Fiona Sampson's 'A Speaking
   Likeness: Poetry Within Health and Social Care'*   163

Selected Bibliography   177

Index   183

ABOUT THE AUTHOR

Omar Sabbagh is a widely published poet, writer and critic. From 2006 to the present his poetry has appeared in many prestigious venues, such as: *Agenda, Banipal, Kenyon Review Online, PN Review, Poetry Review, Poetry Wales, Stand, The Moth, The Reader Magazine, The Warwick Review, The Wolf,* (T&F) *New Writing, New Humanist, Two Thirds North* and *Acumen,* among others. His first collection and his fourth collection are, respectively: *My Only Ever Oedipal Complaint* and *To the Middle of Love.* (Cinnamon Press, 2010/2017) His fifth collection, *But It Was an Important Failure,* was published with Cinnamon Press in 2020. His Beirut novella, *Via Negativa: A Parable of Exile,* was published with Liquorice Fish Books in 2016; and he has published much short fiction, some of it prize-winning. His Dubai novella, *Minutes from the Miracle City,* was published with Fairlight Books in 2019. He has published scholarly essays on George Eliot, Ford Madox Ford, G. K. Chesterton, Henry Miller, Lawrence Durrell, Joseph Conrad, Lytton Strachey, T. S. Eliot, Basil Bunting, Hilaire Belloc, George Steiner and others; as well as on many contemporary poets. Many of these works are collated in *To My Mind Or Kinbotes: Essays on Literature,* published with Whisk(e)y Tit in January 2021. His *Morning Lit: Portals After Alia* is forthcoming in early 2022, with Cinnamon Press. He is currently at work on a Lebanese verse novel, *The Cedar Never Dies,* contracted for 2022 with Northside Press. Sabbagh holds a BA in Philosophy, Politics and Economics from Oxford; three MAs, all from the University of London, in English Literature, Creative and Life Writing, and Philosophy; and a PhD in English Literature from King's College London. He was visiting assistant professor of English and Creative Writing at the American University of Beirut (AUB), from 2011 to 2013. He is associate professor of English at the American University in Dubai (AUD).

For Marcel Proust – The son of well-to-do parents who, whether from talent or weakness, engages in a so-called intellectual profession, as an artist or a scholar, will have a particularly difficult time with those bearing the distasteful title of colleagues [...] The urge to suspend the division of labour which, within certain limits, his economic situation enables him to satisfy, is thought particularly disreputable: it betrays a disinclination to sanction the operations imposed by society, and domineering competence permits no such idiosyncrasies ...

Theodor W. Adorno, *Minima Moralia*

The brilliant man seems more lumbering and elaborate than anyone else, because he has something to say about everything. The very quickness of his mind makes the slowness of his narrative. For he finds sermons in stones, in all the paving stones of the street he plods along. Every fact or phrase that occurs in the immediate question carries back his mind to the ages and the initial power. Because he is original he is always going back to the origins.

G.K. Chesterton, *William Blake*

PREFACE

I have known Fiona Sampson since 2006, when she was assigned as my tutor in a second MA I was starting at the time, in Creative and Life Writing, at Goldsmith's College, University of London. Earlier that summer, having just resigned a PhD under Professor Stefan Collini at Cambridge, I sent in a batch of poems to be considered for *Poetry Review*, where Sampson happened to be editor. I was being, to put it lightly, ambitious. However, at the close of our first group meeting with our tutor later that year in September, as I was about to leave, Sampson mentioned that she had accepted a poem of mine for the forthcoming winter 2006–2007 issue. I hope the present book serves in some small way as a token of personal gratitude as much as of professional admiration.

As I make clear in the introduction, this book is by no means a work of scholarship in the field of contemporary literary studies. It is a work of sustained literary criticism. And, *as* a literary critic, my hope is that, for all the baroque sound effects and rhythms of the prose, my judgment in the way I have analysed then synthesized in and through the chapters that make up this book is as lucid as it might be incisive. Yes, the approach is at times aggressive; but I see no point in merely describing the body of work under study. I chose to study the oeuvre of Professor Sampson, and then write this book, not only because I was a longstanding admirer of her work, but also because I value bodies of writing whose overt signs of high intelligence are palpable and fruitful. The kind that challenge me to find their inner workings, their submerged logic and hidden unities; the kind that challenge me to find 'ways of going on' that mirror some of my own tendencies as a meaning-making or meaning-seeing mind. Work, in short, such as Sampson's, allows me to elicit some inferential load that takes my thinking life forward. I hope the arguments in this book inform, interest, but also 'take the story forward', too, for any students or readers of contemporary literature or creative writing.

ACKNOWLEDGEMENTS

There is a small group of primary persons to acknowledge as having been highly helpful and/or understanding by the time this book will have been completed and released. I would like to thank four editors who were kind enough to publish a very small part of this book, as is, or different, before in fact work on the whole book-length essay got underway. First, thanks to Patricia McCarthy, editor of central UK poetry organ, *Agenda*, for publishing a review of mine, 'The Ways of Empathy', on Professor Sampson's 2016 collection, *The Catch*. The section in this book on that same collection is longer, more copious and more studied, but the original seed of my reaction to that collection is to be found in that short review. Secondly, to thank Professor Clare Simmons, who as editor of *Prose Studies* (T&F) published my paper, 'Animating Places', which in fact remains as first published in this present book. I would like to thank the editors of *The London Magazine* and of *Life Writing* (T&F) who were also kind enough to publish short review articles on, respectively, *Coleshill* and *In Search of Mary Shelley*; these preliminary reactions to two of Sampson's major works proved foundational as well for the more copious writing on said works in this book. I would also like to thank Abi Pandi and Megan Greiving at Anthem Press for being understanding, given certain obsessive and/or manic tendencies that overcome me when in flagrante when at work on a new publication. They were always kind enough not to complain when I would send repeated versions, edited-up or edited-down, of the different chapters of this book as they were written, piecemeal, between fall 2018 and fall 2019. Finally, I would like to thank Professor Fiona Sampson herself. Since coming to know her in late 2006, she has remained like a literary guardian angel for many of my endeavours and many of my follies. Not only has her patience with the same obsessive, manic tendency mentioned above been unequalled, but she was always on hand by email to fact-check those more empirical parts of the book. She was also of course continually on hand to answer queries and to provide as much information as I needed at any one time; not to mention, as I came towards the close of writing the first draft of this book, providing me with many documents, articles, papers, and book chapters, that otherwise would have been more arduous for me to locate, read and use, given my current berth in Dubai. All that said, it remains the case that any errors or slurs of judgement, any waywardness in the way the literary–critical remit of this book is done, remain quite obviously my own responsibility and flaws.

INTRODUCTION

What This Book Is Not; What This Book Is

In the opening part of this introduction I introduce, first: what this book certainly makes no claims to being, its shortfalls and limitations; and then second: some prefatory remarks regarding the mode and the structure of this book-length essay on Fiona Sampson. Some detailing now of what this book *is not*.

I am no linguist, and the first way in which this book-length essay of literary-critical reading and appraisal falls short of the full range of Sampson's work starts with my lack of fluency with (and even in translation) or knowledge of the current literary scene in postcommunist Europe. I mention some of Sampson's work, either as editor or translator in this part of the international literary scene (her work on and with Nobel nominee Jaan Kaplinski a central example here); and, indeed, in relation to other parts of the globe, such as her work with Amir Or (and others) from Hebrew. However, throughout I claim only to read how Sampson's writing in these areas seams with and is significant for the more broadly argued thesis and theses (about her poetics and poetic career) of the loosely interlocking chapters that follow.

A second incompetence comes with my near-zero knowledge of musicology. Again, there is comparatively little conceptual and literary–theoretical grasp in the reach of my readings where musical knowledge or analogy is specifically used. The hope is, nonetheless, that enough has been grasped to illuminate the poetic and literary oeuvre in ways that might be suggestive to later students of the subject who wish to approach the oeuvre from a more rigorous and detailed musical angle.

Another caveat to mention here is that this is a work of literary criticism and of close reading, and that is all that the interpretative weaving work below encompasses and enacts. It has been the case that much of Sampson's oeuvre has been deftly elided, especially the gamut of much of her more workaday reviews and articles, which might have furthered insight into the overriding artistic temperament or sensibility that is the focus of this book; and this, primarily for reasons of economy. That said, part of the aim and purpose of this book has been merely to find salient and cohering reading directions through the oeuvre – rather than, say, some scholarly endeavour to locate Sampson's poetic career (taken globally) within late twentieth century, early twenty-first, poetry and poetics. Of course, there are many biographical friendships in that latter field, which are also critical to the development of her creative (and critical) oeuvre. But those too on the whole have been omitted, again, partly for reasons of economy and focus, but partly also because reading widely as I do and must, it remains the case that I am simply not as au courant with the latter as would be needful. Thus, this book-length essay is just that: a testing-ground, trying what I hope will be seen as a coherent and lucid reconstruction of some of the major elements of a contemporary and ongoing oeuvre that compels its readership in many different, fruitful ways.

Finally, there is little biographical context in many of the chapters that make up this book; as is the case with much of Sampson's highly original thinking about poetry and poetics. If I have delineated any kind of biographical story in this book, it is that of the formal propensities of the artistic talent under discussion – the lifetime, as it were, of a wide and at times dovetailing series (or patterns) of poetic gestures and writerly mannerisms. The life in and of and through the body of work.

Below, however, I outline the structured sections of the book, which configure separate readings into one sustained argument. This book's thesis is that the whole corpus of work(s), whether in poetry or in prose, is ultimately very much *one body of work*; and that *like* one whole body, all the parts needs must interact in seamless ways – perhaps only groped-at in the chapters that follow. Beyond the obvious fact that all the work(s) 'come down' to us from the same individual poet and writer, I hope to show, but in many detailed, textured and dovetailing ways, how *it is* one unified and unitive sensibility at work. How it is, in short, the same structure of feeling that can be descried behind the verse, the creative nonfiction, the critical prose and so on. This literary temperament turns out to be a deeply individual and at the same time deeply communicative and personable, often teacherly, one. And that kind of paradox in turn generates many of the paradoxes and dialectical tropes that appear in the body of this book.

Sampson's searching, Socratic mode of doing literary business, across many genres, is *eminently* poetic, insofar as that last term stands for some conception of the configuration of meaningfulness that is and goes beyond – that is in some important sense *more* than – the sum of its parts. To put it anachronistically perhaps, her literary oeuvre has a (processual) soul as it were running through it, a 'way of going on' that defies the sense of some teleologically closed, established, dogmatic purpose on the one hand or, on the other, the readerly idea that the value and signifying worth of the oeuvre is delimited to a set of finished senses. Insofar as the whole oeuvre – still in vital motion of course – can be conceived as akin to one grand poem, it shimmers and breathes with life, with an inspiration that moves past the more static markers on the page. And it has been part of the central aim of the readings in this study to release some of this very living quality; to have an open mind that might 'catch' the workings of an open mind busy with going on.

The first material chapter of this work, 'Hearthsides and Hospices', starts with a discussion of Sampson's editorial career. 'An Editor's Poetics' aims to relay just that: the ways in which editorial (and indeed curatorial) decisions and positions begin to outline salient aspects of the poetic sensibility more directly assessed and read through in other chapters. After very briefly detailing aspects of her editorial career, the second part of this section makes use of a paper of Sampson's titled 'Practical Measures: Poet as Editor.' The paper (from 2011) offers significant insight into, inversely, the editor-as-poet; indeed, here Sampson defines in some telling ways her conception of what is at stake by the term 'literary'. The third part explores some of the decisions and opinions in some of her editorial and curatorial work in a manner that hopes to tally. 'Hospitable Words, or, Care for Idiosyncrasy' is an essay within the essay that is this book as a whole, addressing the career of a poet and more broadly speaking creative talent within the worlds of health and social care. Here, too, as well as an empirical outline of the achievement, I try to show how Sampson's work in these fields, for all the hospitality engendered, stays as poetic as her paraphrasable stance *on* poetry (which should in her view stay resolutely 'poetic', subject to the same artistic burdens) when working or writing on her work *within* these fields.

The second chapter, titled 'From the Looking Glass to the Lamp', opens with a discussion of Sampson's work as a poet and as a critic between 2005 and 2007; between, that is to say, her first major poetic work, *The Distance Between Us* (Seren) and her next, *Common Prayer* (Carcanet). Tying in with the analysis of much of the verse in these two quite heart-wrenching collections comes analysis of two of her most important early critical forays, namely (co-authored with Celia Hunt) *Writing: Self and Reflexivity* (Palgrave Macmillan, 2005) and *On Listening: Selected Essays* (Salt, 2007). The themes of self-awareness and reflexivity, as much as their correlate in some respects, embodiment, are central to how I am able to draw a beeline or beelines, wavering, fecund, but still steady I hope, across these works. In many respects, it is Sampson's very canniness about (and 'about') the moves she makes as a writer (and about writing), about her (a favourite phrase) 'ways of going on', that allows her to both embody and at the same direct her readership to more authentic or sincere (dare I use the terms) ways of using creative writing for more ultimate effect. Her poetry, as much as her thinking-on of the same at this period in her oeuvre, redounds with notions and conceits of loss, as much as redress, communal or otherwise. There is, too, use in this chapter in particular (given the critical works engaged with) of some theoretical resources that might have seemed outside the pale under normal circumstances, but which, the hope is, serve to illuminate the poetics at hand – even if the poetics feel darkly affecting at times.

On *Rough Music* and on *Coleshill*, duplicities within the home ground as well as haunting ambivalences are registered, as these two collections (from 2010, Carcanet and 2013, Penguin Random House) comprise a period in the writerly career which remains resolutely uncanny (to coin a stranger phrase). Images of violence, liminality and of the underworlds of experience and their mythopoeic transliteration (at times, transformation) make these two collections a kind of end point, from which both the predominant style and ethos change and lighten to a telling, palpable degree, becoming more aerated. Because (to reference only the major works) from *The Catch* (Penguin Random House, 2016) through to *Come Down* (Little, Brown, 2020), the major modal move is one – to use a now old-fashioned trope – from a (dark and darkened) looking glass to a lamp. In these last two collections, ways of sharing, ways of empathy (formal as much as content-driven) as well as more hopeful gestures, from dug-up pasts into now-transpiring futures, are enacted and made. All this is certainly not to say that there is little 'common' ground between the earlier and the later works. (Commonality and community are a very common trope to be elicited across the whole poetic oeuvre. In fact, an alternate title, since discarded, for this present book, was to be *Common Prayers*). But it is to say that there is a very significant change in mood and mode. Of special note is the fact that certain biographical experiences, alluded to with much lyricism from *The Distance Between Us* through to *Coleshill*, experiences such as an early near-death encounter with an accoster, seem to be relieved rather than relived by the time we get to *The Catch*. The verse from now on is more aerated, both in the way that formal properties catch and unlatch, and in the way that there seems to be a more enlivened openness of poetic demeanour. A former (reflexive) darkness goes into the light, freed of some kind of shadowing burden.

In the third chapter of the book, 'Prose Animations', we see Sampson animating places in her tour de force, *Limestone Country* (Little Toller, 2017). Sampson's exploration of 'the spirit of place' is here read under the (paralleling) lens of one of her most telling influences – in this case, Lawrence Durrell. Both writers, in the argument of this section, find uncanny ways of letting different aspects of geography and topography speak up and speak out; and both make use of a wide array of at times fictional techniques of narration, sharing in many ways as they do a late modernist sensibility. However, the irony is that the next section's title, 'Animating Instruments', is about (and 'about') what the quotation from *Frankenstein* with which Sampson titles an early chapter of her biography of Mary Shelley reads: 'The Instruments of Life'. Which is to say, what was a heuristic tallying of two (Sampson, Durrell) solicitations of the 'deus loci', becomes directly relevant to Sampson's *In Search of Mary Shelley* (Profile Books, 2018) – because Shelley was 'the girl who wrote *Frankenstein*'. Place is replaced by self in this second section, that is, converting the animations of this section's twinning predecessor. Self-awareness or reflexivity seem to come most fully into play in a work of biography whose somewhat *autobiographical* mode matches some of the most salient aspects of its subject. As in much of Sampson's work, perspectives and senses from inside *and* outside the frame of the writing in question cross over and speak to each other. To repeat, in part what constitutes the intelligence of the sensibility at hand is that it finds fertile ways to be both (logically) about subject matter and topographically 'about' it at the same time. As in music, taken very broadly, inside and outside prove married in many ways – and it is the implied thesis of this book that this is an effect of a presiding *self-awareness* in Sampson's work.

The closing chapter of the book, 'For the Love of Music', discusses Sampson's monographs on form; from her 2011 *Music Lessons* (Bloodaxe), which were delivered the year preceding at Newcastle University, as public lectures, to *Beyond the Lyric* (Penguin Random House, 2012), Sampson's 'map' of contemporary British poetry, to a striking work of poetic and literary theory, *Lyric Cousins: Poetry and Musical Form* (EUP, 2016). My book's two final sections segue onto and develop each other. They are two separate, if not logically distinct, stages and/or versions of discussion (being about and 'about', again) of Sampson's most recent and developed thinking about what constitutes poetry and the poetic. And it is not just love and music, community and poetics, as they interact and form, that are at stake here. This last part of the book might be read as recouping in more direct, discursive ways much of the preceding material: whether it is hospitality, openness and the willingness to 'listen' with 'attention'; or whether it is the inherently reflexive space of editorial facility (and facilitation), critical self-awareness and/or the kind of embodiment that allows the body to duplicate in its home ground, haunting itself, a spectre to itself; or, finally, whether it is empathy and hope elicited at the last, as they animate other, variegated parts of Sampson's lifeworld with spirit, life. Because these last two sections explore how a kind of friendship, or cousinhood, bonding and fording, work to show how lyricism in the world out there and in the world in here can be so much more than merely individual.

First, though, a brief biographical reconnaissance is necessary.

Fiona Sampson: A Brief Biographical Reconnaissance

Fiona Sampson, as the reader of this book may be aware, is a distinguished poet and writer. As this book will outline, Sampson has also been and remains prolific (and significant) in other literary roles, such as: editor, translator, critic, theorist and community artist, as well as in service as a judge, board member and publisher on the international(ist) literary scene. Her books, in many different, but it is the thesis of this book closely dovetailing, genres have been translated into more than thirty-five languages to date, and she has received a number of honours as a writer (some of which are mentioned below), marking her out as an established literary presence. And yet this book, the first full-length study of this contemporary author, is warranted not only by her distinction; the manner in which the different coalescing commentaries comprising the body of this book may be seen to synergize, should indicate as well the innate *interest* of an author as compelling as this. That said, this second, and final section of my 'Introduction' *will* detail for the reader who may come to this study the overt indices of her accomplishments.

Born in London, Sampson received her formative education at the Royal Academy of Music, as well as in Salzburg and Paris, having already begun her first career as a concert violinist. The impulses that began that early, rigorous artistic career (although Sampson left it abruptly at the age of twenty-three, in the midst of substantial success) can be viewed as very significant for the later literary career; what was left off has proven, serendipitously or not, to be an integral part of the sensibility that is the ground of this book-length essay of literary-critical reading and assessment. Sampson then began undergraduate studies at Oxford belatedly, in her mid-twenties – she read PPE – before going on to complete her doctorate in the philosophy of language at Radboud University at Nijmegen in the Netherlands. Her research, whose thesis was awarded in 2001, was titled: 'Towards a theoretical framework for writing in healthcare'.

As sole author, co-author, as editor or co-editor, she has to date published thirty-seven books. Needless to say, as an active academic in her field, she has also published many papers and book chapters. However, I restrict the remit of this survey to the perhaps more unseen parts of the accomplishment to date – the majority at least of her most central works proving the ground of many of the chapters that follow. Thus, apart from the more strictly literary career (critical, creative), Sampson has appeared, and still does often appear, on radio and television, in venues such as: *France Musique, Culture* (France); *Fahrenheit* (Italy); *Babel* (Sweden); *The Late Show* (Australia); *BBC R3, BBC R4* (UK), among others. Sampson is also a regular reviewer in the National UK press and radio (*The Guardian, The Independent, TLS, Sunday Times, New Statesman* and others). She has also of course been anthologized repeatedly from near the start to the present of her poetic and/or critical career, such as, among others: different and/or successive editions of the annual *Forward Book of Poetry*, *The New European Poetry* (Seren, 2009), *When Love Speaks* (Vintage, 2011), *On Kathleen Jamie* (EUP, 2015), *On Shakespeare's Sonnets* (Arden/Bloomsbury, 2016), *The Long White Thread: John Berger* (Smokestack, 2017), or *From the Hebrew Side* (Hakibbutz, 2017). Sampson's editorial career, an essential element of her literary achievements to date, is also signal, whether as 'contributing editor' to such journals as *Wasafiri* or *Context*, or as editor. Among the latter, she was founder editor of *Orient Express: Contemporary writing from Enlargement Europe* from 2002 to 2005; editor of central, leading UK poetry organ, *Poetry Review*, from 2005 to 2012; founder editor of Taylor & Francis journal, *POEM*, 2012–2019; and since 2013 has served also as the poetry editor for *New Humanist*.

Sampson has held a number of honorary fellowships (of the Royal Society of Literature, the Royal Society of Arts, the English Association, the Wordsworth Trust and the Higher Education Authority). She was awarded an MBE for services to literature in 2017. She has also held academic and writers' fellowships. From 2002 to 2005 Sampson held an AHRC Fellowship at Oxford Brookes University; she was CAPITAL fellow in Creativity at the University of Warwick in 2007–2008; with visiting research fellowships awarded at the School of Advanced Study, University of London (2012–2015, at the Institute of Musical Research & Institute of English Studies; and at the Institute of Modern Language Research in 2018–2019). As part of her literary career, too, Sampson has served as judge for various prestigious literary awards and prizes; among them: the Ondaatje Prize, 2015; T. S. Eliot Prize, 2015; Cholmondeley Awards, 2012–2015; Griffin International Poetry Prizes (Canada), 2012; Independent Foreign Fiction Prize, 2008–2009; Foyle Young Poet of the Year, 2003; and as far back as the Southern Arts Prize, 1996. She has also acted as conference director for various flourishing symposia from as early as 1993 ('The Role of Arts in Healing', University of Glasgow), to the 'Poetry in Translation Summit' at the School for Advanced Study, University of London, in 2018.

While still at Oxford (where she had read PPE), in 1992 Sampson won the renowned (from, in Oxford and beyond) 'Newdigate Prize' for her poem, 'Green Thought', inspired as it was by her attendance at a Hélène Cixous lecture. (Cixous is an important influence on much of Sampson's work as a literary theorist and as a theorist of the literary in care settings, too). This early accolade sets the tone for many equally distinguished prizes won, reaching to the present. In 1996, still emerging as a poet, she achieved a Society of Authors Award. In 1998 Sampson won an Oppenheim-John Downes Award. And then in 2003, indicative of her international(ist) goals and appeal, Sampson was shortlisted for the Evelyn Encelot Prize for European Women Poets Maisons d'Ecrivains, Paris, as well as winning the Macedonian Zlaten Prsten Prize. This last presages Sampson's continual and successful interests and engagement with the contemporary literature of Central and Eastern Europe. A Charles Angoff Award (United States) in 2006 preceded her being shortlisted for the T. S. Eliot Prize in 2007 – as she was again in 2010; needless to say, she has had a small clutch of Poetry Book Society recommendations as well, another index of literary centrality on the UK scene at least. She received a Cholmondeley Award in 2009 indicating, if there was any doubt as yet, how established her poetic presence had become by then. As recently as 2016, again showing her international(ist) appeal, she achieved the Aark Arts International Poetry Prize (India); and from Bosnia, the Slovo Podgrmec Prize. In 2019 Sampson was shortlisted for the 'Biographers' Club Slightly Foxed Best Biography Prize' - an accolade for what seems to be a newfound but central genre for her literary career (Sampson's acclaimed biography of Elizabeth Barrett Browning was published in 2021, on the tail of her acclaimed biography of Mary Shelley, which latter is discussed in one of the chapters that follow). In 2019 as well, her engagement with the contemporary literature of Central and Eastern Europe finds her winning the Ditët e Naimit Naim Frasheri Award (Macedonia and Albania). Finally, as well as winning the European Atlas Prize for Poetry in 2020, it has been announced very recently (at the time of composition, in 2021) that her 2020 poetry collection, *Come Down* has won the Wales Book of the Year for the category of Poetry.

Chair of Poetry and Director of the Poetry Centre at the University of Roehampton (since 2013), Sampson is now Professor Emeritus there. Previously, she was a visiting research fellow at the University of Sussex from 1998 to 2001; and worked as a lecturer in Creative Writing from 1999 to 2000 at Solent University. And she was Distinguished Writer and Professor of Poetry at the University of Kingston from 2009 to 2013. Needless to say, her literary career in real time, abounds.

Chapter 1

HEARTHSIDES AND HOSPICES

An Editor's Poetics: On Fiona Sampson as Editor and Curator

Introduction: Notes on the editorial career

Sampson's first notable editorial role was as founder editor of *Orient Express: Contemporary writing from Enlargement Europe*, which she edited from 2002 to 2005. From 2005 to 2012 she was editor of leading UK-based poetry organ, *Poetry Review*. She was next founder editor of the equally internationalist Taylor & Francis journal, *Poem*. And since 2013 she has served as poetry editor for *New Humanist*.

Sampson had real, palpable success (relatively speaking, for what was a 'little magazine') with *Orient Express*, in that many of the authors she championed there – particularly prose writers – went on to book publication and recognition in the West and the Anglophone world. Names such as: Alek Popov, Alesandr Prokopiev, Peter Zilahy, Goergi Gospodinov, Nenad Velockovic, Sandor Tar, Viivi Luik, Yuri Andrukhovych, Dubravka Ugresic and Drago Jancar, among others.[1]

As it would be later in her editorial career, Sampson's main goal in this role of literary facilitation was to recalibrate various literary scenes, as far as her reach permitted. Editing is and was a global project for Sampson, both geographically and logically. Not only is she an adamant internationalist (and universalist), but editing is for her not merely mentor work, though she has done much of that; it is also, centrally, a way of fine-tuning the 'instruments' of poetic 'life' in whatever editorial situation she may find herself. Like Mary Shelley's 'Frankenstein', as an editor Sampson has built life into many literary scenes, from both the elements on the situated ground and those of her own editorial flair.

---

[1] It should be noted that much of the empirical information made use of in this first part of this section was garnered from correspondence with Professor Sampson. As mentioned earlier, the remit of this book, and its author, are unavoidably shy of any currency with the contemporary literary scene of Central and Eastern Europe. And much of this brief first part serves merely to note, cursorily, some evident accomplishments in the editorial career.

As an editor over much of the last two decades she has provided curatorial space for scores of brilliant poets and writers. And though she has indeed published among them what were and remain 'big names', her approach is proactive rather than reactive. She seems in her editorial career not just to reinstate the writerly establishment but, in part at least, to help (re)constitute the same. Here's a brief list of names of poets whom Sampson helped to emerge during her time at *Poetry Review*: Ahren Warner, Sean Borodale, Kim Moore, Dh Maitreyabandhu, Karen McCarthy Woolf and Ruth Stacey. She became involved in the Complete Works mentoring project for BAME poets from the outset. Sampson was also committed to bringing back into further, deeper circulation many older and as a result often-overlooked women writers, such as Elaine Feinstein, Selima Hill and Ruth Fainlight. These took their place alongside male, middle-generation figures like Sean O'Brien, John Burnside and Don Paterson.

In one pertinent example of editorial flair, Sampson published Paterson's early seminal work, a manifesto for the lyric, 'The Lyric Principle', in two consecutive parts in *Poetry Review* in 2007. These two essays, literary bombshells, would later form the ground of Paterson's far more copious and developed *ars poetica*, *The Poem: Lyric, Sign, Metre* (Faber, 2018). In an international context, an example of Sampson's editorial *nous* and premonition, might be her (first) publication in *Poem* (T&F) of one of the chapters of (at the time, *Poetry* editor) Christian Wiman's resounding work of nonfiction, *My Bright Abyss: Meditation of a Modern Believer* (Farrar, Straus and Giroux 2014). A final, relatively recent example might be her support (again, in *Poem*) for Ukrainian-born, polyglot Svetlana Lavochkina, whose ability and flair in verse (and prose) show deep, distinct promise.

These poets and writers all differ, in age, gender, fame, style and genre. Which is to say that Sampson's editorial gambits have been not so much eclectic, as catholic. As an editor, as in much of her own creative work, Sampson bridges distances, allowing difference to flourish and prosper, but in a manner that also allows for the kind of coherences that I hope to unpack below.

Editor, salvager

> For the literary text [...] knows what kind of work went into the making of it. (PM 11)

> As it moves between detail and principle, nuance and generalization, his writing resembles nothing so much as extended thought experiments through which readers are escorted [...] until they can't help but try out his ideas. (CP 3)

The book chapter from which the first epigraph above is taken encapsulates in some very advertent ways much of what this study explores about Sampson's own writing. These patterns evident in Sampson's poetic sensibility relate here, though, specifically to her conception of optimal *editorial* practice in the contemporary literary climate. As though to enact more globally what she does elsewhere *within the body* of this brilliant paper, Sampson's self-awareness of or about her own thinking-through on the nature of the 'literary' and the editorial function within that remit is in the first instance structurally embodied by the paper's two sections: the first, playfully Tractarian, the second, more simply discursive. Via these two overriding partitions Sampson is both about and 'about' her subject, both telling and showing what she tells, immanently – this very patterning of the paper a small microcosm, thus, of the target of its thesis, on, to repeat, literary aesthetics and editorial roles which might aim to salvage the very existence of such. So that form, as ever for Sampson, is also content. Indeed, in an (2016) introduction to the work of Amir Or as part of her role as chair of the European Atlas Prize jury, Sampson avers: '[g]reat poetry has the smell of freedom about it' and, 'this freedom is the actual nerve and muscle of the poem, not simply the particular thematic task it undertakes' (JWD 2).

As a way in, then, I will paraphrase '2.–4.' in that first Tractarian part which is titled, 'Twelve syllogisms in search of an editor'. A 'literary text' we gather here (starting of course with opening definitions) is more than just an 'occasion' of language use; it is an occasion that has 'a sense of [its own] occasion'. And the performance of this occasion of language use, this occasion that is self-aware of its own occasioned and/or occasional nature (of its 'ephemerality', we will see in a different part of this study, from the close of Sampson's 2007 collation, *On Listening*) is for Sampson 'rite-like'. It is like a 'rite' insofar as literary experience marries in its 'performance' for eye and ear the individual (or subjective) *experience* of the artefact with its more public, objective, textual status. Sampson sees the 'individual experience' of the literary as both 'vested in' and 'produced by' the 'public occasion'; thus, two poles, to be elucidated further, do a mutually reflexive or dialectical loop back: the subjective regulates the objective datum of the text (giving it its meanings) as much as ('produced by') the text regulates the occasional individual (giving him or her the delimited markers from which to generate and then experience meanings (PM 1–2)).[2] Another version of this married contrary comes in '4.3.2.' (PM 2), where the literary text performs its 'symbolic function', its meaning (for the

---

[2] I should say that the page references used here refer to an emailed document version of the chapter sent me by Professor Sampson and are not page references as in the publication itself. Indeed, this applies to many of the articles referred to and discussed in this present section.

reader), but also performs 'its own whole self'. A literary text is its own reader, then, in addition to facilitating a meaningful reading experience for others. And there are many ways in which this kind of structure works itself out in the thinking-through that makes up this paper – key to my understanding of Sampson's work as an editor-poet, poet-editor.

From '7.–8.' onward in this same first partition of the paper, the various deployed notions of the literary are in a way politicized, or at least limited, by the introduction of the editorial function into the equation; primarily because as we are about to see, the editorial role for Sampson is at the heart of what *constitutes* the 'literary' in a practical sense. For Sampson (PM 3–4) in the twenty-first century we live in a world of 'post-literary' norms, within which the former century's death of God has resulted in the present's 'death of value'. It is part of Sampson's brief in this paper to show how thinking about editing literature can locate a way out of, redress or redeem such a death, so that judgements of value can be salvaged – given, that is, the passing of purely 'objective' or of some kind of totalizing, absolutist criteria distinguishing art from non-art. Sampson solves the problematic somewhat by opting for a moving, an almost constellatory model of literary aesthetics, one which, as already indicated, takes into account and attends to *both* the (private) quiddity (unique spatio-temporal axes) and the verifiable, public (linguistic) objecthood of literary texts as they are set in stone, so to speak. Because literary value is not objective in the hard-scientific sense, a turn to the slippery slope of radical subjectivism is *not* the only result left for the status of aesthetic judgment(s). And the editorial function is for Sampson like a metonym for how some mobile middle ground can be salvaged.

In '8.1', Sampson writes that 'literary editorship is a profession under threat' due to the economic collapse of publishing, the squeeze of public subsidising of the arts, their redirection to less-controversial, nonliterary (in Sampson's targeted sense here) criteria and the rise of 'bar-room ready-reaction in the blogosphere, whose central tenet is that expertise in reading and writing cannot be developed because it does not exist' (PM 3). Then, in '8.1.3.' the literary is (implicitly) defined – centrally for how I wish to parse and make use of this text – as a kind of language use that transcends its own contingent, occasional, spatio-temporally discrete nature, *immanently*: by registering the very same in its in(ner)most meaning-ful-ness. Becoming self-aware of the fleetingness of that self, allows that self perhaps to redress, convert the fleetingness. What Sampson goes on now to elaborate promotes a conception of the literary text (as per the epigraph) that registers and congeals its own *constitutive* process in its resultant, finished content – a content that has the possibility of indefinite subsequent dispersal in time and space; its reception, thus, has *its own* 'history' as well. Sampson seems to wish to model what certain critical theorists in the twentieth century dubbed 'dialectical images', literary or cultural artefacts or moments within such which in their stilled, finished content seem to reveal or unveil the very mobile, spatiotemporal or historical features *that went into their making*: again, in congealed form. In other words, a literary artefact like a poem (or a telling moment within one) is, ideally, one that shows up the process of its own constitutive *poesis*. Sampson, however, elaborates this thinking in relation to the 'poet as editor'. So that in '10.' the 'editor' is the 'reader' who brings 'wider', 'non-occasion-specific' sense to the occasion of the literary. In other words (now in the closing '11.2.') the editor acts, I'd like to venture here, *as the reflector* of the specifically 'literary'; (s)he *is* (excuse the near-pun) in this sense the 'sense' of its occasion. The editor so conceived salvages the (value of the) literary artefact by being in a privileged-enough position to essentialize its radically contingent, one-off nature. Passing, losing time, is recouped as it passes (on): the editor as a midwife to this process.

After dismissing, then, 'a grid of criteria' robotically applied, categorically applied, top-down onto literary artefacts as the measure of aesthetic judgement (PM 5), Sampson articulates her conception of the loci of aesthetic value by speaking of 'organicity' and then of a 'vegetable aesthetics' (PM 7). The first opens with a sense of 'spontaneous organic growth', the individual occasion of the experience or of the making of the literary text (reader or writer), as we have seen; and the second formulation adds, or, better, *supersedes* with the equally key 'sense of a necessary, and *useful*, cycle of obsolescence'. Registering *the delimited* nature of the literary text, its quasi-death, dying, is seen as a way of paying honour due to it. Indeed, *as an* editor, Sampson dubs herself 'Heraclitean' and a 'pragmatist of flux' as much as a facilitator (in the more standard sense of editorial functions) of 'fiery literary brilliance' (PM 7). And what I want to stress about the resonance of this paper under discussion here is precisely how such superseding movements of thinking, such 'determinate negations',[3] both show and tell: Sampson is writing here as a practised and practising editor as much as, and at the same time, a poet. Two examples will suffice to close.

Sampson discusses the poet, Pauline Stainer, as follows:

> The way that I experience the words of a Pauline Stainer poem as polished beads in a string has everything to do with a private

---

[3] Indeed, at one point in the paper, extending a metaphor put to use in her argument, Sampson writes with approval of how 'gardeners don't destroy last year's work when they weed the same row again. Rather the reverse' (PM 9). This sense of palimpsest-forming and recursion is also noted in other parts of this study of Sampson's poetics – with parallels to some beginning notions in Edward W. Said's *Beginnings*.

triangulation between the note-beads of her namesake's *Crucifixion*, the rounded double vowels of her name (*au, ai* and the double trace of *ie*), and the perfected images (often religious) and vocabulary of her short verses. From this circumstantial soil grow occasions when I've published, reviewed or taught on Stainer as a vivid miniaturist. (PM 6)

This passage is exemplary Sampson. She not only discourses on the process of her literary experience, as a thinking reader, or as that more pivotal kind, an editor (or reviewer), but it is also the case that this discourse, this (to use a favourite phrase of Sampson's) 'way of going on' does just that: it goes on and *in us* at the same time. Paradoxically, by being so self-aware, reflexive, Sampson is able to facilitate her reader to be able to think-with her, to also *experience* her thinking; because Sampson is not only naming what she does as an editor, but doing it as well. And her telling tellingly 'shows' elsewhere in the same paper – a repeated discursive mode, if not method, in Sampson's toolkit.

For instance, elaborating on how '[i]t wouldn't occur to me *not* to read' literary ephemera of literary authors, such as their letters, say – in the next paragraph, in a nicely stagey move, she pulls herself up, calls herself out, by addressing her just-deployed double-negative, saying how that way of expressing herself *was also* a way of going on, and can be seen to have (just) held richer thought: what she now calls, seeing it, a 'fruitful fuzziness' and a 'good mix in the soil' of her thinking (PM 8). And what my commentary here in these introductory remarks amounts to is that this kind of discursive movement was and is *not preplanned*, like a gimmick. Sampson is thinking on the page before us, in process, as much as presenting us with the product of her thinking borne of practice. Her thoughts on the literary, on the central editorial role in salvaging the literary – from out of a world-in-the-wake of the death of value, expertise – are in a significant sense poetic. She *embodies* in both the complexity and the compositeness of her discourse here some of the ideals she holds for creative literary art. Her dicta about the editorial persona seam thus with other facets of her poetics.

As we will see presently, by discussing other of her editorial texts, Sampson's dialectical sensibility often looks towards the very Wordsworthian paradox, where the exceptional and the everyday (needs must) marry. This salutary chiasmus between deep individuality and equally deep community is after all one of the key contraries between which Sampson negotiates her poetics – accepting mess as much as order. That which is local, concrete, true thus to itself (to its own self-delimitation), seems to be the only bona fide source or root of what just is universal. Indeed, in a recent paper Sampson writes with admiration of Ted Hughes that he viewed the 'audience for poetry not as a handful of metropolitan literati but as unlimited, indeed universal' (TH 2).

And yet, while Sampson is discussing his 'literary legacy' – a very booming, resounding one of course – we can't help but note and know its root in the *sheer originality* of Hughes's vision.

A calling to a calling together of things

> But pause to read them in context, as part of a flexible line of thought, and something else becomes apparent. These are the points where overt reasoning, as opposed to pure description or expression comes to the fore – in a way that mimics how we do in fact think. Their very abruptness resembles 'having an idea'. Through this mimicry, they bring us face to face with a poetic *persona* that is attempting to resolve the essential tension within Wordsworth's idea of the poet as both exceptional and everyman. (PBS ix–x)

> European self-identifiers vary: from common cultural heritage to particular economic scope, from human groupings to geographical coevals. But communities, even world neighbourhoods, are not categories. They're something more intrinsic; more subtle. What Europe shares is perhaps above all the idea of Europe, rethought by the individual and by the discursively local. (AFL 14)

We will see in the section of this study discussing Sampson's work in health and social-care settings that fostering agents (and agency) is at the heart of her poetic advocacy. And if we agree with one of the canonical poets Sampson has made a 'Selected' of, Percy Bysshe Shelley, that being an engaged writer opens one up to ad hominem criticism (PBS xi), or at least commentary – then Sampson must, like Shelley, be in a manner biographically, personally responsible for her poetics. In the present context: her editorial concerns and priorities. Put otherwise, Sampson is as much a 'poet' as editor or health-care worker as she is when writing strictly in verse. This might even be seen as another version of the cohabitation of showing and telling: her choices as editor here about who to let tell or show, by the same token show *her* (poetic) hand. In a 2015 introduction to the work of Sean O'Brien, Sampson writes with admiration of the former's committed poetics; and, as a 'compassionate moralist', the Sean O'Brien Sampson describes here mirrors her own empathic forms of advocacy. O'Brien's 'profound and literal compassion' results in how his poetry feels 'with us', teaching 'us to feel with it', revealing 'our shared limitations and the way we share the experience of having our lives limited by the follies of commercial and political worlds in which we have to carry on' (SB 2). This note eliciting a sense of a sharing collective shows, I want to argue, how Sampson's own editorial advocacy can be seen to be much like

Shelley's 'West Wind' – as noted and elaborated by herself (PBS xiii): 'While a wind may be invisible, its actions in and on the world are palpable. It is present *through or as* its agency'.[4] Tellingly, Sampson chooses to open her introductory to her Shelley Selected edition by stressing how Shelley was not some victim of fateful romanticized myth, passive, but a poet and man who stressed the importance of agency and a poet deeply concerned with (the invisible?) arrival of moments 'of change' (PBS vii).[5] The agency Sampson embodies, as much as facilitates, then, is a complex one. As we are to see, this very un-stuck, musical conception of it ('*through or as*') parallels other tropes of *active* ambivalence in some of Sampson's editorial work.

Much like in her searching Mary Shelley biography (discussed elsewhere in this study), by taking a typically fine-combed approach, Sampson out-romanticizes Romanticism (with that Upper-Case 'R'), insofar as she searches the individuals in question (here, a batch under her editorial scrutiny or elaboration) with a more *infinitesimal* individualization. Indeed, in a recent paper contextualizing the work and legacy of Sylvia Plath, Sampson analogizes Plath with Mary Shelley and again: *alerts* readers to the dangers of undue 'romanticization'; and especially *on behalf* of any of our (perchance) romantic leanings. Making Plath's writing some kind of effect of 'spontaneous' genius (independent of technique or a technical-poetic growth curve,) or, as a direct, therapeutic kind of confessional pathology, pacifies the truer individual truth (SP 3). In an article on the legacy of the last hundred years of women's writing in the *Times Literary Supplement* Sampson makes an analogous point: women writers of the last century *are not* to be seen as having 'reacted' to a preceding canon of men writers – as passive, victims, thus (TT 3).

Another strand to be found woven across some of Sampson's most revealing editorial (or curatorial) work has to do with her persistent and overriding (phenomenological) concern with the 'experience' of consciousness, a notion that dominates not only her (editorial) interests, choices, but also how she goes about doing her poetics – whether in verse or discursively. To keep 'making meaning' requires a certain, radical 'openness' to being, Sampson avers in a 2004 afterword to a book by Amir Or (P 77). And such

---

[4] See here a comment Sampson makes about Sean O'Brien, whom she deems a 'compassionate moralist'; the commentary on responsible agency here is of a similar pattern to Sampson's descrying (above) of Shelley's. O'Brien shows by his poetry that 'human life is made collectively, not *within* a society that one might use as a series of convenient facilities but *through* society, which is to say together' (SB 1).

[5] Even writing in 2019 of Elenkova, Sampson remains concerned with the senses of change and of mutability: 'This mystical verse dives repeatedly into the given and discovers there a world of symbol and – perhaps above all – movement' (TSC 2).

openness can be indicated by the very *formation* of a work, whether in verse or in prose. Writing of the same Amir Or, but in 2016, Sampson notes that, though many poets describe the physical world and pose existential questions, 'fewer describe the thinking process itself'. Or integrates many elements, 'not to mimic but to reproduce a stream of thought' (JWD 3). Not for nothing, again, does Sampson choose to highlight the same motif introducing Shelley, a poet who does more than 'describe' 'rapture'; a poet who 'demonstrates' it (PBS xv). Under Sampson's lens, Or, or Shelley are not passively reflecting their visions; their poetic burdens present as much as represent. And this, as it were, aesthetics of immanence, is something we will see, repeatedly in this book-length essay, close to Sampson's own practice, as much as to those she chooses to work on or with in an editorial capacity. Editorial or curatorial work is a forming, a work of configuration, I venture here, as much as direct literary creation; their poetics are not, however, some simple thematic or stylistic range; they are a way of being, being open (and to openness).

As with some of the concerns elucidated earlier, Sampson conceives of the relation of the objective (language) and the subjective (human experience) as a kind of dialectical chiasmus, language guiding experience, as much as vice versa (P 74). To really try to capture the elusiveness of your true experience, Sampson writes, pursuing Or, involves 'self-resistance', where what is resisted by language, in language is 'not its grammar or capacities, but the closure of its logic' (P 75). Sampson again and again resists the fallacy (anthropomorphic) of trying to be categorical about the experience of meaning, or its inverse; her kind of dialectics, by resisting facile totalization or closure, is a negative dialectics. Since 'literature is', essentially, and emphatically, 'language set in motion' (CP 5), she resists facile romanticization, mythologization (forms of essentialism) of (the sense of) the past – but she does so on behalf of a celebration of what the romantic, Keats, called 'negative capability'. This will continue to be seen as a temperamental feature, noted repeatedly in other parts of this study, of Sampson's oeuvre.

Sampson writes of Or, in a manner similar to her searching conception of 'Europe' in the second epigraph above, placed at the head of this partition:

> [S]hifts of position sometimes suggest ambivalence […] and sometimes the importance of boundaries. Earth, root, tree and leaf are in a relation not of difference but of continuity with each other: with the experience of which they form a part. It's not identity but presence which patterns being. (P 77)

And what I wish to show again here is that such 'openness' is Sampson's, too, even or perhaps especially in editorial mode.

In her recent acclaimed Mary Shelley work, Sampson's sensibility is very much open to the counterfactuals of the past as much as of the present – another kind of modal multi-tasking. Praising Percy Shelley for it, Sampson highlights how 'Shelley is an elegist, a narrative poet, a poet of ideas and a rhapsode' (PBS xv). Of Amir Or's *Poem*, she writes, choosing to celebrate just as much:

> Sometimes the narrator explains, sometimes he leads the reader through their own experience, sometimes he brings the reader into his: we see a lover through his eyes, we experience his memory, desire, even his difficulty in waking up. The effect is of the collisions and colliding consciousness of life itself. A calling together of the nature of things. (P 75)

The choices an editor makes, the things she chooses or is called to call together, reveal much: ad hominem. However, we can't be too quick with the 'openness' in question. Sampson writes in a recent foreword to a Brazilian edition of William Empson's classic, *Seven Types of Ambiguity*, 'biography is not a routemap of the intellectual life, merely a set of clues to its development' (CP 10). Equally, we might say that the intellectual or writerly itinerary or oeuvre is not a carbon copy of the biographical individual. But perhaps all we need be concerned with is (as with her construal of Percy Shelley above) the editorial '*persona*': the mask(s) *she chooses* to wear, vicariously, around and about, via this facet of her writerly career. As an editor, after all, though she has advocated scores of literary artists, launching them or further establishing them, the catholicity of her editorial tastes is quite evident. In a simple empirical sense, the writers she has supported over the years *are not* all similar or cognate in temperament or aesthetics; which is to say they are not merely writers who write according to Sampson's own singular take on what is good or true or beautiful. That said, such range, however ranging, is range from one editorial centre, a kind of 'still point' of 'a turning world'.

In her introduction to Tsvetanka Elenkova's *Crookedness* (2019), Sampson writes: '[t]he best poets take you to a conceptual world you have otherwise never visited, although when you see it for the first time what you feel is recognition' (TSC 1). By Amir Or, we read, if only three years earlier, '[w]e are seduced as well as engaged', *and yet*, 'more importantly, the world is brought closer to us, rather than squirreled away in an arcana of erudition or of poetics' (JWD 1). Sampson's striving to salvage aesthetic values *is not* elitist in essence; it serves as universally in principle as her own very catholic, internationalist tastes – because the kind of exposure Sampson has facilitated for poets and writers in her editorial or curatorial capacity is not one domineered by that very editorial presence. Like some of the poets (such as Shelley, Amir

Or, or Sean O'Brien) we have seen she praises, curates, celebrates, Sampson is a reflector for the being of other writers' variegated works. So that, editorially, she presents as much as represents. She allows the poets and writers she advocates – being open to openness as she is and has been – to be radically idiosyncratic while, now curated, they commune with the everyman of their readerships.

Hospitable Words, Or, Care for Idiosyncrasy
Fiona Sampson on creative writing in health and social care

> Individuals are not interchangeable: this, I would argue, is one of the very lessons creative writing in health and social care teaches as it enables patients to 'find a voice.' The many skills which practitioners, in particular, bring to the field are characteristic of its multi-faceted character, I suggest, rather than indications of some kind of failure. Instead of thinking of more and more precise – and perhaps narrow – definitions of creative writing in health and social care, it may be more useful to map the range of good practice which makes up the field. (CWHSC, 17)

In a foreword to this 2004 volume, *Creative Writing in Health and Social Care*, edited by Sampson, Christina Patterson, then director of The Poetry Society, details the 'Poetry Places scheme'. Within the remit of the latter, the 'Kingfisher Project' had resulted in Sampson's pamphlet, published in 1999, *The Healing Word* – one of a number of projects in community- and public-art settings. The Poetry Society's 'Poetry Places scheme' also entailed the facilitation of a poetry residency in health care (CWHSC 10), as well as the (perhaps more well-known) 'Poet in the City' project. These ventures were part of a relatively recent upsurge of work in this field, where cross-pollination between the skillsets of arts professionals and the needs of those in different care settings became an increasingly established domain. Indeed, writing in the introduction to an earlier volume (1998), co-edited with Celia Hunt, *The Self on the Page*, Sampson (along with Hunt) discusses how over the decade preceding in the UK there had been

> a growing interest in the practice of autobiography and creative writing as a means of gaining insight into oneself, of coping with difficult emotional and psychological problems, or as a way of dealing with difficult life experiences such as emotional traumas, illnesses, ageing and death; indeed, writers were found to be increasingly working in institutions

such as prisons, hospitals and day centres, working with client groups with mental health problems, learning disabilities, older people, stroke victims, dementia sufferers and terminally ill people. (SP 10)

And the volume in question, introduced as such, reflects in the variety of the chapter contributions such 'a wide spectrum', or mapping 'range', as the epigraph to this section has it.

Nearly two decades later, in her inaugural, 'Wellcome Trust Annual Public Mike White Memorial Lecture', Sampson stays the course by speaking again, but in a more innovative, less overtly context-bound way, of the need to find (discursive) acceptance in our lives, to all find ourselves 'bade welcome' – especially, emphatically in times of personal discord, when 'dwelling' (Heidegger) makes itself felt as a more pressing need. And this eminently humane need relates both to our relationships to our own selves and in relation to others. 'We need to make sense of bad experiences in a way we don't of good ones, which speak for themselves'. And then, 'when we see *other* people struggling we feel an impulse, somewhat akin to hospitality, to do what we can to put them at ease' (SL 2–3). These are the basic parameters of the shared experiences and processes of creative writing in health and social care settings; and as detailed below, of some of the most common ways of human sharing, or community – of 'speaking likeness', more generally.

Before proceeding to reconstruct some of Sampson's thinking in this area, it seems apposite to provide some basic biographical context, which will emphasize both the centrality of this part of the arts field to Sampson's earliest practice, and the centrality, by turns, of Sampson's work to this area in the UK in toto, as well. Sampson was one of the main pioneers in the UK in this area. Having started her undergraduate work at Oxford belatedly, in her mid-twenties (after an earlier musical career), she then went on to doctoral research in this area (at Radboud University in the Netherlands) at a stage in her career when most aspiring arts practitioners at the same are busy writing and hustling their way into publication. Thus, not only was Sampson present and active at the beginning of the upsurge of work in this area, but her own literary endeavours and accomplishments to date also seem to find their beginnings in this same field of arts practice.[6] Indeed, the history of creative writing in health and social care grew, seminally, out of the hospital arts movement, and the reason (as per the above citation) Sampson was asked to

---

[6] Sampson's PhD research work was titled, 'Towards a theoretical framework for writing in healthcare'. It should also be noted that in addition to the main texts discussed and referenced in this section, Sampson has, as an avid researcher and worker in this field contributed a series of conference and periodical papers in this area of study.

give the inaugural Wellcome Trust lecture – on the occasion of the hospital arts movement's archives being given to the Wellcome Archive – was precisely because Sampson had pioneered in the practice in the UK.[7]

Sampson held the very first creative writing residency working throughout health care in the UK, on the Isle of Wight; and those three years, Arts Council England funded, produced a national report for the National Health Service 'Writing in Health Care'. Thereafter, she was involved in a series of long-term projects, including five years of work for Swindon Age Concern, several months in a psychiatric prison unit based in Hampshire and much sustained work in care homes and hospitals, such as, for instance, three summers of work in the Lord Mayor Treloar Hospital, seven years with the Salisbury Health Care Trust and a one-year stint at Addenbrooke's Hospital in Cambridge.

Having spent much of the first, key dozen years of her practice as a creative artist researching and working in this area, understanding the scope and the significance of this biographical experience to her more globally considered poetics and poetic itinerary seems both necessary and apposite. And this would apply to her other literary roles, especially perhaps to her position as an influential editor both in the UK and elsewhere across Europe and beyond. An editor is a facilitator almost by definition. But Sampson's work as a creative writing specialist in health and social care has been just as much work of facilitation – and that, not necessarily only with the beneficial effects of this work with those in care. What is central is that both of these roles, editorial and arts practice in community settings (not to mention her roles as a teacher, mentor, translator and critic), are part of a deeply embedded belief that poetry is not and should never be an exclusive medium, or the provenance of an elite. Sharing, radical communality, as seen in other chapters of this work, are like beelines through or keystones for the complex and composite literary achievement to date.

Via reconstruction and minor elaboration in the main, in the next part I discuss Sampson's thinking, borne of her more than decade-long practice, on the roles and functions of poetry and creative writing more generally in health and social care settings. There are many strands to what remains a consistently coherent and cohering approach to these practices and subjects – including notions that discard writing in such settings as merely, flatly 'therapeutic'; nothing so banal and, more pressingly, so reductive. Another dominant motif in Sampson's thinking and practice in these areas, parallels artwork, poetry, or whatever kind of literary configurational practices may be at hand, with the individualized nature of discordant experience: the idiosyncrasy and autonomy of these literary practices match the same of persons being worked with by

---

[7] It should be noted that there have been conferences aimed at the study of Sampson's work in this field as otherwise in Sweden, Norway and Spain to date.

facilitating writing professionals. The notions of empowerment, and more precisely, of agency and its sundering of passive states for sufferers are also key to how Sampson's dynamic thinking in these areas enlightens both sides of the predicament, the literary art and the personal suffering or disability of whatever sort. And I will close this reconstructive discussion by showing incipient ways in which Sampson's thinking (after practice) in these areas marries quite neatly with other areas and roles she deals with and embodies in her poetic career, speaking globally.

As with many formative discursive gestures Sampson is wont to deploy in her critical writing, her pamphlet, *The Healing Word* (1999), opens with a couple of dichotomies whose contrariety will facilitate fertile reconciliation in the thinking-through that then follows. First: one has 'the expertise of someone experiencing illness or difficulty (what we call "vulnerability") or involved in personal development', and then one has 'the professional poet'. Another contrary that spurs her discussion is between 'institutional processes of health and social care and the individuality which both poetry and healing may promote' (HW 9). However, part of the manner in which Sampson begins to mediate or process these starting difficulties involves noting how 'the practice of facilitating poetry workshops in care settings that emerged out of the Health Care Arts movement' has (or had) emphasized poetry in formal health-care settings 'as an arts activity which complements a care setting rather than' as 'in the medical model'. This entails 'advocacy – poetry and healing has more to do with individual and active voices than with prescribing what the nature of a patient's experience will be' (HW 8). Finishing this opening of the pamphlet, Sampson highlights the centrality to her work and its reflection in this small book 'designed around shared poetry and healing activities' of the fact that 'it's important to get things right when we're enabling other people's experience' (HW 11). This note of responsible and responsive recognition of others will persist into her latest work in this area as well; insofar as we are representing and representational animals, Sampson seems to be saying, we have a basic human right to 'care'. Not for nothing does she open her 2016 Wellcome lecture with a citation of George Herbert's 'Love'; and certainly not for nothing does she make use of citations from the Universal Declaration of Human Rights and then the European Charter (SL 4–5) there as well. But to return again to 1999.

Towards the end of this pamphlet penned at the turn of the century, Sampson highlights the fact that if '"healing" includes the idea of enhancing a fuller way of being' then the 'basic right' of 'people who take part in poetry and healing activities' 'not to be harmed' should be 'respected as they should be anywhere'. As shown below as well, part of Sampson's humanizing mission in this field has been to make the more vulnerable part of the same humane continuum as those perhaps less immediately so. For in workshops where patients' senses of self may well be revealed, a 'risk of emotional harm' is entailed; in 'therapeutic contexts', of course, any participant 'is already vulnerable' (HW 63). This caveat noted, what I think is clear now – apart from Sampson's insistence on the persistence of artistic norms throughout health- and social-care settings – is that it is also the case that the vulnerabilities in such settings are on a likening spectrum with the vulnerabilities of persons who either engage in creative literary activity beyond such settings, or those, more generally, who suffer the hardships, anyway, of the human condition. Indeed, as elsewhere in her critical writing, poetry stays poetry, not some cheaply conceived, direct or transitive form of 'therapy'. This ennobles the sufferer, by recouping him or her into the remit of poetry practiced by all, poets, sufferers of the human condition – and not necessarily only in a health- or social-care setting.

> But poetry itself is not a magic medium. Much of the value of such projects lies in the skills and sensitivity of the poet-facilitator who leads the process of opening up and of creative engagement. If this is not done with due sensitivity and care, then it may be of no value at all. It's a process of trust. If the trust is not there, then it may be better to watch telly. Poetry as therapy, like any kind of therapy, is as good as the person doing it. (CWHSC 11)

After Patterson's comment here, Sampson continues in the 'Editor's Introduction', that in her view there is no (final) tension between 'formal provision and the development of individual experience' (CWHSC 14). Arts practices in care contexts 'ha[ve] to speak to both arts and care discourses; and about each discourse to the other'. However, '[a]n arts professional may be wary of an arts practice which seems to talk about itself in any terms except the artistic' (15). Indeed, six years earlier, Sampson (with Hunt) puts to use an opening citation of Virginia Woolf (often invoked in Sampson's critical writing) by suggesting that whatever 'therapeutic benefit she may have derived from her writing came by default rather than by design' (SP 9). The obliquity, the (Dickinson) 'telling it slant' that literary art allows for, 'makes discussion possible' (64). Engaging in poetic (slant) activities, viewed as authoritative and privileged by many sufferers, empowers them, Sampson notes (65). However, this latter, precisely *because it is* 'poetry' or literary art in question and at practice, and not some facile reduction of the latter to 'treat' 'patients' in need of some transitive unloading of some negative experience or state. Again, nearly two decades later, Sampson writes in her inaugural 2016 lecture:

> Of course, every individual, including the artist-maker, has a psychological prehistory. But human rights legislation – and the practice of care itself – acknowledge that our human-ness *encompasses and is prior* to such prehistories, just as it is to a broken leg or a blocked artery. So art in health and social care, an intentional, human practice, must be art *in the same way* as if were produced in any other setting in order to *be art*. (SL 11)

For Sampson here, 'there *is* no separation between what poems do within and beyond health and social care. Poetry in health and social care is not instrumental: it works *as* poetry' (21). However, she continues with strong and signal intent, 'perhaps because it's positioned precisely here, at the nub of what both art and human nature are', that the hospital arts movement has been somewhat of a battleground. Thus, concluding this seminal lecture, Sampson argues against the idea of hyphenated identities for art workers in health and social care; they should be seen rather as '*doubly* skilled', not as 'half-and-halfs'. The brief of creative writing in health and social care in Sampson's estimation should thus be seen as a positive sum, not a zero-sum, endeavour. For such practitioners 'need to remember to integrate their practice in health and social care with the rest of their artistic practice and their working [...] lives' (22). And although this is about the established literary practitioners – this is also a (closing) injunction because the patients at hand are to become agents, too, in or along the continuum of the same arts field. It is after all 'a speaking likeness' that Sampson is eliciting in this inaugural lecture – as though patients and poets were similes of each other; as though the optimal practice of poets with patients (turned agents) might be poems in themselves.

In *The Healing Word*, Sampson cites the poet Selima Hill with praise. Hill writes of how it is not the case that 'a poet is a special kind of person, but: each person is a special kind of poet' (HW 59). This begins to highlight how Sampson's thinking in this area of her poetic career emphasizes in a radical way the common, shared idiosyncrasy between the literary art form and the human condition in its most human state, vulnerable.

> [P]oetry is often unexpected in the therapeutic context. It's newer and more conspicuous than a chat with the social worker. It's more permanent than a conversation with another user at the drop-in. It's more public than a diary and more attractive than a feedback form. It's

oblique: it doesn't have to deal with 'issues' and in any case it can do so indirectly. (HW 18)

While the field under discussion is built out of a 'three-way pull' between '*systems of provision*' and 'the *vulnerability* of the human *individual*' – *that contrariety* is reconciled by Sampson's parallel(ed) notion of '*art*',

> by which we mean, let us say for now, a certain kind of man-made experience and way of going on which avoids what is reductive and which often exhibits an urge towards transcendence of particular circumstance and individual experience. (CWHSC 17)

This note about a 'way of going on' 'beyond' the particularities of the individual, debilitative circumstance, is a repeated notion in Sampson's approach after over more than a decade working and thinking in this field. '[A]s we know from our experiences – health care needs are individual' (SL 4). After opening this inaugural lecture with a citation of George Herbert's 'Love', a poem which outlines a 'hospitable principle', Sampson recoups by later speaking of how this principle is 'an interlocutor, not merely a provider', one 'who approaches, questions and smiles at the narrator', and whose response is 'memorably' '*reactive* and *individual*' (15). This latter teased-out-use of her opening citation maps onto Sampson's notion of 'dignity' for the vulnerable person, a notion which is an 'elastic concept', and which 'allows us to leave what a person *is* as something underdetermined; as a *principle* rather than a *definition*' (5). This reflective underdetermination, as elsewhere in Sampson's poetic career, and this undercutting of teleological statement in favour of a course of literary action that is questioning, Socratic and, as with Herbert, 'quick-eyed' – is part of an agenda that prioritizes empowerment, (new) ownership of discursive space, (new-found) authority and the kind of recuperative agency that flies in the face of an obedient or spoon-fed passivity of the patient in care. And this active acquisition of an active voice would apply even if the patient forewent actually writing his or her own poem or literary artefact: '[S]ince reading and writing are equally important in the life of a poem, we can say that everyone who joins a poetry session is "doing" poetry' (HW 19).

Along with her deployed notions of 'hospitality' and 'dignity', Sampson adumbrates a third, drawing-forth from Spivak's conception of 'translation' – whereby the target language needs must come forward to meet and accommodate the 'guest', its precursor (SL 11–12). Such garnering of agency makes service to patients in care settings, '*the repository of an individual's way of going on*' – instead of a mere '*form of provision*' (CWHSC 13). The aim of the process of facilitation of creative writing in health and social care settings 'isn't primarily to allow' the patient 'to believe in the process offered by the facilitating writer. Rather, it is to allow the participant to experience the accessibility of a form of writing whose status is empowering, both within and beyond the care context'. Indeed, the 'authority' or 'ownership' thus bestowed, taking the patient seriously in the artistic sense and setting may well then involve, in Sampson's view, the 'passing up the opportunity to publish' his or her work (SP 76). As elsewhere in Sampson's paradox-prone thinking and writing, the dialectic evinced is enabling, if nominally counter-intuitive. Bestowing dignity in these settings is not good manners by the facilitator, which would keep a patient passive; rather it '*is* a capacious (re)definition of being human: one that leaves growing room and that says, in effect, nothing more or less than that "humans are intrinsically valuable"' (SL 5–6; 7–8). The burden of agency in Sampson's way of thinking works in both directions.

Indeed, in that same final section of Sampson's article in *The Self on the Page*, titled 'Celebrating Ownership', the notion that the professional poet at practice, the facilitator, should leave editorial dues unpaid is rubbished; not only would this be immediately condescending, but also unproductive. 'Editorial discussion reinforces the identity of the text produced. It underlies its separation not only from more conversational moments in the session, but also from other pieces of transcription, and facilitates '"literary" judgement' (SP 74). For Sampson the editorial role takes on a truly (re)productive and configurative status, but it is also the case that Sampson's notion of 'attention' (musical or otherwise) found peopling other areas of her critical writing, is also enlisted in this part of her critical domain. In health care settings, '[p]rompt, accurate diagnosis can require radical *attention* to, and brilliant *interpretative* skills in, what a patient – inexperienced in their body's new forms of behaviour – hesitatingly reports' (SL 8). Just so, the poet or working literary facilitator at hand in the now-combined setting has, always, to account for and respond to what is radically 'our own way of putting things. This means that to listen, really to pay attention, to what someone else has to say requires us to step outside our own native idiolect and try on another way of thinking and speaking' (12). This move, health-giving on both sides of the artistic equation, can be driven by the basic human need and/or desire built into our 'curiosity' – the epistemological version, if you like, of what elsewhere in this study I have descried as Sampson's (well-nigh systematic) 'empathy'. But this move can also be engendered by what Sampson here calls an 'ethics of recognition', parsing the Kantian categorical imperative – perhaps more in its sovereign 'kingdom of ends' version, than in its other in the second *Critique* (13).

Chapter 2

FROM THE LOOKING GLASS TO THE LAMP

Into the Looking Glass: Fiona Sampson as Poet and Critic from 2005–2007

Introduction

The four parts of the writing of this opening section segue on from each other, but also revolve around their central concern, which is to descry and elaborate on Sampson's modernist metaphysics (an oxymoron, perhaps). Both in conception and in execution on the page, about and 'about', the hope is that the insights, readings, samplings and so on commune in a way which is like the conception of an 'oceanic logic' that opens what follows. All this is to say, that the interwoven and interweaving form of the discussion of the communities and the distances in Sampson's critical and poetic oeuvre between, in the main, 2005–2007, hopefully lives out, embodies, its discursive content, to a certain extent at least. My hope has been, constructively, to mirror the various mirrors in Sampson's poetics, closing distances between only seemingly separate works, genres, modes. What holds is that in Sampson's writing at this time there is indeed a community of viewpoints that close in, but which do so, not like the closing of a circle, but like the spiralling of a spire. The ability to be universal and concrete at the same time seems to be a kind of never-ending project, an insuperable middle. And the purpose of this section is to show that conscientious middle-ness – in what is still the (early-) middle of the Sampson oeuvre to-date.

A possible framework, or, a framework of possibilities

> Clarity can be demanded of all knowledge only when it has been determined that the objects under investigation are free of all dynamic qualities that would cause them to elude the gaze that tries to capture and hole them unambiguously.

In a recent work, *Theories of the Logos*, the contemporary philosopher Ermanno Bencivenga allies 'poetry' with 'dialectical logic'. Before this, though, he explains the nature of 'analytical logic', the 'Aristotelian framework', as that which aims to pin meaning down to one final and irrevocable sense. The next chapter continues by saying how analytic logic does not necessarily mean a kind of meaning obtained by a 'process of breaking down' (TL 25). No; it is

> rather that this process is irrevocable, for both words and sentences: what is obtained at the end of it is indeed an end – nothing further will be learnt about a meaning, and certainly nothing that contravenes what the process has taught us. (25)

By turns, 'dialectical logic' 'cannot be formalized' (33) in this way, because unlike analytical logic, which can disregard and abstract from content, it 'needs to "explain" the nature of identity in the connectedness of a discursive path', one that 'will make you *understand* what allows the identity to be maintained across [...] difference' (33). This hospitality of dialectical logic for ambiguity, contrariety, difference, the mess of contingent life, coming-to-be-comprehended in what is still described here as a monist narrative, leads Bencivenga to associate it with 'poetry'.

> Poetry, after all, is what makes language move away from its entrenched settlements, from its clichés; so poetry is as immediate a presentation of dialectic – of the liveliness of delineated projects – in the verbal world as spacetime continuants are in the physical one. A poem is a pulsating organism – one that proclaims its vitality on the page, rebelling against the inscriptions in which is it is locked, affirming a meaning that supersedes them – and a spacetime continuant is a poem incarnate, a physical structure that, like a poem, keeps defying any attempt at reducing it to a formula, any 'definitive' characterization of it (analytic definition as such). (35–36)

It would seem, on the face of things, that Fiona Sampson's own conception of poetry would tally. Her conception of the poetic hungers for 'discursive plurality', which, dialectically, is the product of 'sites of conflict'. Insofar as 'forms of knowledge cannot *live up* to their objects of study' (*OL* 14), she would seem to be at odds with the same irrevocable (thus overdeterminingly authoritative) nature of purely analytic logic. Whether, in the same work, she praises Sean O'Brien for 'embracing ambiguity' (6) or Jaan Kaplinski for evincing perceptions in his poetry that are continuing and 'uncompleted', (32) Sampson has her critical sights here targeting and critiquing 'totalizing discourses' (25). For instance, making use of one of her most central critical tropes, 'listening':

> What is built into the life of present participles is the significance of what is uncompleted or continuing. 'I am listening' is not the same as 'I listen' or, especially, the dismissive 'I hear you', which has always already *moved past* the moment of listening. Reading, writing, speaking, making a case, listening: all are forms of process, movements of discovery. (21)

Poetry and/or poetics (and that conflation is part of the purpose of this prolonged discussion) at their normative best embrace irreducible antagonism for Sampson; they afford 'the chance to mix-up discourses: the domestic with the exotic, the frightening with the beautiful; fiction with fact' (100). All that said, however, and while Sampson does evoke, invoke and evince an often Socratic maieutic in her work, her poetics as critic and poet share a dialectical space with the third theory of logic, which Bencivenga outlines, namely 'oceanic logic'. At the start of her co-authored work on writing, the 'self' and 'reflexivity' she (with Celia Hunt) pressures a question about creative writing, a 'contradiction':

> [C]reative writing is deeply personal, deeply connected with the writer's self, but it also involves moving away from the self and becoming impersonal. How are we to understand this?

Under the brief, copious indeed at this period in Sampson's oeuvre, of the concept of 'reflexivity', Sampson (and Hunt here) essay a way of understanding what Eliot called 'impersonality', a distancing from the personalized, confessional mode, with novel fruit:

> What Eliot calls impersonality is more usefully understood as *adopting a different stance towards* the personal. It involves relinquishing, even if only temporarily, the deep personal connection we have with our material; it requires a kind of internal distancing, allowing a space to open up between ourselves and our material, so that it can develop a life of its own in our imagination. (*WSR* 2)

The self-duplication intended by the notion of reflexivity is at the core of some of the readings woven together in what follows; indeed, in the poetic works discussed and sampled below, Sampson's poetic voice often addresses her self as 'you' – such apostrophization directly inhabiting and indicating a reflexive sensibility. However, what I want to pick up on here, is this notion of 'adopting a different stance towards'. As outlined below, 'oceanic logic' would better the serial developments of dialectical logic as a way of opening out a discussion of Sampson's poetics at this period in her oeuvre.

For instance, for Sampson creative writing needs both angles of vision: a need 'to develop *a stance* towards' any 'work in progress that allows our material as much freedom as possible whilst also taking into account the need to hold and shape the material' (52). These are two angles of vision on the discipline of subjectivity that writing is; two perspectives, control and freedom, only seemingly in conflict, on the same process; for such doubling self-awareness is, as per the opening epigraph of the first chapter of this work of Sampson's, from the cognitive psychiatrist, Antonio Damasio, the 'underlying prerequisite for creating great art' (1).

Subject formation – where 'subjects' are both one's creative material and the creative mind shaping it into form – is for Sampson at this stage in her career as later, a way of accomplishing which is not directly or transitively a form of mere 'self-expression', or indeed, 'therapy'. The reflexive, self-mediated self, bares his or her accomplishing and accomplishment in the accomplished artefact (a text in this case), which is not and should not be seen as an unmediated 'symptom' (*OL* 110–14). The (regulative) ideal artefact in question marries the distance between 'our own personal needs and the need of the writing to have a life of its own' (*WSR* 3). In different, but substantively dovetailing places, Bencivenga is also enlightening in this respect, framing as he does here the liberating coincidence of control and freedom.

> I am (my freedom is) a connective. A variety of behavioural structures are appropriated wholesale, and what I am is the particular capacity that belongs to this being (that *is* this being, that constitutes its 'essence') of combining them in certain patterns and not others, of reacting from one to the other along certain specific paths. And my growth, the deepening and expanding of my liberation, consists of appropriating new structures and creating new paths. (*DS* 100)

> [N]o rule or principle will ever conquer and hold all of us: in spite of whatever training and conditioning we are subject to, there will (or perhaps may? or should?) always remain a 'soft core' of our being that is inaccessible to, and independent from, the training and the conditioning, and that is ready to take the most varied shapes, the most fantastic directions. (*TDS* 50–51)

The 'dance' and/or the 'discipline' of subjectivity means that analytical logic as our rubric thus, is out of the question, eschewing the movements of (such) paradox; in that framework, 'to unambiguously define', for instance, '"safety" and "freedom", clearly state their opposition, and then bring out their respective pros and cons and comparing and contrasting them', is in effect 'to become a staunch defender of the one or the other (but, crucially, not both)' (*TL* 51). However, dialectical logic insofar as it is seen as purely serial will also not be wholly sufficient to account for the poetics descried and discussed in what follows; because that 'theory of the logos' 'would judge one of the two values (e.g. safety) to be more mature than the other, a later stage of dialectical development' compelling us to 'work on safety, as the necessary actualization of the promise involved in freedom' (51).

'Oceanic logic' overcomes confrontations and contrarieties, however:

> [N]ot by reducing everything [...] to a bland common denominator [...] but by exploring the porousness of reality, the flexibility of borders, and the sudden familiarity the unknown acquires when you move toward it. Everything will recognise itself in its other, not because it will see the other as a phase of its own development but because it will see the road between self and the other as one that can be travelled without impediment and in both senses. (54)

So, still using the same example from above, for the oceanic framework, 'when people talk about safety and freedom, they are talking about the same thing: they are foregrounding two angles of the same desirable state' (51–52).

> What there is in life is an infinite gradation of nuances, and whatever nuance might apply to our situation it will never, in and by itself, determine which of those opposites are here to use. It will always be how we see it; and we could always choose to see it differently. Which means: we could always choose to *act* differently, depending on how we see it. (59)

As we will see below, just as 'water' (not to mention 'light') is a recurring and often-reprised image made-use-of by Sampson, oceanic logic is named as such because like a wave in an ocean where it (the wave) begins and ends is a matter of continuous, abyssal and fuzzy perspective (46–47). Reflexivity in Sampson's discursive writing and thought, as embodied in her poetry of this time, often portrays a healthy writing practice and thus a healthy poetics as a kind 'attention' or attunement to differing perspectives and, most pressingly, where they blend and blur, vanishing into each other at their mutual thresholds. Paradox is rife in the work of Sampson at this period; and by paradoxical we mean a poetics that bares itself as targeting a reality, of self or world, that infinitesimally eludes direct naming, analytical pinning-down – hence, the need for the fluid convolutions, ambiguities, contrarieties, a living-with that Keats called 'negative capability' (*WSR* 62). Like the unnameable remit or domain of a wave in an ocean, Sampson's thought and poetry between 2005 and 2007 is eminently metaphysical. And what is intended by this term is articulated by Sampson herself, admiringly. She speaks of the seventeenth-century 'metaphysical poets' in a way that is highly revelatory about her own poetics. 'The metaphysical poets of another expansively scientific age, the seventeenth century, used paradox both to approach what cannot itself be put in words and to suggest the doubled, or reflexive, nature of experience' (*WSR* 114).

However, for all the metaphysical animus ratcheted in her work, we don't quite achieve the wished-for 'communion' with Sampson; not wholly at least: 'prayer is continuing failure' (*CP* 25) in her poetry at this time; and if the humanistic, essentialist god-particle in 'our common name' (68) remains un-'touched', it is perhaps because the kind of belonging Sampson believes in is not like a wholesome sense of ending, but immanently plural: 'You don't *belong*. / It is about the landscape / as confessor' (26); or the 'Trace / of the leverage / self exerts on its surroundings' (12). Self in both these citations seems nonidentical to itself, dispersed by (confessing-to) its bodily situations. And recognizing this, naming the not-fully nameable is the brief of reflexivity and the self-awareness that is 'attention'.

Reflexivity and embodiment

> Psychotherapist Donald Winnicott was of the view that in order to be able to use our aloneness effectively, we first have to learn how to be alone in the presence of someone else. (*WSR* 79)
>
> The threshold of the self's a large lit room. (*DB* 35)

For Sampson it is always, or should always be the case, that 'a grammar of thought underpins a poetics' (*OL* 2); there is an 'intimacy' between 'thought and language' (3). And, as we have seen, at this period in her oeuvre at least, she favours a poetics (by conviction and also as embodied in her verse) that is playful and thus 'transgressive' of 'the unitary authority of a particular way of going on' (*WSR* 175), that 'destabilizes' 'ideas about identity' (176). The specific dignity of the 'literary' for Sampson 'undermines' as much as 'supports' itself (140). 'Cultural mediation is transgressive':

> When we borrow or mediate against the grain of our particular cultural limitations, we engage in dialogue with what is repressed in our own ways of thinking and writing [...] At these moments we are in fact listening *over the margin* of our own text. (142)

The reader beyond the 'margin' of a 'literary' text is just as much the source of reflexivity, or at least, as above (or below), can be seen as a metonym for the self that can mediate it-self.

> In other words, despite the individuality which we celebrate in reading and writing practices, what *contains* this plurality of meanings and versions like the waist on the hourglass of a text, is the mutual embodiment of reader and writer: what they can cope with and enjoy *as a result of the way they are embodied*. *Textuality* draws these embodiments together. (*OL* 149)

'Ways of thinking', another modal term picked up and attended to by Sampson, which doesn't embrace or attend to its own limitations, can lead to 'discursive violence' (*OL* 17). By this she means a discourse that dominates other, minority positions by way of a false claim to objective validity – for a discourse that is still, ultimately, inevitably only in fact one of many. Speaking of translation as a working metaphor in more than one sense, Sampson seeks at this period in her thinking to preempt and disarm such violence by an 'active listening' (14). This involves empathy, which is an 'unconscious metaphor' for 'embodiment' (*WSR* 105). The link between the empathy of or with the real (out there) and the empathy of the poet (in here) straining or stretching the line of attention towards such is articulated here:

> You're right. To enter you
>   or me
> is to enter a forest
> where everything's alive.
> Leaves stirring with private gesture.
>
> Presence is a vivid scent [...]
>
> moving through as if native
> we find
> how form opens onto form,
> bulb into fern into tree. (*DB* 39)

Subjects and objects blur here, clearly; the worlds of persons and of selves and the worlds of nature and of culture all dissolve into each other, like different waves of the same ocean; without, though, losing their ('vivid') integrity. This commonality of things is also intelligently toyed-with of course in *Common Prayer*, a short distance of only two years on. Many of the poems there invoke, with irony and with mourning, a central instance of 'embodiment' and radical empathy – namely, the mythos of the 'incarnation'.

In 'Body Mass', one of many sonnets strategically peppering the dovetailing sequence of, in the main, longer poems in *Common Prayer*, Sampson plays, eponymously and within the piece, on the notion of incarnation as well as incarnation and its vanishing. It starts its playful erotic with 'Each bone's a chalice', but the 'he' 'asking why' is asking 'not of you'. 'Not of your bones, // which pour themselves between these sheets / of skin with practised cool'. His arrival is imaged quite beautifully as a 'chasing flight of angels', before he 'tumbles to earth himself' (*CP* 28). 'Re-ligere', reconnection, to the matrix, to the earth ('Anchorage' is the title of yet another sonnet nearby), is toyed with here in this sonnet, as much as another in *Common Prayer*, the gospel-invoking, 'Take, Eat' (24), analogizes the closing distances between erotic and spiritual loves, devotions. And like with the paradoxes and chiasmi of this latter, in 'Body Mass', the 'you' who is departed from is ambiguous and ambivalent. It could be a fellow mortal lover; it could (also) be referring, but in lower case, to the more expected, transcending person of embodied mass, the 'incarnation'. The poetry here is 'about' empathy (like some godly incarnation) in two simultaneous senses, logical and topographical. It stretches across and about the immanent lines of the verse and also makes a point by the execution of its conception. The poetry in its concretion and the critical mind of the poet marry across the only nominal distance between them.

Indeed, poetry, speaking globally now, is a specifically resonant and poignant mode of this living-with, and this (material) self-delimitation thus — either because of its obvious reflexive indication of its 'man-made origins', as opposed to some so-called 'objective' 'logic' (*OL* 18), or because it adverts emphatically to aural components of language which are semiotic and presymbolic, bodied moves which shift 'the meaning and experience of texts *further into* the physical world' (*WSR* 148). In both cases, the practice of and the working metaphor of 'active listening' is a way of allowing for 'potential spaces' of meaning (61–62), plural, othering, almost by definition, to develop. And again, this is accomplished because the discipline of active listening demonstrates its own situatedness and materiality, undermining ironically any totalizing claim of representation, and permitting the emergence of the 'non-identical' (*OL* 19).

> In this model, tradition, culture, the local and the personal can move in to take their place at the international table, unseating silence and unshrouding whatever they locate as the sources of meaning. (15)

This reflexive or self-aware attention allows voices to 'multiply' (*WSR* 43) and by doing so makes responsiveness into responsibility; for 'the capacities for reflection and selection' that literary use of language demand make our writing a practice, after active listening, one of moral agency (153).

> Writing, and the *move into form* of thought, teaches us about rights and responsibilities as thinking agents; it records our individuality. Without this, we cannot achieve insights and changes which we might call therapeutic. However, writing itself is not therapy [...] writing achieves what it does because it is built out of both process and product, in continual dialectic. (*OL* 110)

After empathy, a kind of now-recognized embodiment, a here not there that allows a here to be for there – 'authorship is seen as an ethical responsibility to say what we have to say because we occupy a unique niche in history' (*WSR* 54). Our inevitable material finitude takes on the dignity of a categorical imperative, precisely by the quiddity of our, or anyone's, position. The poet's 'grammar of thought' then, by being transgressive of, disobedient to uniformity, totalization, becomes, as Sampson descries in her admiration of the work of Jaan Kaplinski, a meta-obedience (*OL* 4). Such 'conscientiousness' carries the individual (voice) into a 'generalized space' (3). The responsible poet enters a no man's land between his or her empirical poetry and his or her thinking, which is the 'shared space' of difference (10). The 'grammar of thought' behind responsible poetry, then, is, 'if not prior to, at least simultaneous with the poem' (6). And this conscientious poetic stance is therefore not a posthumous justification or apology for the poetry in question, a kind of selfish special pleading; it is rather, as it were, its constitutive ground, that which inhabits itself discursively at the same time as the breath which transpires through any poetic artefact. If thinking and language, critical stances and poetic sensibilities at work are intimates, then their oneness in Sampson's view is oceanic, different waves of the same body of water. And this is a way of understanding a transcendental deontic space that is very redolent in later critical works by Sampson, such as *Music Lessons* (2011) or *Lyric Cousins* (2016). There, among other things, music, which is before and beyond denotative presence, is seen (heuristically) as part of the constitution of the whole poetic enterprise, synchronically, structurally and not as some empirical, chronological or indeed biographical inkling that spurs the first phoneme of a poem.

Listening (whether the notions of 'music' or of 'translation' are specifically at hand) is a practice and a metaphor in Sampson's thinking at this time for the fidelity to infidelity (29) (paradoxical, again), a 'resistance movement' that 'acknowledges the place from which it is listening' (22) and 'selects' 'what it wants to pay attention to' (23), demarcating here from there. Indeed, discussing her early editorship of the *Orient Express*, a pivotal and seminal journal originated by Sampson that published translations of poetry from postcommunist Eastern and Central Europe, Sampson's nonreductive 'oceanic logic' is named by her as 'palimpsest communication', 'where traces of one context overlay but do not obscure those of another' (41). By embracing the situated embodiment of our perspectives, what, closing *On Listening* Sampson calls, the 'ephemeral' – which is material delimitation itself – goes dignified like time, passing, timing itself. And it is a way, not of thinking 'round', but of thinking 'through' perspective (64). As Sampson writes in *The Distance Between Us*: 'But the body / inconsolable/ is the burnt mouth the closed eye / everything passes through' (*DB* 16). Indeed, in *Common Prayer*'s 'Attitudes of Prayer', a shard from the end (a threshold after the first sex scene) of the first section of the first novel, *Justine*, of Lawrence Durrell's own 'palimpsest' narrative, *The Alexandria Quartet*, is inserted into the text (*CP* 58). This gesture is both a formal and substantive wink to the endurance of the ephemeral. Towards the end, the frontier, of *Common Prayer*'s 'At the Sex Frontier' (a doubled and doubling threshold, again, placed as it is at the meeting-points of desire):

> When your face
> comes puckering up,
> so that I lean across the shiny space between us
> towards the image of me
> floating in you
>   like a palimpsest. (*CP* 44)

This empathic distance is only a short distance on from *The Distance Between Us*.

To recoup, like the responsible poet, thinking in Sampson's conception of poetics at this time does not provide a fixed agenda for any one poetics; it is, in its free motion, the constitutive ground of her (or the) whole conception of poetics; which is still a spaciousness.

> As we relinquish names [...] we move into a certain spaciousness, which is to say something under-determined. Unidentified, we're free to reinvent ourselves and the world of our experience. It's like going to a party where no-one knows you. Without being able to name something, we're forced to open up our attention: to glimpse, as well as we can, what something is *in-itself*. (*OL* 155)

Reflexivity thus undermines identity-thinking, or overdetermination, allowing for 'the possibility of something else' (62), like 'travellers, caught between homesickness and the provocations of the new' (63); a liminal space then, so redolent in her verse of this period, which is even more othering than sheer or facile dichotomous othering. Indeed, in this same piece, in this same space, where Sampson reflexively identifies with the 'Viola' of Shakespeare's 'Twelfth Night' (a small passage of which is used as an epigraph feeding-into the main text, blurring the frame), Sampson speaks of her self and the other whom she identifies with, using a demotic simile (as in the last indented quotation) that typifies much of her empathic critical writing. Viola 'turns away from the new country; turns her attention backwards – to shipwreck and sea. Hers is the classic adolescent shrug which, taking the form of a question, refers responsibility backwards to something or someone *else*' (61). However, by Sampson's reflexive and immanently duplicative descrying of sense here, we see, rather, at a meta-textual level what she calls just below, 'the sign of newly-approaching adulthood' (61). Indeed, this piece is titled, exilically and, tellingly again, after another poet, Shakespeare: '*What country, friends, is this?*' And the dialectical and/or oceanic movements in this piece, between then and now, here and there, writer and other (now-internalized) writerly presences, such as Woolf, Conrad or Lawrence, among others, speak to the infinitesimal nature of the reality of experience in question. The truth Sampson is targeting by the palimpsest of her movements (as elsewhere in *On Listening*) between frames of discourse, aims to try at least to capture the elusive nature of the felt reality (past and present) at hand – which, however, lies in the (unconscious) interstices, like music. For the 'Mediterranean', which is viewed as the 'British Unconscious' in this meditative piece, ends by being: 'Like a music always just below the surface of the words' (67). Similarly, for Lacan, a huge implicit influence on Sampson's thinking at this time, the truth of the reality of the person is presymbolic, caught-up in or with the discords between words and the presence or (re)presentation of denotative meaning.

Reflexivity, the awareness of and attention to the other, of and in time or space, means understanding the way misunderstanding may well be inexorable. But this recognition makes a home at a higher order of understanding; and so on, ad infinitum. Allowing for the nonidentical, undercutting some totalizing or wholly necessitated discourse, means that in 'rendering something ephemeral, we render it – if not immortal, at least enduring. The market creates *waste*; we create meaning in the ephemeral'. More pressingly, by giving up 'its claim to permanence' 'the ephemeral gains a continuing identity in-itself' (154). It is as if to say the contingent becomes essentialized as the locus of a (de)limited berth in the world. The changing, passing, endures, thus, only because it is reflexively self-named and known as such.

And if the ephemeral is associated with materiality, some-thing that is present in the positive world of time and space, and is thus inevitably susceptible to slippage and, ultimately, absence, passing (for reasons elaborated below) – it's no wonder that Sampson (and Hunt here) praise Kristeva's notion of the prelinguistic, presymbolic, 'semiotic' (*WSR* 16). Whether we call it reflexivity, attention or active listening, Sampson (and Hunt here) wish for a poetics that combines what psychologists have called the (prelapsarian, in Sampson) 'core self' (before language-acquisition) and the later, symbolizing 'extended self'; because this working combination allows for a writing practice that evinces a stable and continuous sense of self that is at the same time, from a different angle of vision, continuously in the process of change and development (16 & 65). In Kantian terms (his third *Critique*), the underdetermined, nonteleologically closed poetics at hand is 'reflective' rather than 'determinant'; this is what Kant meant by 'purposiveness without a purpose' (*CPJ* 105), or, as one of the titles of Sampson's pieces in *On Listening* has it (after, and an after that is telling again, T. S. Eliot), 'home is where one starts from'. There, Messiaen's music (significantly themed: 'Vingt regards sur l'enfant Jésus') is admired, reflexively by Sampson, as a 'sound that is both powerfully reassuring and the mark of absence' (17). In particular, this seemingly contradictory phrase speaks about Sampson's reimagining, after listening actively to the music, of the relations or distances between fathers and sons – whether, as themed, godly, or closer to home, regarding the composer himself. This heuristic and deontic reimagining and listening, between past and present among other blending distances, typifies the oceanic logic of all descried so far, and below – a kind of oneness, a kind of homeliness, that is immanently dispersive, plural, uncanny, not dominative or authoritarian; that is paradoxical, distance-giving. And all these modes and themes can be found peopling the two main works of verse in the period in question, *The Distance Between Us* (2005) and then *Common Prayer* (2007).

Reflections are homonymous in these works, speaking to material reflections and the more contemplative kind; or, better, Sampson's rigorous, but always limpid, reflexivity pits mind and body as two angles of vision, two stances towards, the same oceanic reality. They share as it were the same 'grammar'. Indeed, towards its close, 'meaning' in the first, *The Distance Between Us* is likened to and embodied as a 'fish', all 'muscle' and 'shine' – 'fluid power' – like rhetoric (*DB* 65). And the closing image of the whole work has 'doors // like water //' going or passing, 'through the long indifferent corridor' (67). So that's where we'll start, enter again, enduring the ephemeral – with the 'real presences' (in *Common Prayer*, now) that can only 'flicker' (*CP* 32); evincing and soliciting an 'Obedience' only 'to this given world, / whim after shining whim' (42).

For while there may well be in Sampson's oceanic poetics, metaphysics: 'A hundred keys to the human body / in a hundred drawers'. And while she or her poetic persona may well strive, endlessly – 'I'll open them all / until I find you' (66) – nonetheless, we are left, inevitably, 'still asking the mortal questions: / *Where are you?* (67). At the last: 'the hunt for the human, / for what secures us' results in finding only 'the other / who sets up an echo in the self' (65).

Into the looking glass

> Indeed, I suppose that impressionism exists to render those queer effects of real life that are like so many views seen through bright glass – through glass so bright that whilst you perceive through it a landscape or a backyard, you are aware that on its surface, it reflects a face of a person behind you. For the whole of life is really like that; we are almost always in one place with our minds somewhere quite other. (Ford Madox Ford, 'On Impressionism' 41)

The epigraph to *The Distance Between Us*, from Aleksandar Prokopiev, runs, 'Always be hungry! Then you'll become like each other' (*DB* 7). It speaks to the theme of desire, which is the presiding motif of this work. Because in Sampson's responsible hands, desire, often bodily, straining for or towards 'touch', is never arrival or rest; it is immanently distance-giving. This is so of course, independent of any biographical experience. After a Lacanian insight, where presence, the 'phallus', is the signifier of lack, because it is the signifier of signification itself, as such, we must realize that the 'desire' for at-onement, what elsewhere Lacan puns as 'copula-tion', is natively impossible. For Lacan, the workings of 'desire' are modelled on those of language, hence the pun on 'copula-tion'; indeed, perhaps Lacan's most telling, most global adaptation of his Freudian inheritance was to pick up on and make universal Freud's only implicit recognition of this; sexuality in Freud after all is psycho-sexuality. Thus, insofar as each presented word only indicates the next, the other (endemically, endlessly associative), but never fully pinions the motive and infinitesimal nature of the real, whether of self or world, desire for consummation (of desire, too) is aporetic by nature. So, in 'The Plunge' (another water-infused title, like the prize-winning 'Trumpeldor Beach' in *Common Prayer*), we read of how,

> Your illness is a pact;
> to bear it
> is to bear even death
> in this name – *love*. (*CP* 33)

The communion, pact, is in, with loss; there is a vital gap in this pact, a (loving) distance. And this distance of mortal intents is apparent earlier as well. 'Impossible to touch each other / impossible / to touch each other here' (*DB* 14). Even if we might hope for a love, 'where meaning / comes to rest' (66), the next phrase is a question: '*Where / are you?*' (66). On the same page, just above, 'Meaning multiplies itself / with every hungry bite we take'. Even if 'We live towards significance, / it calls us in', 'Word branches to word' (64). So that 'we struggle / the many headed stranger / growing in our arms // out of and beyond our bodies // pulling our truth out of our selves out of reach / into pain' (67). Similarly, the 'urgent narratives' (urgency, another threshold) of 'water' – that seeming image of totality and rounding and closure – are 'from' only 'the middle of the world'. 'Water / always pressing towards water // as if it could dissolve the skin of the known world' (*CP* 22) – cannot. Narratives are 'urgent' because they'll always be pitted by slippage, 'pain', by that common, failing 'hunger' whose failure makes us all similes of each other in our continuing incompletion.

Language for the attentive Sampson falls short of truth, or the real: 'Impossible to emulate /the unaccountable give of growth', as the willow tree's 'petalled fall' is of 'what can never be concluded' (26). To recognize 'a distance', thus 'between self / and self' is 'where relief blossoms' (*DB* 31). And yet, re-leaf, too, it would seem, via verb choice; and that relief is like a reflexive recognition of self-limitation. Because even if 'What we desire / is to arrive. / We move as towards rest //' but 'life' still 'is motion / animate / as we are' (63). Indeed, the epigraphs for *Common Prayer* only two years later, come from Virginia Woolf and Jacques Lacan, two writers and thinkers (professionally) obsessed by language. Woolf suggests there that the 'real world' is silenced by the 'habitable world'; the 'core self', perhaps, by later, slippery symbolizations trying desperately to pin it down. And in the second epigraph Lacan berates 'eros' in its Platonic sense we must assume, no doubt because hope for achieved harmony is outdated in a modernist and in Lacan's (specific) case post-Freudian world. (As with the title of her next Carcanet collection, Sampson can only offer 'rough music'.) Relapsing like a wave again across a short distance, however, to the 2005 work – this note in question is already struck: 'The deep beauty is in fracture' (*DB* 41). 'Odd how lazy the eye is […] / […] Odd / how it lingers on disharmony, / broken patterns' (24). And that 'eye' may be a reflexive image of the person, the 'I' – an embodiment of it, so to speak. It is also true to say that throughout Sampson's poetry at this date, as elsewise, her metaphysics of presence and absence is copiously embodied by repeated abyssal, aporetic or just paradoxical images of 'light' and 'dark'.

'Home / is the bare room of attention' (25) in that same (2005) work – as much as the highly reflexive image of the 'wren' in (2007) *Common Prayer*'s 'A Sacrament of Watering' is 'the stretched line of attention holding itself, / breath stilled' (*CP* 18). It would seem, with that final image, silencing song, that we'd only achieve true communion then at the moment of ineffable totalization, the 'death hour' (*CP* 53), the barren, bared. Sampson's persona tells and 'reassures' her 'students' that what gives us 'form' is 'The stories we tell, /the voice we tell them in' (*DB* 47). But then the 'body' is 'like music', and 'form opening through time / in a breathing line' ends up as 'a cry' (*CP* 60). Hope weeps here, as Sampson's discourse finds a bodied home in her contemporaneous verse; the 'reassurance' is also, simultaneously, the 'mark of absence'.

For 'history's like that. Takes with one hand, / gives with the other' (52). Indeed, ending this poem, 'The Archive', the zero-sum ethos of the given or the immanent world runs: 'We hadn't drifted apart it was hard we kept in touch'. No punctuation here enacts the closing of the gap. But then, the last line, after a telling line break, widens it again, in different staggered ways: 'Who saved my life. Whom I persuaded to volunteer' (54). The death of the saviour in this context is segued onto the survival of the narrating voice; there is no positive sum scenario where all transcend together. For the self to live, the other must die and live again in the self that lives, but as his or her own failure.

> Disapproval like a gasp
> outside this minute
>
> the minute of presence before its image
> closes on it
>   before the circling of mouths
>
> kissing their zero sums.
>   Before subtraction. (*DB* 57)

Even when poesis is named as not quite discordance, 'story connects' only 'what's half-seen, / half-imagined'. Again, story does not romantically transcend here, rather it 'sifts down / its fine grit / connecting this, to that, to you' (*CP* 31). Which is to say 'obedience' only 'to the given world'. After the opening of *The Distance Between Us*, in question mode 'Who's this?' we 'follow the line', of attention we must assume, 'the pointing finger – / in the desert presence bares itself' (*DB* 12). And this baring is a moving homonym: presence bares, shows-up, itself as bare or barren; presence presents itself in its own denuding:

> Can I touch you?
> Putting my hand into the wound of presence
>
> because I don't doubt this truth
> that is a lie. (16)

The reflexive duplications of paradox are telling here; and the fact that they cannot be wholly resolved is the point. 'World', like self in Sampson of this period, 'burns: all edges and corners / burnished with leaf' (*CP* 38). To burn is both a verb and something that does away with itself, not to mention the 'threshold' images of 'edges' and 'corners', vanishing points which populate Sampson's verse. The relief of dissolution, though, is also re-leaf, as in the play between 'burn' and 'burnish'. Some-thing, but something not concluded. In 'Mid-Journey': 'How life constantly turns outwards – / unstoppable forest', 'I hardly know where to begin / or end / do you?' (*DB* 39). And then, the reflexive play between the 'core self' of the real and the 'extended self' is articulated when Sampson writes, 'You tell your story / or it tells you' (51); 'What matters / makes you in its own image' (49). Which is to say: matter, embodiment, is the God in this context. God, meaning, what matters now, is the distance between. Of course, both aspects of selfhood, patient and agent, are happening as two angles of vision or stances towards the same lived, felt life. As in the Ford epigraph quoted above, Sampson's metaphysical reflections reflect in the real, literal world. Ending 'Turkish Rondo', one of many (continuously discontinuous) internationalist essays in this work:

> Beyond the picture window
> faculty buildings graze
>   among trees
> and out of a listening dark
> I gather my face. (52)

Similarly, opening *Common Prayer*'s 'The Looking Glass', we read of: 'Darkness at the window / holding your reflection / dark-lamp turning its bowl of warmth / onto the table // and here's your face, / its pale / shield / blurred at the edges' (*CP* 12). Indeed, at the start of that same *Common Prayer* 'Messiaen's Piano' 'throws notes like handfuls of stones / to clatter / against a glass- / house God'; and at the close of this opening poem, just after the Lacanian epigraph demoting Platonic 'eros', we 'hear what bodies do: / suspension, / interruption. / That long, perfect fall' (11). Not only is the idea of God, the whole, total, implicitly shattered, but this (paradoxically 'perfect') fall from grace is a fall from the semiotic core self to the world of symbolization, which is endemically pitted, being presence, by absence. And then, near the close of *Common Prayer*:

> Setting off
> into the invisible, beyond music,
> you strain at something
> glimpsed –
> but the retina's
> all fog and shine,

light curtained by water.

> How to catch what you're looking for
> in the mind's
>   tricky lens? (74)

Both 'here / and absent-minded' (13), 'the secret mark of grace' of the 'looking glass' when 'you look through it', and 'see something flawless', 'thickens to white / only at the cut' (14). All of which suggests the framing of things is what lets us see. And the framing of things, the liminal space between inside and out, are like waves in an ocean, when attended to responsibly, and change with each different 'raid on the inarticulate' (T. S. Eliot).

Via self-awareness, active listening and/or attention, the self in these works is distant to it-self, finding itself in that distance, 'a cushion of faces / on my lids' (*DB* 25); 'a chorus / of selves' significantly triggered by a 'susurration of language' (21). At one point in *On Listening* Sampson quotes (having listened to: another overlay of discursive frames) the psychologist Bruno Bettelheim as stating that it is inaccessibility and distance that is the true guarantor of proximity (63); or, perhaps the distance between, temporal now, communes as, rather, 'the echo of what *might have been*' (67).

Coda: Wits at mo(u)rning

> Suddenly for no earthly reason I felt immensely sorry for him and longed to say something real, something with wings and a heart, but the birds I wanted settled on my shoulders and head only later when I was alone and not in need of words. (Vladimir Nabokov, *The Real Life of Sebastian Knight*)

> Your fear
>   and mine
> make a verse with no answer. (*CP* 35)

In his much-earlier book, *Hegel's Dialectical Logic*, Ermanno Bencivenga creatively out-Hegel's Hegel, clutching-at and using the form of his insight rather than its biographical substance. Here, then, a dialectical logic opens out onto what Bencivenga much later calls an 'oceanic logic'.

> Think of the past, of history, as a repertory of diversity, in the specific sense of *projectual* diversity. We must see a lot going on there besides the official line: a multiplicity of false starts, of crushed hopes, of sidelined, forgotten dreams. And we must insist that, for all their being forgotten and sidelined and crushed, those projects are still there, and their

> presence *in the past* is an indictment of the official line – as much of a substantial incarnation of a normative stance on it as we can get but also, maybe as much of one as we need. We must feel the cutting corners of the little rocks to which those (never realized) majestic boulders have been reduced, and sense that they can still draw blood. (*HDL* 88)

And if 'home' is only 'where one starts from' (according to Sampson, as we have seen), perhaps it is accurate to say that

> one is not 'always already' human. Humanity should not be understood as automatically including bodies of a certain shape; 'humanity' should not be used in a lazy 'referential' way. Humanity is indeed a project: the project of making certain bodies temples of diversity. So, if I favour (and I do) certain bodies, I favour them becoming human (their becoming what they are), their struggling to conquer and maintain humanity, to justify the definition I want to be true of them. I favour the disciplined, painstaking effort of building enough structure so that deviance can happen inside those bodies without taking them apart; ultimately, I favour the constitution of a human self – and an arena for transgression that is not purely negative (destructive) of that very self. (*TLM* 54)

Which is to say that Sampson's central, pivotal trope of 'distance' can be seen as a humane acknowledgement of the paradox that to really attain our humanity, that 'common prayer' – as yet, a 'prayer' only 'shadowy with life' (*CP* 31) – would be at the same time to eradicate that same humanity. We would become what Sampson calls in her prize-winning 'Trumpeldor Beach' 'the fictional angels' (23), which we are not. To paraphrase the modernist philosopher, Theodor Adorno, adapting Marx at the start of his *Negative Dialectics* – a work thoroughly modernist for its pan-logism, its oceanic reaches across faculties and domains; a work, too, rigorously critical of 'identity-thinking' – 'philosophy' continues, goes on, because it certainly hasn't as yet 'realized itself'. In this case, though, the philosophy at hand might not be Reason, but rhetoric, Sampson's configurations, her 'starry combinations' (*CP* 13). Thus: 'Scars on a map. // The distance between us' (*DB* 31), indicate that 'What must be said / is far off' (13). The true 'ought' remains distant still from what 'is'.

Indeed, far off, in 1992 Sampson won the Newdigate Prize for a poem in four parts, 'Green Thought', published in her *Folding the Real* (Seren, 2001). It was written as a reaction to a lecture of Hélène Cixous, given at Oxford. (And Cixous is a critical presence in Sampson's critical thinking of the period in question here, as later.) Here, then, Sampson phrases in brief the amphibian polyvalence of what has been highlighted (after Bencivenga) as an 'oceanic logic'; while adverting in a manner to the impossible reaches of 'copula-tion', Sampson writes:

II
The last thing you
see isn't white
or blue. It's

pubic fuzz, the soft scrim
of trees going
left off the picture. (*FR* 59)

Last things, margins, leaving off, the fuzziness of boundaries, the fuzziness ultimately of the problematic of emergence, are quite apparent thus from the opening strophes of Sampson's poetic oeuvre.

Whether it's by time or by space, Sampson's modernist poetics, metaphysics commune, hone, home, by distances, distancing. It might be seen as similar to what Adorno, again, at mid-century dubbed in his *Minima Moralia* – an inversion of Aristotle's *Magna*, as I understand it, as much as its 'melancholy science' was an inversion of Nietzsche's 'joyful' one – a 'refuge for the homeless'. Sampson's 'metaphysical wit' – a phrase George Steiner uses to label the then-still-fresh approaches of Jacques Derrida in his honorary lectures from the late eighties, *Real Presences* – are wits in mourning. When one enters into the looking glass of Sampson's poetics at this period in her oeuvre, one enters a hall of mirrors, whose paradoxical reflections, for all their precision still nod to an abyss. But that very recognition may be the only hope, the only common prayer at hand – all her wits, thus, geared, too, at morning. And yet, the wave goes on, relapsing. Because about Sampson's poetics as descried and elaborated on above, we might also say that 'mourning' in effect 'becomes the law' (Gillian Rose's late titular phrase). In order to know and to let others know where she stands, falls.

Homely Duplicities: Reading Fiona Sampson's *Rough Music*

Beyond the ash-tree
Caesar waits.
But these words won't render to him. ('Nel Mezzo')

A trip to the unheard

starts noisily ('The Door')

Just as reflective distance gave us control over our animal nature, so maybe reflective distance from our self-control could give us control over it. (Christine M. Korsgaard, *The Sources of Normativity* 160)

In one of the poems in Fiona Sampson's *Rough Music* (Carcanet 2010), 'Amal and the Night Visitors', we read of a boy who 'breaks your heart', but who 'is breaking it still' at the poem's close. Strangely, among many poems that play with closure and its lack in this collection, strangely, that is to say, among many poems that end with rigorously inconclusive marks, this ending on a present participle actually embodies in its argument and cadence a kind of rendering of accounts. The heart or hearts may be breaking still through the end of the poem, but there is nothing in the way this poem ends that does anything but still the breaking. However, the main reason I begin by adverting to this long-lined poem, a poem in its shape and indeed in its continuously storying intention, which is not prototypical of Sampson's poetics, is that there is an image and/or argument near its middle that seems to me to capture much of what is going on at different levels and in different modes throughout this collection.

We read of 'Amal' that 'his destiny is his own life, which seems to mean / not his home in the known but an unknown of his own' (47). The seeming and paradoxical formulation are of course some of Sampson's tell-tale gestures, being a (broadly construed) metaphysical poet, with deep reflection in and behind her verse; but it also picks out in the aporetic framing of its argument the many ways in which Sampson homes in and hones her insight as a poet via duplicities. Whether the mode is temporal, spatial, a mixture of both, contemplative or descriptive and a mixture of both – whether it's by deft lineation or syntax, or indeed punctuation, allowing for registers to shift with the shifting of the poetic mind behind the verse – Sampson takes great pains to elide overdetermination or teleologically closed answers. However, this way of going about her thinking and living in verse finds its revelations in the reader, nonetheless; there is something so much more reassuring and indicative of her poetry at her best, about being able to question with a sure hand – which means, thus, and at the same time, to question that same questioning.

Throughout the verse in this collection, cognitive awareness or rational processes are subordinated to more embodied, realer ways of knowing and being. However, as a deeply reflexive poet and thinker, Sampson is able to achieve this shearing away of discursivity and/or ratiocination, not by an accumulation of unadorned images, no; rather what she does, with a kind of hale duplicity, is to reflect in such a way as to reflect upon and debunk thus any traces of reflexive surety or resolute homecoming. In fact, for all her charms and magic (the collection is peppered with some songs, ballads, folk songs, sonnets), this book of 'rough music' evinces most of the time gestures of disenchantment, whether it's lithe snipes at patriarchy or logocentrism, or whether it's a speculative and counterfactual attitude directed at memory and experience, among many other homely duplicities.

Indeed, we read in 'Crow Voodoo' three consecutive quatrains which do a counterfactual dance, typical of Sampson's intelligence all the way through to her more recent biography of Mary Shelley:

> You're the knife
> whose blade
> tickled my life
> one day
>
> or you're the man
> holding the knife –
> my life
> in his hands –
>
> or you're my life
> cut open
> by this knife,
> and woken up
>
> to wonder. (50)

Even if this poem picks up on an early, pivotal and highly traumatic near-death experience of Sampson's (discussed elsewhere), the play at play here both tells and shows, in one immanent flowing movement, wondering, but also wandering.

But to loop back in a filmic way, now, to the collection's own filmic opening – the opening poem, 'The Betrayal', starts with the line 'Something is broken'. The opening of the second stanza (of three five-lined ones) informs us that 'Something has broken through / what was clear'. This breaking through (of) clarity, purist argumentative pellucidity perhaps, is hinged onto images, very filmic, of the fleetingness of experience, but a fleetingness which endures because it is reflexively named as such. As in some of her earlier work, the 'ephemeral' nature of temporal experience, when poetically reflected upon, begins to time itself. And this canniness is a salvaging of sorts. And then, after we learn of the broken thing, we read in a kind of cinematic loop back rewinding movement of 'Milk not rising from the floor / to resume the shape of a jug'. And we end this note on irretrievable mutability, a *via negativa* of sorts, with, 'the next moment/ comes racing back / along your glance' (11).

By the sureness of the self-awareness of the poem, the images linger as more than what their discursive contents indicate. Indeed, at the start of one of her critical works published close in time to *Rough Music*, namely, Sampson's *Beyond the Lyric* (Chatto & Windus 2012), such reflexivity points out a very similar kind of aporetic paradox, as follows:

> At times it seems like a kind of club: only if you're already a member can you locate the entrance. Only if you already know lots of contemporary poetry will you be able to guess where it would suit you most to begin. (BL 1)

This is as it were another example of Sampson's homely duplicity; while being open-palmed in her approach to her readers, using throughout her discursive works demotic and welcoming similes and gestures from everyday experience – still, she shows the inevitable complexity that attends a serious-minded approach to contemporary poetry. Teacherly, her introduction to 'A Map of Contemporary British Poetry' sets the stage or scene for a reconnaissance that is a 'way in' to the contemporary gamut, which at the same time, however, refuses to talk down or bowdlerize the depth and complexity of that moment in 'vibrant transition' at question.

From one filmic loop back, to another now, back in *Rough Music*. Towards the very middle of the book, in 'Nel Mezzo', we read,

> There's a path, of course.
> Chequered red and grey
> it disappears in grass,
> reappears near the kitchen
> as bricks leading backwards –
> these are old plots –
>
> or forwards to now
> and the yeasty smell of elderflower. (32)

It's the same play at play; what's happening, typified by that parenthetic intervention from the commanding present ('these are old plots' – pun no doubt both operative and intended) is that the dialectic (as throughout the collection) between then and now, now and then, here and there and so on, is not only what we read later in the same poem of 'what Hegel called history' applied to the individual personal life (itself a fresh idea) but, more emphatically, the shifting registers that unsettle overdetermination; a kind of syntactical and/or modal stop/start that keeps the movement of thought and image ever fresh, moving. Indeed, this is shown more overtly by how the citation above is mirrored later in the same poem, where Hegelian (teleological) 'looking on' (which comprehends all empirical pasts into their notional essence) is controverted by a more colloquial looking on:

> The future seemed clear
> as Menna and I climbed trees
> beside brackish water in Yr Waun –
> or sunbathed on the pebble-dashed bunkers –
>
> the deluge was coming –
> and we knew we
> wouldn't be lifted or tumbled. (33)

The two girls, looked-upon from the present, are looking-forward to looking-backwards, already. And so on. A similar transgression against too much clarity and distinction, Cartesian idylls, is proverbially indicated in 'Out of the Attic' by how 'no philosophy / were necessary to joy'. Opening the poem:

> Things we love go with us
> like marginalia,
> those detours
> early illuminators made. (30)

But to contrast with and to complement this mixed metaphor of mutable passing and the enduring, in the poem's final stanza:

> The intimacy of father and son
> unravels, as a child grows to equal
> the man who was his measure. (30)

As ever with Sampson, here it's not just the paradoxical or homonymous sense of 'unravelling', indicating both coming apart and growing into or developing, but it's also the dexterous way early parts and later parts of the poem unify via alterity and juxtaposition. The unities of Sampson's verse are never monochrome or uniformed unities; they reside very much below the surface, awaiting the sensitive reader to reconfigure them.

In 'The Code', we open with two stanzas which indicate and enact two kinds of critique against essentialism or, as it were, the more Apollonic kind of music:

> How each thing gathers to a whole,
> the leaven in its heart

holding a pattern before it shows
capacity —

the tree inside the feathered stamen
the egg inside the bird
are infolded, not unthought —
like something heard. (23)

Sampson seems to want to 'catch' processes in their processing; (her later, 2016 collection of verse is titled *The Catch*). However, the catch is that she wants to catch turning points in a way that allows them to turn in their points still – caught in a way, but also uncaught, still unstill. The punctuation, or its lack, in the citation above, as throughout the collection, serves this nondominative gambit, an attempt to let process happen without its overdetermined stilling in verse, words, logoi. The reflective nature of Sampson's poetic intelligence is also evident here; she is meditating, as it were, or contemplating about, and about, the way things are, or better, how in their becoming they become what they are. Moreover, the 'infolded' nature of natural process(es) are not in some facile way suggested to be 'unthought'; no, Sampson's manner and intentions are always too honestly reflective for such an attempted foil or fakery. Rather, rational pinioning processes, essentialist pinning-down in some analytic endeavour to decipher a once-and-for-all truth of the matter, are replaced by, or 'like', 'something heard'. And hearing truth is different to trying to pin it down. One would think that to hear truths allows, by (modal) definition, said realities to remain their own realities, without being grasped by the poet with a violence of finished naming. As in earlier poetic works, the hopes in Sampson's music are just that: musical, rhetorical and configurative. She constellates sense and senses, which means that there is always a liveness and breath in the way she represents and/or reflects upon the lived realities surrounding her. In a way, then, Sampson's poetry does the equivalent of what she praises in critical 'close reading', which is reflective rather than determinant in her view:

Any critical writing which doesn't proceed from close reading muffles, rather than clarifies; it damages the very thing it claims to promote. (BL 4)

Indeed, staying briefly with this introduction to one of her near-contemporaneous critical works, it's no accident, in fact it's very telling and significant that the way Sampson frames her 'rationale' for the pursuant book in question here – 'because British culture itself is in vibrant transition' – seems to pick out, again, her efforts to 'catch' change and mutability in their processes, without that rationale being a reductive reasoning-away or whittling. She gives many examples preceding this comment on early twenty-first century 'British culture', examples which are or were analogous, such as: the new movement of nonfiction in the eighties, philosophy and theory in the wake of 1968, the Harlem Renaissance and so on (BL 2). By trying to 'get' (7) different sensibilities in their analogous differences as disclosed by their texts, by trying to create as much as reflect a 'balancing variety' (8) in this critical work, her reflective bent merges into that kind of alterity-promoting, juxtaposing that is so redolent in her verse, by turns. Here, as there, Sampson's unities are universal and universalizing – precisely because she never discards, omits or forgets the concrete base of any reflective adventure. Her unities are like music's, speaking very broadly; they try not to subordinate content to formal reduction, nor penetrating insight to concrete dispersal.

For it's not just logocentrism that's critiqued in *Rough Music*; it's also of course phallic patriarchy. In two dramatic places, 'Zeus to Juno' and the eponymous 'Rough Music, or Songs without Tunes', which latter is equally myth-based, male figures are seen to be eclipsed in different and nuanced ways by female ones. In the former, the dramatic repartee is between 'He' and 'She'. He, as it turns out, starts in special pleading mode, making excuses for his infidelity. 'You saw the way her body looked at me / all address / calling me down'. Zeus here is implicitly emotive; it's Juno, the betrayed female, who takes on the truer voice (of reason). After her first more fact-of-the-matter intervention, Zeus continues, but in a richer, deeper vein.

> When I entered her
> > her death became my life
>
> in her death swoon
> > she fell away from me
>
> the more she fell
> > the deeper I pursued her
>
> the deeper I went
> > the more lost she became
>
> her body
> > became a forest of echoes
>
> hills and valleys
> > echoing each other, a language
>
> I didn't know. (12–13)

It's not just the echoic language that's alien to the patriarch here; no; what's most pressing here is the way the argument of the drama develops and has developed. Yes, the story gets fuller here, but the reader will have had the distinct impression that it is the impact of the female, Juno, in the interstices of Zeus's failing dictions, that is the truly telling factor. Sampson then says, again, seemingly with far less emotiveness:

> The discarded body
> lies in long grass,
> flies and wasps
> fumble there.

Then it's she who ends, closes the parley with,

> The scavenging crow
> knows she's beautiful,
> outgrowing her name
> in the noon heat. (13)

Juno's 'voice' here is ambivalent, which, because of its implicit truthfulness and roughshod honesty, actually becomes the more authoritative for it. She is showing female solidarity even in the passing, fading, of her female coeval(s). In short, by closing the drama, she holds the reigns of the dramatic tension that still lingers beyond that last line, echoically.

In a similar manner it is 'Eurydice' who opens and closes the second dramatic poem. She closes her first entry with 'Hurdy-gurdy heart / lead me / down-river', and that river is both the notorious 'black river', an image of experience through time and, as we will see, conjoining both, of Orphic music. When Eurydice says, 'I'm the lost girl',

> That half-articulate blur
> glimpsed in the blink
> of your eye. (25)

She is able to take command of her losing or lost position; and that liminality so self-named becomes through some of the imaged logic of this poem, a metaphor for music itself. Which is to say she commandeers it from Orpheus, perhaps. Here, Orpheus seems to be describing the literal elements of the mythos, but he is also describing, it might be ventured, how the 'she' who eludes him is the she who takes on the mantel of his music:

> Hold her in your arms
>   she slips away through the dark

> Hold her with a ring
> > she slips through a magician's scarf
> Hold her with a knife
> > she slips away
> > she slips away. (26)

In a sense, here Orpheus is losing his ability or 'capacity' for music, as well as her. Hades by turns marks the berth and final dock of her, music, as that 'black river' which is death, absence: 'I brought her home – / I bring them all home'. The home of death, like that of music, may be rough – and yet even Hades is outmatched by Eurydice's volition:

> Love is an eclipse
> I wanted to step into the light –
> the vast silence
>
> free of fists and hearts and rose tattoos,
> flotsam and jetsam
> of his need
>
> Every girl wants to be free
> When the snake bit
> I offered my arm (27)

Just as the rough music of the argument of this poem is led through by Sampson's deft versification, Eurydice, the lost, ends the piece showing who, in truth, was and is in command.

> It wasn't love, the second time
> I disappeared
> The water shone black and white
> like a choice.
>
> I swam upriver to my heart
> looking for harbour
> till Death took me at last,
> like a lover. (29)

The harbour or home of death becomes the music, in at least two senses.

There is also much about Sampson's verse that conflates inner spaces and outer ones, as much as it shifts with strategy between descriptive and prescriptive registers. For example, such doubleness is embodied in the second stanza of 'First Theory of Movement':

> In the window
> I glimpse my page turning
> and mistake it for a gull. (14)

The poem, early on in the collection, 'Skater', is also a case in point in this respect. It starts,

> Out into the cold
> goes the line you draw
>   across this pond.

But this description begins (while still being representational) to be infused with more illuminative intents, skater's line and poet's lines synergizing into more than their addled parts:

>   When you move and break the silence
>
> alarm thuds an ice drum
> tuned tight as the skin
>   that binds your bones.
>
> In an elegant
> enlarging lens – silver, *ornée* – you
>   and the moon must drown
>
> together. Go on, then,
> where glass
>   waits to splinter
>
> and every step's new,
> your skates *hush-hush*
>   your water-double
>
> through that broken mirror
> where moonlight
>   hurls your shadow forward. (17)

The doubling here is not just between moon up there and her down here, but the shadow of she, no doubt moon-forged, is also emphatically not maudlin and retrospective, that kind of romantic sense, that is, but rather that sense's romantic shadow, of adventure into the 'new'. The skater is a heroine, as:

> The line behind you brightens
> with crystal, then darkens
>   as you draw it out
>
> of your perfect future.

It's the skater, here, who draws the chiaroscuro and the temporal tides (much like the poet observing and embodying her in a manner). Earlier in the poem, 'Night is its own weather'. And now:

>   Night, dark water
>
> and this is you, slicing
> the dream membrane
>   that holds them apart –
>
> when out into the pond's
> cold eye
>   you go alone. (18)

Skating on and through and past its ending, the heroine here goes alone. She has no more need, we sense, of the paraphernalia of the moon and its lending light. And it's she, after all, who slices the membrane between worlds; she who 'goes', if alone, on.

'At Käsmu' is a more continuous, straightforwardly told tale, which nonetheless holds married duplicities in its texture. Even as a more straightforward verse-gambit, it still shows Sampson's musical unities by the way it offers tensions and antagonisms across its distance, but seems to seam and gather them in, under the surface, by the end. 'I'm a visitor here', the poem's persona says,

> while I drink my coffee and wonder
> how to phrase this problem,
> this matter of dwelling –
>
> or, more precisely, of not-dwelling (19)

The people of the eponymous place, ruled once during the Soviet era, were forced to learn 'to be liars'. And as elsewhere in this collection, the discourse shifts and permits parenthetic interventions from the present. And even if, 'Existentially, such a split is bad faith', 'it's how we live' –

> isn't it? Draw the curtain
> and path, pines and painted villas disappear,
> but they could all be *here*,
> and my hand on the seam makes the difference. (20)

Existentialist, forced unilinear willing, is subordinated to the homelier duplicities of narrative and its humane exigencies. And this minor split is emblematic of how the second colonizing theme layers with the first; this second, more personal one, has to do with the poem's persona and the sometime impact and/or influence of a mother figure. Now, however,

> walking down to the beach
> beyond the trees, I'm still practising,
>
> neither Alpha-*femme* nor dyke
> but as it were *entre-deux-guerres*. (21)

Though the persona – who's spoken and speaks of these two-placed wars about, ultimately, identity – dreams 'of something fixed', it remains the case that 'history completes me too, / and I dwell on water, / that endlessly-adapting ground'. As in some of her critical work, Sampson's ideal is a self and sense of self that is stable but also rigorously susceptible to change and growth or development. The poem's last three lines, invoking a father now, by contrast and/or complement:

> *People who have minds can change them,*
> my father used to say.
> I love whatever changes. (22)

Earlier in the poem this salutary split, or duplexity, is named as, rather, and in, quite good faith:

> Look how each bird's double,
> reflected beneath it,
> completes the fraction. (21)

'In A Chalk Landscape' ends with the 'confounding' of 'imagination', which is to say, suggests the unreachable reaches of some targeting and/or targeted configurative endeavour; but the middling-named 'Nel Mezzo', by turns ends:

Instead, I listen
for the weather warnings
that will make sense of this
as we were promised –
We were promised it all. (34)

That last line conflates optimism with scepticism in an ironizing doubling act; we'll never know if that promise was fulfilled or not – we're promised that ambivalence, as it were. Much as in 'Communion', not only is God questioned and doubted as the mere giver of death rather than wondrous life, but the ending, by keeping steadfastly inquisitive, continues, goes on, past the last line with a questioning that also questions itself:

You who are animus
and blood,
who make me dust

from this table
blown into glass
invisible –

is it you or me
I pass
and cannot see? (16)

Or, much later, the last three stanzas of 'Vigil' evoke the amphiboly of a liminal place between, so to speak, nightfall and dawn:

but make me sleep –
hopeless, whole,
attended
by each nightly ghost –

to wake at last
in borrowed skin
clothing a shame
that Love let in

You whose daylight
thrills the nerves –
burn me now
as I deserve. (58)

The Deity addressed and apostrophized here is not, again, a clear and distinct one; He is rather, as is His implicit is-ness, texturally complex. Ending 'The Door':

> But even as melody's
> atomised,
>
> losing its memory
> in the plural
>   beat of the city,
>
> you hear that low C pedal.
> Buried tunes
>   like grief, but walking. (40)

The roughness of the music endures through the terrors of that kind of victimhood that is intended by that same, proverbial term. While the first epigraph to the collection is a paragraph-long parsing of the phrase, and in different traditions and tongues, 'rough music', from E. P. Thompson, the second comes from Emily Dickinson: 'I cannot dance upon my Toes – / No Man instructed me' (9). That note of defiance undergirds this collection, without ever being brash or overly forthright. Because, as in 'Charivari' (another version of 'rough music'), it's

> [d]ifficult
> to keep hidden,
> bad blood leaks
> around what's given. (41)

Sampson's way of going on, goes on despite the roughshod nature of a disenchanted experience, opting instead to be like rain on a window, lucid, of course, but also truthfully waylaid. In 'The Rain-glass' the 'Flawless water – blank, like a lens – / lies where it's least expected'. And the poem closes with the lie or lay of the unexpected – of what was out there, being described, becoming an illumination for self, in here and as disclosed:

> some drop of you
> undressed and new. (46)

The 'ought', thus, emerges from the 'is' and 'will be' from 'was' – without however conflating the vital distances between them.

Haunting Ambivalence: Reading Fiona Sampson's *Coleshill*

> demonstrating beauty
> is a kind of humility (*'Bee Samā'*)

> where the self echoes entire –
> the outer to the inner call ('The Soloist')

> *What gives you life's the thing that kills.* ('Psalm of the Coleshill Washing Lines')

Introduction: a genealogy of shadows

Let me begin with a genealogy, but a genealogy that starts from the future. This inverted metaphysical mechanism proving true to much of the haunting, ambivalent paradoxes that people Fiona Sampson's 2013 collection, *Coleshill*. In her 2018 biography of Mary Shelley, the notion and working conceit of chiaroscuro is put to use in at least three interlocking ways, blurring the line between being inside and outside the frame. The play of light, lucidity and dark, murkiness is noted as a feature of Mary Shelley's changing dwellings from childhood through youth and age; this insightful note is seen to potentially shape a creative and intellectual mindset close to the incipience of the occult and Gothic (Shelley's *Frankenstein*); and these two layers are cast into relief as two interlocking layers by Sampson, the biographer, noting how such light and dark plays out in her own illuminating and searching biographical endeavours (SMS 118).

Having made that note from the future, I want now to return to a dominant theme in Sampson's 2005, *The Distance Between Us*. Because in the section titled 'Brief Encounter' there, the verse mediates an early experience of Sampson's, a near life-threatening one, of being accosted by a stranger with a knife. And this experience, we will see, finds itself shadowing through the spectral poetics of much of her later work, including *Rough Music* (2010), as well as the central purport of this section, *Coleshill* (2013).

The opening (islanded) line of 'Brief Encounter' is 'Scars on a map' – thereby indicating the map of the body and the map of the mind – the mind of a poet who poetically maps lived experience and its metaphysical fruits much later in the mapping of places of and in and about *Coleshill*. The experience in question (still in 2005) is represented like this:

> time stepped out of its daily clothes: [...]
> leaving a distance between self

                    and self
where relief blossoms. (DB 31)

So far, then, the experience indicates how the eponymous 'distance' of this book-length sequence is not only between self and (many different, eliding) others, but also between past and present selves and selves. However, one key feature adverted to here, which will be relevant in this section, is how the problem of evil, so to speak, in Sampson's poetic mediations of her experience is always illuminated by a kind of metaphysical gratitude, eliciting survival and winnings from the painful episode(s). As elsewhere, it's a kind of loss and gain by which the poet's words nod to, but certainly don't wholly ratify in any way, the notion of Logos or, if it's preferred, Ratio. For when the 'kitchen knife' of the attack in question is detailed, we read of how 'Its blade has no shadow' (DB 32). Enter the paradox: how the blade, shadow-less, would seem to be thus in a literal sense more fulsome, more wounding; but not having a shadow might also indicate the redress which verse is enacting, rubbishing the trauma's echoic stain. Later in this same section, Sampson sets herself the problem:

   and
how to close this gap?
How bring *He* and *I*
into the same story? (DB 32)

Then, we learn of how the blade at her throat 'is a word / in the present' (DB 34):

it's the precision
with which the distance between us
the distance between living and dying
is measured. (DB 34)

Insofar as the word of that wound is still in the present, it seems to have a shadow; but insofar as that present word is negated by her present words, in which attacker and victim unite into 'the same story', it's the 'precision' of Sampson's representational formation that lifts the experience into 'relief', re-leaf. The distance, between life and death, is 'measured' here – which might be seen as a knowing metaphysical gesture. Indeed, if we look at 'Crow Voodoo' from Sampson's *Rough Music*, we read of how

[a] shadow
passes like rain

and leaves me
whole again. (RM 50)

It's not only the jaunty tune here that 'leaves' her 'whole again', but it's also how in a lower stanza the 'knife / whose blade / tickled my life', uses that lightsome verb. Indeed, in three consecutive stanzas we witness a poetic manumission of the shadow. The 'he' in question is seen, serially, as either 'the knife' itself, then 'the man / holding the knife'; but then he's seen, potentially, as having become her, so to speak – how in effect: 'you're my life' (RM 50). It's both a vertical and a horizontal movement here. The speculative options are parallel possibilities and they also lead onto each other in a progressive process of deepening and individuation – making Sampson's autobiographical tale-telling a parallel to her much later biography, where the speculative counterfactual probing of a life marries into the progressive definition of what is an intriguing, compelling and definitive stance on the life and significance of Mary Shelley.

The discussion of Sampson's *Coleshill* that follows will detail the multifarious ways in which Sampson continues her metaphysical probing, searching, of self and world; will continue to delineate the way she conflates inner and outer spaces; will analyse the 'precision' of her often homonymous word use and word choice, which serve the searching metaphysics in question; will see how literal and figurative registers and domains also marry, often abyssally, like Russian dolls or Chinese boxes; but also how the cogency and coherence of Sampson's poetic intelligence is able to keep rigorous unities intact between all the conceits of nontotalization, of healthy antagonism; will show how patient and agent are another binary shadowing each other across the metaphysics of this collection; and, finally, most specifically local to *Coleshill*, the dreamscapes, surreal at times, by which Sampson is orphic in the way she shadows the conscious present with repeated explorations, outside chronology, of the unconscious – such shadowing, collection-wide, such juxtaposing and analogizing, served by all the foregone features, as well.

Haunting ambivalence

When Sampson dedicates *Coleshill 'for my good neighbours'*, the community in question is the literal remit of the village 'Coleshill', but also, as we will see, the communities between her and herself, between her and much flora and fauna and between different differentiations and divagations of the same. In the 'Prelude' that follows, we read, continuing the use of neighbourliness, of how '*November / makes blue smudges / between trees* [...] */ drifts down the lane / familiar / as the neighbour / I call fear*'. Past the impressionist detail of 'blue smudges' we can notice how two abstract nouns of very different sorts, 'November' and 'fear' are personified in a way that makes them both neighbours and familiars of each other in the unity of the lyric. Instead of 'walking' in Byronic 'beauty', we might say, the temporal token, 'November', 'drifts' like 'fear'. Community, that hale notion, is married, both formally and in the elicited content, to a surreptitious violence; and the fact that it is a temporal token, seems to make fear (and ultimately death) the 'calling' of experience. A kind of sublimity opens the collection. Then, we read in the third stanza of this opening sonnet: *'Again this occlusion / this instability / of light'* (CH 1). And the light here (picking up in a synergizing way the earlier impression of 'blue smudges') is both out there in November and in here, in the familiar, fear. Occlusion and unstable light are illuminated and, in a manner, signpost the predominant features of haunting and ambivalence that mark this collection with shadow(s). The familiar in question is not just 'fear', but something Sampson's persona 'calls' 'fear'. Which is to say, for all the errant sublimity, control is also evinced, if perhaps only with retrospection. As throughout her oeuvre, Sampson's reflexive self-awareness makes all that's embodied about her work, all that would normally be viewed as effects of subliminal force, quite knowingly deployed. A bit like Nabokov's insider joke against Freud (whom he thought of as a Viennese witchdoctor), where all the narrator's perversions in *Lolita* are very much known and accepted, nay, well-nigh gloried-in by the pervert in question – Sampson speaks from and about unconscious domains and forces with nearly full cognizance.[1] Indeed, the first three poems in the collection following the 'Prelude' all-knowingly invoke kinds of underworld, 'Canto' (Dante, thus), 'Little Virgils' (Dante, too) and 'Sonnet One – A Dream' (the thoroughgoing unconscious).

In 'Canto' the first stanza starts with the poet 'suspended' above 'a dark pool'. When she plunges a hand in, the water 'breaks' into a 'splash / of black mercury'. The mirror is black as much as it is mercurial and hermetic, reminiscent of Narcissus's dooming pool; both features, that is, the blackness of the mirror and the mercurial texture, speaking directly to the infernal gift of being an artist. Then, starting the second (shorter) stanza with the in-gathering gesture of 'All of us', the archetypal significance of the black mercury, each of us no doubt having our own infernal underworlds, is parsed by seeing us all, more humbly now, as 'insects' like 'water-boatmen / dimpling the dark' (3). What I think is pivotal to pick up on here, at the start, is the haunting ambivalence at work and/or at play. She, then we, are both designated as hell-bound by our own 'dark pools' of 'black', but also are the shuttling messengers, mercuries

---

[1] For some pertaining perspectives of Nabokov's on Freud, see for instance, Bryan Boyd, *Vladimir Nabokov: The American Years* (Princeton: Princeton University Press, 1991), 160–61, 221.

and water-boatmen. Perhaps this conjunction is about how self may come to discard self, like cells, in the way they individuate through the experience of loss. Indeed, the 'dark' here is lightsomely 'dimpled'. As throughout this collection and Sampson's oeuvre more generally, it is the choice precision in word use that elicits the (im)plosive effects of her metaphysical imagination.

In 'Little Virgils', though the poet is 'seen' and seen-through by the 'night voices', they are, opening the poem, 'guides'. It seems to be a kind of transferential relationship, whereby unconscious aspects of selfhood are made one's own by hale displacements. And the poet is as real to the night voices in question 'as one of those on-screen heroines // [...] her eyes filling / with the world's tears –' (4). The deft homonymy at play here toys with agency and passivity. The eyes fill with the (hyperbolic) burden of the world's suffering; but this risky melodrama is averted when we notice the second, punning sense, whereby the 'crying' of our 'heroine' reaches out to and is multiplied by the literal viewing masses, her community of familiars, her neighbours. The weeping self seems (also) to be a mirror (a black messenger) as much as a microcosm of the world. Even if the sentiment is one of sadness, community as elsewhere in Sampson's poetics is a vital resource.

A similar conflating conceit occurs when, later, in 'I Was Glad When They Said Unto Me', we read how the birds are 'carrying the air / or carried by air' (28). And the birds, like us, readers, are caught by this 'sweet flurry // into time, / the shadow passing / through the barley // like a word' (28). It is, again, the implicitly fuzzy logic of the verse here that plays, in a second gambit pitting passivity and agency with each other – as the spatial shadow passes in a rustle through barley we can imagine ('sweet flurry'), to a more temporal shadow of the experience of loss, which passes 'like a word' (another 'sweet flurry') 'to race away / to disappear'. And at a deeper level, two antonymous senses are also pitted against each other here. First, we have perhaps the notion of serial word-slippage, an endless associative track that races away indefinitely, a feature of 'presence' indicating the inexorably vanishing-points of any satiation of desire – what Lacan would call 'the phallus' as the 'signifier of signification as such';[2] but also, the other sense of the sweetness of words giving relief, like a 'talking cure'. The Freudian inheritance seems aptly bifurcated here, in a collection one of whose major themes is dream and the murky world of the unconscious. And then, as another instance, late in the collection, in the twelfth of fourteen sonnets marking its progress, we read of how 'we' are mirrored by 'World, too' as 'something poured / and endlessly pouring

---

[2] See Jacques Lacan, 'The Signification of the Phallus', in *Écrits*, trans. Bruce Fink (New York & London: W. W. Norton & Company), 575–84.

itself' (55). Both victim and agent, judge and judged; still points as much as turning worlds.

In 'Sonnet One – A Dream', the shadow of Sampson's past is then dubbed 'the incubus'. 'The incubus is back / half-absence, half beast'. This phrase in a unitive way aptly names the modality of the whole sonnet, where Sampson's poetic persona is both inside and outside the frame of the dream. The 'formless dark' in question here is presently part of the formation of a sonnet. The half beast 'grown fat on lack' settles in, in the final line, 'to break you: break the dream' (5). It's not just the sense of her trying to wake herself up at the end which lives out a focal ambivalence, but the shadow or beast of the unconscious haunting grows fat on lack, absence. This is another paradoxical formulation playing with an inversion of senses, aptly surreal for a dream lyric. But it remains the case that redress, partial at least, is proffered by the naming and thus filling-out of those unconscious presences in the interstices. Which is all to say that the sonneteer's intelligence here constructs, appropriately, a deep-bedded unity to the form, but does so without easy or facile totalization. The orphic music of the unconscious accompanies the conscious logoi, like their neighbour and familiar, but neither like the conquered nor like the conqueror.

By the time we get to the next page, with 'Orphic' the shadows are established. The symbolic 'vixen' opening this poem was a 'silhouette' – so that the spectral poetics continue, abounding. We read of this vixen in a narrative that picks up on the earlier-mentioned central traumatic experience, that 'Her mistake was forming / like shadow in the muscle'. Three senses partake of each other here: the mistake was made in a way felt to be intimate; the mistake of the vixen is literally and spatially imaged by the shade-producing movements of 'muscle'; and the 'forming' in question may also refer back outside the frame, to the poet forming the mistake about to be redressed, or at the least a fear made more familiar – as the 'signals' of the night are 'coarsely drawn / with ink'. In the third stanza we read of how she is 'Propped akimbo / the soiled fox seems to mouth / some vast affront' (6). Ambivalent homonymous effects here, too. The sexual scenario speaks of the sullied body and sullied mind or spirit, dirtied by an affront whose vastness picks up nicely on the 'limitless' 'dreaming mind' of the previous poem, 'Sonnet One – A Dream'. But the soiled fox might also have redemptive senses to her: soiled may indicate grounded or earthed fruits from the erstwhile sullying. As indicated above, relief is just as much a feature of these mediated experiences, ambivalent in space and in time. Indeed, some of Sampson's titles in this collection overtly nod to Christian romance-tropes, such as 'Resurrection', 'Conception', or 'Annunciation'.

'Sonnet Two – The Death Threat' starts like many poems in *Coleshill* – in 'Coleshill', with a description of the night-setting, only to move from description to blended poetic burden of prescription. The night out there becoming a vehicle for the night in here. The 'threat' is from 'A window at the road's end', which is to say, an image of light in the darkness of life's end, death. But the verb choice to describe this window 'like a gaze', typifying Sampson's poetics, is 'gleams'. And the 'autumn nights / permit this, with their mint of smells'. Smell is a shadowy not a pinpointing sense, but mint is positive in its connotation. And the closing couplet has the threat in person, 'with a knife' like a 'plumed and gleaming angel' (8). These paradoxical formulations between light and dark, pejorative and positive, reflect as it were a kind of wisdom literature; as per notes above, they seem to welcome loss and risk as the source of re-leaf and growth or individuation. But this effect, it should be repeated, is effected mimetically not discursively on the whole, via the formal features of the verse, such as line breaks, line endings, lexical choices and so on – making poetic form(s) more poignant to the complexity and textured ambivalence of any individual experience.

> When we met, myself and I,
> each cast the other into a kind
> of shining shadow. (33)

The Borgesian conceit here is made Sampson's own, as we witness another paradoxical lexical choice, pitting the verb against the sense of the noun in that last line – another way, perhaps, patient and agent checker as part of the process of individuation. And then, speaking of transformation, towards the end of the 'The Changes', we read:

> Is it right –
> to be the lamb
> who must trust the shepherd,
> which is to say death?
> Your blood is honey. (11)

Here, victim and agent, self and the resolute reality she must face, blur like blood becoming honey. In the third 'Sonnet – The Night-Drive', we read of the 'hallucinatory' that 'like a dream / [...] brings you back to yourself // then lets you slip away again'. 'Things seem to swell and stall – / blooming into close-up' (12), before reality or chronology continues. Which is to say, again in the dream world underworld, night-like, spectral and shadowy imaging have the positive connotations as well of interstices where epiphanies happen – such ecstasies between the notes, as it were, pivotal to any selfhood that hopes to develop or grow. After all, in 'Hymn of the Coleshill Orchards',

> What the wasps spoil
> is the sweetest;
> they sow the ripeness
> in the plum. (25)

But these moments of clarity in the dark, where we find 'sound filling the space of sound' 'trembling and calling / itself out of the dark / ceaselessness of itself, / unendingly re-forming // dark in the darkened clearing' (15), are clearly, here as elsewhere, ambivalent and/or more grammatically speaking ambiguous experiences, and haunting ones. And the spectral effects are elicited by lineation which toys with the darkness of self and the darkness 'out there', the one lighting up the other in its otherness, so to speak, back and forth. The 'dark' is both an adjective put to use and an abstract noun, with the two slipping into and between each other via the canny enjambments. Moreover, this last poem, tellingly titled '*Bee-song*' compounds all this with a metaphysical sense of the loss and gain in 'being' itself.

Indeed, in another bee song, the sky-invoking '*Bee Samā*", the later speculations of Sampson's *Lyric Cousins* are prefigured. We read of a hypothetical God: 'If he could be glimpsed in the pattern / of limitless addition – / but were the not the pattern' (16). God here is wished for as both inside and outside the frame, marrying empirical indefiniteness with transcending infinitude. In a way the pattern is poetic form – an abstract content which feeds into concrete content, but is not reducible to it. And then, reminiscent of a famed and paradoxical theme in the father of confessional writing, Saint Augustine, Sampson writes in 'Dreamsongs', complementing the above while remembering that's she's forgotten: 'If only form / were language, / if only these dim shapes / would form that word / you can't remember' (35–36). Perhaps that forgotten word is the Logos itself, the whole, or a thoroughgoing rationale that ratifies loss, absolutely. And if what Sampson as a modernist is indicating is very much the absence of the whole, making hers what George Steiner distinguishes as an 'epi-logue' in his honorary lectures from the late eighties, *Real Presences* – it nonetheless remains a failure she is able to name.[3] She remembers, paradoxically, what, or at least that she's forgotten. Or, earlier, as we read in the fourth sonnet, 'Conception':

---

[3] See George Steiner, *Real Presences* (Chicago: University of Chicago Press, 1991).

> Grace is a secret clockwork...
>   Which is true –
> we'll never arrive at that truth.
> I mean, we can never undress
> right down to how we were
> in our conception's new caress
>
> when the membrane spilled the dreaming yolk;
> when self first broke and entered self. (19)

'Grace' or the 'plenitude' of Sampson's earlier *Music Lessons* is as elliptical here as being itself. Our 'thrownness' (Heidegger) and the resultant problematic of 'emergence' is a repeated motif, not just in this collection, but across Sampson's oeuvre. And it's significant for our purposes here that the antechamber of being, where 'conception' happens is, like the poet's other conceits in this collection, 'a dreaming'. Note, too, the internal rhyme in that last couplet: the break between selves is matched by the happy, intentional falling-short of end rhyme and/or some perfectly mapped euphony. Ambivalence is truer, and more graceful, as it happens. As in 'The Art of Fugue', when Sampson speaks about her past as a 'girl' she misses, that past self is as much produced as discovered or found ready, waiting: the girl 'Whom I so nearly / and never was' (22). Sampson's fugal artistry involves just as much artifice in the art as the art itself. She is remembering a past self that was nonesuch – which may be seen as saying that the past is as elusive as the words deployed to find and pinion it. Shadows, shadowy, again.

Then, in the fifth sonnet 'Coleshill Resurrection', the road in question, 'now dark, now bright' offers 'clues [...] too vague / to make a neat Freudian riddle'; indeed, the sonnet starts with 'The dreams start in the middle' (23). Paralleling such ineffable paradox, elsewhere the world of outer nature is melded onto the world of inner: 'In the sweet growing season / something bubbles up in me' – the growing of flora blending into a more seasoned self. For 'Sometimes skin / weeps, when you can't bear to' (24). Here, the ambivalent shading-into of different spatial perspectives is compounded abyssally by how even one of those perspectives, the self itself fissures into surface (skin) and what's beneath; and the suggestion seems to be that this fissuring could go on indefinitely down, making the problem of emergence, which is the metaphysical problematic, again, central to some of Sampson's poetics.

In 'A Game of Cards' the poet starts in bold declarative mode:

> This is a poem
> about windows – and doors –

> that open and open
> on another story
> > just beyond
>
> the velour and gilt-braid drapes. (30)

Partly by line endings and line breaks we sense ambivalence between a more epiphanic 'beyond' for the self and the one more prosaic describing a feature of the room and its limits. And then later in the poem, after juxtaposing the present to 'Poznán's Old Market Square',

> cobbles and arcades,
> > where they speak tourist German
> because of what happened
> in the squeezebox of history:
> compress – release –
> we should understand this,
> our own lungs work air
> that thickens
> > because we grieve. (31)

Apart from making world history and the self familiars, blended neighbours; and apart from the very Sampson-like teacherly-ness of 'we must understand this' – note how that last image can be read in antagonistic ways. The air thickens with loss; we lose by air thickening in our lungs, clogged, perhaps; the air is also life-giving 'because we grieve'. And these two counterpointed senses are summed up, perhaps by the play between ending on the note of difference in a way which is formally unitive: 'what a disappointment / it is to wake / from a dream / […] of difference' (32). She is awaking here, but disappointed, waking. Later, the last line of the last poem in the collection, before the 'Coda', the ending of the fourteenth sonnet, 'Tremor', runs, '*If you're not dead you're doing alright*' (63). It's as though ending at times on such conclusive notes gives them more intension, as themselves, as endings – by being 'disappointed' in the one case and by eliding an end-rhyme in the second, despite being the closing of a closing sonnet's couplet. Again, that is to say, as per one of the epigraphs of this section, loss and gain seem to twin and tango in Sampson's poetic visions.

In '*Wait*', one entry of 'Night Music', we see

> fear
> like dirt
> under the daylight –

> fear not cancelled ever,
> but shadow-struck
> by happiness. (48)

It would seem that music of the orphic kind can bear such surreal paradox. What is it to be struck by shadow? Well, it's as ambivalent a notion, we might say, as 'waiting': a participle which is going on, perhaps, but neither forwards nor backwards. And though the fear is not cancelled, happiness still strikes a chord – this antagonism a bit like an amber traffic light, that (waiting, fuzzy) ecstasy between red and green. Or, in the eighth sonnet, 'Summer Dusk', we close with:

> Dusk's a wide, blue table
> and we're numberless as the settling dust –
> little souls, barbed like pollen
> with selfish, unassuageable dreams. (38)

Here, the 'we' in question are named humbly as particles of dust; but also 'barbed like pollen', so defensive and 'unassuageable'. Our wishing dreams, Sampson wants to say, desire itself, are replete with what Freud descried as 'beyond the pleasure principle', namely, the death-instinct.[4] Strangely, in this poem where the dream is less a dream in its literal sense, more a waking desire, there is less optimism; it's as if the underworld were more promising.

The surreal play between beneath and above, inside, out – or these dreams that start in the middle, are recouped again in 'A Charm Against Knives'. Opening the poem:

> She lies under the earth; that earth
> lies under your skin
> like a bruise,
> or the way dirt
>
> seems a quality
> of skin itself. (42)

Then, closing:

> How urgent it is,
> this never being free

---

[4] See Sigmund Freud, *Beyond the Pleasure Principle*, in *The Essentials of Psycho-Analysis*, ed. Anna Freud, trans. James Strachey (London: Penguin Books, 1991), 218–68.

> of soil beneath your skin,
> of dirt on your skin. (43)

The lying (pun, too) here juxtaposes the sense of a troubled past whose urgency traps one, unfree, precisely because it has become a part of you; now and then, inside and out, move (us) in a reflexive dialectic. In the second section of 'Hawthorn Milk', this clotting and melding of difference runs:

> You were a breast
> where I drank rusty milk
> making me yours. (49)

The poet here is marrying a kind of absence or death. For 'The taste of blood in milk / is like rust; the smell of death / is like hawthorn blossom' (50). It seems that nourishment is being scandalized, if by small dovetailing associations: 'Hawthorn stars the sky, / black against daylight' (50). Which is to say death illuminates both sky and, more figuratively, constellating destiny; which is to say, compounding the paradox in more than one way, simultaneously, the light of stars is black against daylight.

Mimicking this effect, the end of the eleventh sonnet, 'Separation' runs, 'out beyond the boundary / where the trees drink down the light' (51). Again, 'the trees' (which had jumpstarted the collection and remain a consistent image put to use in Sampson's poetry as a whole) blossom here by drinking down the light; but the light, by being drunk down, must, we feel, lose something and darken. Loss and gain, again, move and move us in a reflexive dialectic. 'Jerusalem' makes an analogous binary, pitting a local place like 'Coleshill' into, or as, a pivotal place – making here there and, well, everywhere. It is in effect another kind of 'common prayer', a kind of 'revelation of scale / as it moves through the local' (CP 25). Because when we read (in as world-pivotal a place as 'Jerusalem') of how 'White stone in sunlight / baffles the eye' (CH 52), we discern how light, facilitator of the sense of sight, is occlusive here – but also, we scent, occludes that clarity of sense associated with the principle of personhood and individuation, 'I'. For Jerusalem to be contained in Coleshill must certainly baffle the eye, but it also destabilizes the 'I'. Indeed, close by in '*Glissando*': 'To watch myself / is to slide across myself, / like pushing past a stranger' (57). And on the page preceding, cannily grouped nearby, in the tellingly titled, 'The Soloist':

> Beyond all the technique is a prayer
> that, when I need to, I will act –
> only a part of me feels free
> to shape the words I lack. (56)

It's ambivalent here, whether the poet as freer agent is freer with language and the shaping of words, or, perhaps, freer with their lack. In a way this verse, speaking of lack, also enacts it. The ambivalence in this argument is like (a) lack (of any closure), and part of that effect is produced by the enjambments and the way syntax is used. The ambivalence of 'action' in its truest sense, that of truly effectual 'decision', is like the liminal and problematic space of emergence itself, where the inarticulate, so to speak, is raided. Or, put otherwise, and in a manner directly pertaining to the above citation, the space of poetic choosing, intending, is a mystery, but a mystery, if not solved, duly shriven by the extant words which refer back, rigorously, to their absent ground. As the opening of the final, fourteenth sonnet, 'Tremor', has it: '*The metals of the pipes do not agree*' (63). And, opening, ending, it is this eminently tremulous music which refuses to totalize into conclusive or at least unidirectional sense, while remaining compellingly meaningful throughout, that at the last haunts the reader past the last page and the closing of this book.

Ways of Empathy: Reading Fiona Sampson's *The Catch*

> Rationalism can live on air and signs and numbers. But sentiment must have reality; emotion demands real fields, the real widows' homes, the real corpse, and the real woman. (G. K. Chesterton, *Robert Browning*)[5]

Introduction: Catching grace

> being complicit ('Collateral' TC 23)
>
> Dickinson's virtuoso play with metrical conservatism suggests what I'd like to call *a rule of poetic density*: a principle according to which, the more complex a poem's ideas are, the less baroque its versification may be. (ML 36)

The epigraph of Fiona Sampson's *The Catch* (2016), from Sir William Cornwallis, runs: '*Like a singing catch, some are beginning when others are ending*'. Opening with this quote serves the usual function of epigraphs: it both speaks to much of the poetics of the poetry that follows as well as to much of the poetic structuration of the unitive architecture of the collection. With a metaphysical sense about the life cycle, shared across Sampson's oeuvre, it also 'catches' onto (early on here, but also on behalf of the whole collection as well, as we'll see) specifically, Sampson's previous full collection, *Coleshill*

---

[5] G. K. Chesterton, *Robert Browning* (London: House of Stratus, 2001), 28.

(2013). And both effects, within and without, prove true more locally of the enjambments, steps and fluent borderlines of Sampson's poetics as a whole. Even though the predominant moods of the two consecutive collections are in stark contrast, that between light, joy on the whole and shade, melancholy, I want in this introductory section to hook the two in ways that may put into relief the oneness of the poetic sensibility in question, despite the very different subjective states behind the verse. Something in the way Sampson's music moves remains constant across very differently coloured stages of her life.

Emblematic of this 'movement' and these movements, I'll sample here, starting in the middle, with two passages that catch onto each other implicitly in the first (of two) section(s) of *The Catch*. In 'Leap', tellingly titled, we start with:

> Like autumn when it
> changes when
> the breeze begins
> its new idea.

Then, later, 'a copy / of themselves / the hollyhocks / freckled with bites:

> meaning that summer's
> over meaning
> that things change
> but you love change. (TC 35)

There are many things to be gleaned here, catching onto Sampson's poetic sensibility in general and in particular onto her previous, 2013 collection. The enjambments in evidence here, though far more forcefully and consistently employed throughout *The Catch*, echo some of the kinds of effects noted already in my discussion of *Coleshill*. Meanings catch onto each other here in a way that speaks directly to Sampson's predominant ways of creating meaning. Apart from the argument, where autumn (deathly, of course) is beginning ('its new idea') and at the beginning of the poem's formation too, where summer (bright and lively, presumably) is 'over', it's also apparent how the movements of senses, as in *Coleshill*, echo and catch onto something essential about Sampson's sensibility. Indeed, earlier, in (again, tellingly titled as passageways) 'Arcades', we start in a way that catches, if in opposition, to many of the nightlike openings of *Coleshill*: 'In the morning air / voices fill and empty [...]'

> one continual linked pouring
> the way arcades go

> linking and pouring linked
> and poured their speech is one
> continual discourse. (22)

The arcades here 'leap' or 'link' as well as flow; as elsewhere, the discrete juxtaposing between there and here, poet ('discourse') and her deployed perceptions ('walnut trees' like 'arcades') are – I want to continue to show in this introductory – at a meta-textual level part of one 'continual discourse'. Here and there within that global sensibility are enacted by here and there within the particular poem. And the two levels of this continuous discontinuity, textual and meta-textual, are often portrayed, aptly, in images from the world of experience that somehow also catch onto the very verse framing, forming them. In the same poem:

> speaking on and on
> in the shade under
> the cypress trees they do not
> know the morning or the evening
> when it comes
> they only know this speaking
> that rises and falls
> in them like song. (22)

Catches abound here, too (some inter-textual as well as meta-textual). The poet's (perhaps) 'raising hands', which are doing the speaking here (on and on) are meant to be unknowing of the catch of light and shade, but still, rising and falling in them 'like song' by the end, it would seem they know full well. Which is to say, there is a continuous dialectical movement, beyond the enjambments, between outside and inside the frame of the poem, making outside and inside one continual discourse – as in some of the paradoxical unities that were seen to pertain in *Coleshill*. Between collections, collection-wide and within poems themselves, Sampson is creating a moving (two senses catch onto each other here, as well) architectonic of mutual echoes. It's as if with this collection, a watershed in her life and in her poetics, to a certain extent at least, Sampson collates many of the inter-penetrating gestures of her previous verse into one book. The things that 'change' in the earlier citation above, those elliptical movements of the seasons ostensibly, are also captured – because at the same time (in the next line) Sampson loves 'change' or, put more emphatically, otherness finds itself: 'loved'. A parallel with the opening 'November' of *Coleshill's* 'Prelude' – which 'drifts' there like its 'familiar' 'fear' (CH 1) – is also a contrast. But as with all analogies, to make the contrast there has to be some continuing communal ground.

Of course, there are many more strictly speaking thematic appositions between the two neighbourly collections from 2013 and now 2016. In 'Birthstone' Sampson's grandmother's 'opals' with their 'touch-me-not mystery – // the stuffy interior out of Doctor Freud', are seen by the younger poet as 'dirty / too: foreign, vulgar even, I thought / with a tremor I didn't realize

> was sexual, was shame because I saw
> how the colours shone inside […]
>
>   the stones
> were stained by something, rumour or violence, she found thrilling;
> opals that are my birthstone, that I
> inherit with the rest of it. (TC 30)

The 'tremor' here picks up, like a rumour upon rumour, on the fourteenth sonnet closing *Coleshill*. And this catching movement is made emphatically meaningful when we notice, at the same time, the sentiments of the same kind of fear and sublimity already read into that preceding 2013 collection; that, that is to say, Sampson here 'inherits' from Sampson there. And yet, there is more self-distancing in this collection from the younger 'shame', 'stain'. Though Sampson inherits the pejorative burden, it is portrayed with palpably more empowerment as more throwaway here, 'with the rest of it'.

Before I detail more catches within the collection, hoping to tease out some fruitful reading directions, it might be best to start with the catches of the very 'beginning' and 'ending' of *The Catch*; or at least the ending before the final poem, 'The Catch', which in a manner of speaking eponymously resumes the whole collection and thus in an architectonic sense at least is lifted out of its chronology – an end that is also a centre.

The collection's penultimate poem, 'Here' ends with 'cicadas // in their eternal present / no dream / but limitless clarity / the promise

> that you will go on here
> even after
> you have left although
> you just arrived. (65)

The self-named 'you' is caught up with the cicadas out there, her music 'here' with theirs in an 'eternal present'. And apart from the evident paradox of arriving at the end, where arrival is both literal and more figurative (like a ghazal signing itself off), the 'promise' here is also quite clearly paradoxical. However, this last note will seem more potently significant after I now read the beginning of the collection in a bit more detail.

Like a double bluff, the obvious paradox of starting a collection (one titled *The Catch*) with 'Wake', is only the irony on the surface. Yes, 'Wake' opens with 'Wake again to first light', thus capturing opening and ending in the verb itself, but also, *within that same* opening duplicity, capturing the duplicity collection-wide, because of the way the near-ending of the collection 'arrives' as though to start, as already detailed. And whether we choose the final 'arrival' of the penultimate poem, or the eponymous title of the final one, it's clear that the duplex 'Wake' at the start nods to the ending of the collection in quite an adhesive manner. But there is more and more nuanced artifice and artistry in this opening poem than that typical Sampson-like nod to brainy structuration as much as mindful insight(s).

The first thing to say is, 'Wake again' is telling. It's not just the starting *in medias res*, which is very Sampson-like; but the gesture of 'again', too. It's central to the dialectic of the poem, but catches (again) on some of the 'agains' in *Coleshill* – notably the turn of the first poem, sonnet, of that collection, 'Prelude': 'Again this occlusion' (CH 1). The attitude is plainly collusive with either the reader and/or a former self; as if the poet's felt life were indeed one 'continual discourse'. But to see the full complexity of this poem whose catchy last lines are: 'feet fall feet lift / nothing to it', I want to cite it, being relatively short, in toto:

> Wake again to first light
> it's like a slim cat
> coming home through Top Field
> through high barley scarcely shifting
> tassels scarcely
> parting stems that stay half hidden
> in a dark
> that won't give up the night
> where roots go down
> any which way here's another
> feet fall feet lift
> nothing to it. (TC 1)

The notes towards the humdrum 'any which way', 'nothing to it' are foils on the surface of what's 'half hidden'. The deft, half-hidden end rhymes of the poem, the way the 'barley', 'the dark' and its play against light echo against *Coleshill*, are buried lucid signs: half-hidden, but also revealed by being named as 'half hidden'. Which is to say the dialectical movement of senses is not only caught up with the formal use of enjambments, but also the abyssal nature of this (poetic and literal) movement ('feet fall feet lift') indicates again Sampson's metaphysical sensibility, where 'being' (opening, ending, here, there, inside, out) cascades, devolving, as though 'nothing' to it – when, that is to say, there is quite a bit to it.

Other features here which catch onto Sampson's previous 2013 collection are: senses of neighbouring and fuzzy borderlines; the sense of sacrifice as the source of value, or the relief (re-leaf) produced by poetically mediated loss; as well as the (very dialectical) synecdoches that are so pressing a feature of Sampson's poetic intelligence. And whether she deploys such synecdochal imagery intentionally or not is neither here nor there. It is enough that such plosive images can be noted and noticed by the objective critical eye to indicate the intelligible oneness through difference of the sensibility at hand.

After starting the second poem, 'The Border', with 'One after another' – we can notice how it's not just the analogizing of the 'creatures great and small / all of them strangers / all of them naked as the white / moths' (2) – the 'familiar' insider play between strangeness and community, in-gathering, 'great' with 'small', 'one after another'; but that such features are also summed up *and* instantiated (serial and structural) by how at the closing (at the) 'border' of the poem, the last quatrain reads,

> haven't you arrived
> once again at
> astonishment
> at the brink of dream? (3)

Once again, the arrival at the end here, early on in the collection, will be caught up with the near-end, already cited, of the whole collection; but also, the spatial juxtapositions between flora and fauna in this poem are married with temporal ones, as in *Coleshill*. The 'dark' in this poem is caught, too, in 'astonishment'. Then, 'At Bleddfa' (4) starts, 'Back and forth', thereby enacting the same not only within the forthcoming poem but between itself and its neighbours: 'nudging each other', 'familiars' (4). And whether or not this kind of signalling from within the text to inter-textual as well as meta-textual continuities is biographically intended is not quite to the point. Again, it is enough that we can sustain such a compelling case; enough that is to say, that a common sensibility behind different moments of verse is being demonstrably effected by noticing the continuing similarities of image use among many other poetic tics.

Staying within 'At Bleddfa', the recollecting in this same poem of how 'I was afraid / and not afraid' (5) catches onto the ending of the next poem, tellingly titled 'Neighbours': 'these were new / as I was new' (6). The next poem, whose title, 'Daily Bread' picks up on the 'Hymns' and 'Psalms' of *Coleshill*, as much as other, earlier 'common prayers' – ends with some beautiful music, syllabic play as follows:

> and the word lying below it
> waiting to be spoken you can't

quite make it out what it is
humming all day out of hearing. (7)

The notion of words being elliptical or elusive is a typically Sampson-like note of self-awareness and speaks to some of the movements in her previous 2013 collection, as well as to others before it. However, it should be noted that the syllabic play in this collection is more emphatically a feature of the verse. Another example might be in 'Street Music':

Wind in the streets wind
that you remember
under the bedroom window
wonderingly. (17)

The reflexive movement here between outside and inside ('under the bedroom window' catching against 'wonderingly') typifies as I say much of the imagery in the collection. Another instance comes in 'Bora' where the argument about sound inside the verse maps onto that of its honing or 'homing' structuration:

and in your mind's ear
sound of distance and of home
making its promise that the breath
you hear is your own. (40)

Another way in which this 2016 collection catches onto its predecessor is by the way sage tropes about loss and gain are as ever cannily deployed. Indeed, in 'Cob' we have a newer 'kitchen knife' at play, one differing from that which had shadowed Sampson until close to this point in her poetic career:

the mysteries
of domesticity

are also sacrifice
each kitchen knife shining
like joy. (52)

The 'shining shadow' of *Coleshill* has now become a kitchen knife more 'like joy', a touch domesticated. So that even if in 'Stone Fruit':

My trees are troubled by a wind
that blows from the heart

> of each, a troubled wind
> speaking the word *loss* (41)

It remains the case that there is 'community' here, consolation ('a wind / that blows from the heart / of each').

In 'Insulin' Sampson elegizes a passed and former close friend ('Fran', in the dedication) from her school-time youth. From the opening: 'A face like her own / in the darkened window. Night / where the eyes should be' (32), the sorrow in this poem is compelling, with notes of the enduringness of commemoration: 'As if / the smell of her conception / were still on her'. Or then, 'She smells of salt. As if preserving / cold salt spray / the cold of her birthplace' (33). And yet the closing parts appear slightly more ambivalent: 'Little vixen / with her hot breath / and cunning' (34). One might read this 'vixen' image (an image Sampson uses, symbolically, for her 'silhouetted' self when treating her experience of sexual violation in *Coleshill* – CH 6) as speaking across the years very much like 'a face like her own'. Indeed, in one section of this poem Sampson writes, speaking perhaps of her writerly mediation of this passed friend in a way that furthers a somewhat partial identification, perhaps, while still indicating the difference of distance a poet's verse permits:

> Blood underlines the cut
> approvingly. Out of fleshy pallor –
> this scribbled response. (TC 32)

There are many ways in which the thematic apposition of catches play out, beyond or beneath all of the above, within the collection's dynamics. A few cursory examples might be: the ending of 'Night Train' on 'as if unconsoled' (46) and the title of the next poem on the page opposite, 'Unconsoled' (47). Or the way 'Cob' speaks of 'The way we used to live / in the old house a house' (52) catches onto the next title 'Stone House' (54), which river-like movement emerges into the next title, 'River' (56) – such touches and touching then named paradoxically in 'Noli me Tangere' like this:

> wanting to touch
> something that's shifting
> out of sight
> even as you
> recognise it
> if you do […] (58)
>
> for what is moving
> there already

> passing so close
> it could almost
> touch them
> as it goes. (59)

The notes here of loss in desire, where what is closest is farthest, are nonetheless written and 'righted' in what Elizabeth Bishop would call 'One Art'.[6] In any event, by now we have indeed recognized, caught onto or caught up with, some of the special effects of *The Catch*. In the pursuant part I hope to re-explore this collection in more thematic ways, discussing different kinds of sharing and empathy that Sampson seems to express and solicit. *The Catch* holds just as much sophistication and metaphysical wit as earlier collections, but the mood from this point onwards in Sampson's writing is palpably more trusting.

The ways of empathy

> The acting out of articulation is dance. Dance is the pure profile of freedom, for spatiotemporal beings like ourselves […] In dancing we make angles, strange ones, surprising and unfamiliar (to others and to ourselves); we show by doing how far our freedom reaches; sometimes we create new joints altogether […] And all this newly found freedom must be supported by solid muscles.
>
> [F]reedom is […] a connective […] A variety of behavioral structures are appropriated wholesale, and what I am is the particular capacity that belongs to this being […] of combining them in certain patterns and not others, of reaching from one to the other along certain specific paths. And my growth, the deepening and expanding of my liberation, consists of appropriating new structures and creating new paths […]
>
> [T]o be really playful and creative, one must let automatisms take over, and just intervene at key times to redirect them ever so slightly, to have

---

[6] The heuristic use of reference to this celebrated poem of Bishop's here, or below, should not indicate closeness of poetic styles. In a recent causerie, Colm Tóibín writes, 'In Bishop's work, much was implied by what seemed to be mere description. Description was a desperate way of avoiding self-description; looking at the world was a way of looking out from the self. The self in Bishop's poems was too fragile to be violated by such mentioning'. Colm Tóibín, *On Elizabeth Bishop* (Princeton and Oxford: Princeton University Press, 2015), 143. And it is of course part of the main thrust of the analysis in this chapter, that Sampson, at least by this point in her poetic career, is far less fragile than is suggested of Bishop in the citation above.

them cross each other's path [...] This of course takes a lot of trust. (Ermanno Bencivenga, *Dancing Souls*)[7]

sometimes they pause
and seem to gesture
or they could
be dancing ('Rite', TC 13)

The first impression any habitual Sampson reader will have on reading *The Catch* will be of a woman who's come into her own; a woman who – either overtly, as poet on the page, or implicitly as person behind or beneath the new effects and the new tint and tone of (what is still) the (same) sensibility – is just more *answerable*, and primarily to herself and those parts of herself she loves: flora, fauna, persons, memories and so on.

This response-and-responsiveness, for all of us, let alone that particular tuning fork known for a poet, involves trust in certain ways – trust of oneself and trust of the world in which that self is bevelled, of which it is a part. So when I invoke the concept of 'empathy' as the beeline of this second part of my reading, I am not lapsing into some trite notion of femininity; in fact – *though not* thematically or in terms of attitude and feeling – technically or stylistically, Sampson's footsteps in this collection are the boldest they'd ever been to date; the path she walks down, her avenue, is perceptibly more adamantine.[8]

There are many senses of 'empathy', taken poetically, which I hope to show are evinced in this collection: from syntactical, grammatical, verbal, conceptual, experiential both in time and space, and holding all these together, the birth of what is some respects, but only some, a new style. The 'brightness / between the trees' (66) that ends both 'The Catch' and *The Catch* can be seen to stand in vital contrast to the 'blue smudges' between 'the trees' that had jumpstarted her 2013 *Coleshill* (CH 1). However, one way it seems to me of eliciting this dominant play of sameness and difference, and all that's in between, is to think through Sampson's aesthetic here, her more revealing and answerable sensibility, by showing the interplay of pattern and structure with the unravelling or of new experience in new forms of representation. As elsewhere in Sampson's oeuvre, this means being both topographically about and conceptually about; or, put otherwise, serial and structural simultaneously. And this is actually a mirror for how empathy works, built as it is on trust. You needs must allow a certain distance of respect, be it with the outer world, or

---

[7] Ermanno Bencivenga, *Dancing Souls* (Oxford: Lexington Books, 2003), 99–101.
[8] Indeed, the second, shorter, section of *The Catch* is titled 'A Path Between The Trees'.

with your-self, in order to truly be 'complicit' with either, or both.⁹ To be with something or someone, on the inside, is premised on a healthy recognition of distance. And this might also apply to the distance in time between past experience and present. So, beginning and closing 'Bear Dancing', almost like a liturgical question and response:

> What is bear and what
> is the dancing man
> inside the bear skin […]
>
> […] and who dances whom
> when like a hand
> dipped in a wound the fear
> is danced over and over (TC 25)

Whether the 'fear' here, like the 'doubt' spoken above it, is danced over and out or (still) dances through the persona in question, is an ambivalent note ('who dances whom'), certainly, but the attitude of the verse is bold enough to suggest that for all the angst, it is being relieved via its poetic mediation. And even if we opt for the second option, seeing the 'fear' in question as continuing to play out, there is even in this case the sense that, over and over, it is or will be soon petering out.

Throughout, the above or the beyond and the below or the beneath find places in this collection of mutual trust, mutual empathy. In the opening poem, 'Wake', again, the night sky goes down into the earth like 'roots' (1). In the second, border poem, which ends on 'the brink of dream', creatures across 'your bright path' are

> knowing themselves seen
> in the headlights
> but not by whom staring through you
> as if starstruck. (2)

The poet, too, we learn, arriving 'once again at / astonishment' (3). Indeed, this 'starstruck' might be contrasted fruitfully with *Coleshill's* 'shadow-struck'. (CH 46) And even though the mutual staring-through in the citation above is also partly anonymous and ends on 'the brink of dream', the poet's

---

⁹ The idea expressed above is *a form of* the central thesis argued for in T. S. Eliot's 'Tradition and the Individual Talent'. And we know Eliot to be a definite influence on Sampson. See T. S. Eliot, *Selected Essays* (London: Faber & Faber, 1951), 13–22.

'astonishment' is nonetheless a revisiting of common ground ('once again'). What is familiar ties with, or neighbours, what astonishes. Indeed, in that same latter poem, the small things of the world are given what would seem on the surface of things a far higher dignity than would seem natural, named as 'emissaries'. Much as in 'At Bleddfa', the 'dogs / wander like clouds', 'familiars // of the kitchen / as of the wet and sunny grass'. (TC 4). Not only do dogs do a very humane business here, wandering, like clouds above, but they 'settle things / into place'. You see, as we learn towards the end of this poem, the poetic persona holds and beholds enough trust to admit fear of newness, enough trust, thus, to admit it in and to let it out, there becoming here, here becoming there, 'nothing / but a stilled sky'. So, closing this third poem:

> I was afraid
> and not afraid
> of how the day hung
>
> above the still house
> how in my mind
> there was nothing
> but a stilled sky. (5)

And then, in 'Neighbours', further happy conflations between above and below, between now and then, continue apace:

> the voices
> of my neighbours
> at the paddock gate
>
> arrive clear and baffled
> by grass
> as they sounded all my life
> singular
>
> and clear
> voices in the great room
> of outdoor voices
> that will guide me
>
> when I'm old as when
> in early memory

they arrived
while I was lost. (6)

The world of time and the world of space are not only neighbours to each other here, but permit neighbourings within each other's own separate realms. To be, Sampson seems to indicate, is to be 'complicit'. And, that sounds and voices, listening and what Sampson calls elsewhere 'attention', are overt features of the experience(s) in this poem is telling. Music is not just put to use in Sampson's poetics, but is also one of the most strident features of the way she perceives the surrounding world.

There is very little punctuation in this collection.[10] It results in both continuity and discontinuity, simultaneously: the labile music catching between endings and beginnings as much as their inverses. In a simple sense, when the reader is confronted by lines like, 'Sometimes it's just the daily bread / of thought just the visible / being itself', (7), he or she can read ambivalent senses. While literally or empirically continuous, the lack of punctuating marks spurs the reader to make distinctions, even liminal and blurring ones. As one title has it, we are 'Visitors' (15) in this collection, both new guests (visiting) and made to feel at-home, well-hosted. And both are empathic sentiments, even if superficially opposed.

Or, to return to 'Daily Bread' – all it implies of sacred liturgy is directly associated with 'just the visible', 'a cup of coffee' (7). In 'Stucco', equally, a 'bright patch of wall' speaks with its 'light on the yellow wall' a voice 'speaking to you quite distinctly' (11). The empathy at work is animated just as much as it animates. And it's somewhat evident that Sampson seems less to be trying to master her surrounding universe in this collection, seeming more to seam and be complicit with it – even more 'negatively capable' than previously:

[R]olled by an imperative
deeper than sleep
he rolls over like a wave
that turns itself over

sleepily within the sea's deep (12)

Here, in 'Drowned Man', perhaps one of the most powerful poems in the collection, the syllables enact the conceit. Sampson's music, like music more

---

[10] Indeed, the vast majority of the poems in *The Catch* are single-sentenced, unpunctuated poems, each with, on the whole, a regular number of beats or stresses.

generally, has no inside or outside. Indeed, 'his dreams swim among hers where / she hears his breathing far'. And then to end, at the beginning of day, we read how she drags him up 'out of deep tides crossing / their legs once more and morning lies / motionless to the horizon'. The use of line endings (or their lack) is essential to this music. The use of the catch as it were. For, evidently, there are many peripatetic senses which overlap or dovetail in that last quotation, and this polymorphous effect is yet the effect of a strident artistic intentionality. The morning for these lovers 'lies' in both senses at the same, both senses' legs entwined. The sensibility here, metaphysical, is anything but 'dissociated'.[11]

There is a similarly complicit music, within/without, in 'Rite' as well. Again, like Bishop's pun at the end of 'One Art', between 'writing disaster' and 'righting disaster'[12] – here's the oneness of a humane condition, conditioned by beginning and ending:

> [F]rom here it's too far
> to see too cold
> too long ago
> our forefathers
> and mothers
> making their way
> as if towards
> us as if
> towards some other
> destination. (13)

The homonymous effect, for instance, of 'us as if' being placed on the same line is exemplary of the whole collection, making there and here the same, making them and us the same – like music; 'being complicit'. Indeed, when the 'end is air' ('Dante's Cave' – 14) it's no wonder that (back in 'Visitors') 'the smells of sleep / still clinging to us /

> half awake
> we saw ourselves as they had dreamt us
> walking between them
> as they walked between us. (15)

---

[11] See T. S. Eliot, 'The Metaphysical Poets', in *Selected Essays* (London: Faber & Faber, 1999), 288.

[12] See Elizabeth Bishop, 'One Art', in *Poems: The Centenary Edition* (London: Chatto & Windus, 2011).

Distinct positions between here and there, now, then, waking and waking, seem to be aerated in this poem. And yet, the repeated 'walking' 'between' seems also to be like a spatial symptom of a deeper community between them and us and/or between wakefulness and dream. Or then, ending 'Street Music' with another touch of ambivalent music:

> [S]o the lamplight from the street
> breaks
> so all the shining things
> tremble and break. (17)

Which is to say two logics, or two grammars for the two 'so's' – complicit in how they break from each other (in order to share in each other.) In 'Song of Those Who Are to Come', we are always ending with a kind of beginning, making the (chronologically) inverted empathy and trust of the argument here internal mirrors of the fluid, surfacing enjambments:

> [W]e bless you
>
> our parents wandering
> the valley as if you
> have just arrived as if
> you understand nothing. (21)

The reader is deftly caught again here; still, though, allowed to wander and to wonder. As earlier, in 'Arcades', while 'they do not / know the morning or the evening' (22), the rising and falling 'in them like song' seems to work quite like a question and its response; just so, here, understanding nothing seems also to be covertly controverted.

Conclusion: Dwelling, or, one art

> [S]mall things reveal to you
> how you're alive and how you live. ('Daily Bread', TC 7)
>
> All the same, just as in Socratic dialectic, its one-step-at-a-time oscillation between approach and standstill leads the mind to *something beyond itself*. (ML 20)

In his early twentieth-century seminal 'contribution' to the 'psychology' of artistic 'style', *Abstraction and Empathy*, Wilhelm Worringer argued that abstract art (then, c.1920, quite deftly on the ascendant) was rooted in fear or anxiety in or at the cosmos, the world of space and time. The rigorous patterning of abstract art was like a compensation for, or reaction formation against, that feeling of dispersal, panic – the 'dread of space' contained now by the rigorous ordering of the felt and threatening chaos. However, empathic, 'representational' art for Worringer was sourced precisely in the kind of complicity, or at-home-ness, we discern in much of Sampson's verse in this collection.[13] And that this new sense of dwelling is indeed a kind of fresh start in Sampson's life might be read into the following passages from 'The Kingdom':

> [T]he fine morning smells
> meanwhile beyond and in
> all of this the stillness
> which means a start which means
> that everything is changed
> and yet it stays the same
> [...]
> as if in a dream
> of plenty as if the beasts
> hungered and fed as easily
> as the soul
> among its imagined
> fields woods and farms. (20)

Beast and woman, nature and its sublimate, the animal kingdom and, perhaps, the kingdom of heaven conjoin both 'in' and 'beyond' the lines like a fresh start; and though everything is changed, we still discern in Sampson's poetry 'the same' deeply accepting metaphysical imprimatur – an 'imagined' community, as it were. And just as in that last citation the beasts out there become vehicles for the poet and her poetic nourishment, so, we read in 'Morning', another fresh start:

> Giotto painted world over
> and over being young
>
> in that young moment of our minds –
> centuries old by now –

---

[13] See Wilhelm Worringer, *Abstraction and Empathy: A Contribution to the Psychology of Style*, trans. Michael Bullock (Chicago: Elephant Paperbacks, 1997), 4–23.

when morning was God everywhere
and all at once. (37)

The artist, Giotto here, serves as a metonym for all artists and for Sampson, too. The young moment of morning is both old in world history and old for Sampson, if we take the juxtaposing sentiment literally. As in *Coleshill*'s 'A Game of Cards', 'our own lungs' are conjoined with 'the squeezebox of history' (CH 31). Which is to say, us, 'too' like 'World', 'poured / and endlessly pouring itself' (55). And, yet, the morning here of a fresh start is very apparent in the joyousness of these verses. Because if Giotto has aged as Sampson has, both are equally young by the very same token. And like many moments in this collection as elsewhere in Sampson's poetry – poetry, which, to repeat, remains highly self-aware but also deeply responsive and accepting – the 'God' at hand here animates everywhere in time and place, honing, homing, making poems we might say that are microcosms of a more global poem.

Falling into Hope: Reading Fiona Sampson's *Come Down*

> The object of verbal paradox, then, is persuasion, and its principle is the inadequacy of words to thoughts, unless they be very carefully chosen words. But the principle of metaphysical paradox is something inherently intractable in being itself; in the Thing. Its immediate object is exegesis: its ultimate object is praise, awakened by wonder. Paradox springs in general from inadequacy, from the rents in linguistic and logical clothing; paradox might be called the science of gaps. (Hugh Kenner, *Paradox in Chesterton*)[14]

> The contemporary reader needs, more than readers of previous generations, the general reassurance that poetry is susceptible of analysis. Without this, the confidence to take pleasure in any particular poem can be sapped, producing a generalized anxiety about possible failure of response and interpretation [...] Demonstrating the power of analysis, as a general practice, is, therefore, not the enemy of a properly emotional response to poetry, but its necessary backdrop. (Stefan Collini, *The Nostalgic Imagination*)[15]

---

[14] Hugh Kenner, *Paradox in Chesterton* (London: Sheed & Ward, 1948), 17.
[15] Stefan Collini, *The Nostalgic Imagination: History in English Criticism* (Oxford: Oxford University Press, 2019), 110.

Introduction: Successful cubism perhaps

We can best lay hold of these pictures' overweening ambition, it seems to me, if we see them under the sign of failure. They should be looked at in the light of – better still, by the measure of – their inability to conclude the remaking of representation that was their goal. (T. J. Clark, *Farewell to an Idea*)[16]

Come down where a bridge
narrows
the fast-moving river
two movements
contrary and conjoined 'Come Down'

Fiona Sampson's *Come Down* opens with a welcoming and an invitation. This is apparent in the grammar of the phrase that forms the title of the collection and the opening poem. But it is also lived out in how the end of this invocation in that first line starts with a 'bridge' which 'narrows'. The bridge in fact speaks to the many ways in which this collection is more than the effect of one signal poetic sensibility and more than the effecting of poems that dovetail and hang together in synergetic ways, fording through and onto each other. The narrowing, which is far from pejorative, indicates the way in which this book is one long poetic meditation, though composed of separate poems. In fact, this introductory will restrict itself in the main to this opening poem, whose own opening is the second epigraph above. The deep community Sampson elicits between times and places, selves, selves and others, immanence, transcendence, sensations and sense making, among many other poles of significance, bridges the manifold natures of 'two movements' by which contraries are conjoined.

By discussing this opening, eponymous poem, I want to begin to illustrate that for all the oneiric gusto of much of this work, Sampson's cubism (at times), her multifarious folding of realities, is far from a record, however illuminating, of failure. Even in Sampson's first collection from 1993, *Picasso's Men*, the representation of the very makings of representation has an air of success. Using Picasso to help delineate what she feels and thinks about what seems to be a lover, Sampson writes,

The whole thing collapses inwards to a medina like a whale bone
in the middle. It's this basin I often stroke,

---

[16] T. J. Clark, *Farewell to an Idea: Episodes from a History of Modernism* (New Haven & London: Yale University Press, 2001), 187.

and think it should be used for snuff
or aromatherapy oils [...] You have a harem bottom,
it sticks out like a pleased child's
and reminds me of how it would feel to model you.[17]

And over twenty-five years later, a far distance from such comparative juvenilia, the movements between times and places, selves and worlds, succeed in their mutual and reflexive illuminations on the whole and the invocation to come down also ends up being successful: description and prescription, falling, fallenness and transcendence dance in a way which is to my mind a poetic tango evincing real hopefulness. Indeed, already in Sampson's eponymously titled, 'Folding the Real', from her 2001, *Folding the Real*, she writes of how

> while
> the given is a folding over into itself, a
> repetition, registering the possible and what's
> beyond it and drawing up to the surface, up through the
> wood and wire and stain, the print of self: that is, of what is.[18]

This, again, far earlier poem reflects on and about Sampson's earlier musical career; and even though the sublimity of a violinist – specifically redolent of some of Sampson's lifelong themes – is or remains a matter of being alone, even here the poem starts with: 'The *voice* – a print of self – which is already in / the unmade sound'. The Lacanian real,[19] that which undergirds, well-nigh noumenally, symbolization into words, seems to fold upwards here, into presence and some kind of comparative success.[20] And nearly two decades on

---

[17] Fiona Sampson, *Picasso's Men* (Newbury: Phoenix Press, 1993), 11.
[18] Fiona Sampson, *Folding the Real* (Bridgend, Wales: Seren, 2001), 39.
[19] Indeed, apart from Sampson's use of Lacan and his cognates in much of her critical work, as seen in other parts of this study, two poems in *Come Down* are titled, '*Langue*' and '*Parole*'.
[20] See here, for instance, Ellie Ragland-Sullivan, *Jacques Lacan and the Philosophy of Psychoanalysis* (Urbana & Chicago: University of Illinois Press, 1986), 131: 'Lacan increasingly stressed that the Real order stands behind and outside the Imaginary and the Symbolic.' Or, 183–95; for instance, 192: 'The Real is the kernel at the heart of psychic experience'; 193: 'The challenge to the analyst, then, is not to understand the analysand's Imaginary discourse, but to expose the Real hiding behind the dream navel'. In a way, then, Hugh Kenner's 'science of gaps' (which serves as one of the epigraphs of this whole section) – reading as he is Chesterton in what was and remains a seminal work – is endemic to true metaphysical representation (by way of paradox), and finds a more souped-up version in Lacan.

from this, Sampson is able to retrieve and recollect in *Come Down* in a way that gives the intelligent reader a sense of the purpose of poetry.

As in the epigraph from *Come Down*, above, the collection at hand has no punctuation, continuing in the same manner from Sampson's previous, *The Catch*. And the rigorous flowing of the lines throughout the collection are like stigmata of the interpenetration of the elements that go to make or configure self, selves, world, worlds; or, as Sampson titles the first, longer section of her biography of Mary Shelley (only two years prior to this collection), we have here what are very much the 'instruments of life'. Breath seems key. Indeed, enjambments – which are the predominant mode of instrumentation in this collection – themselves conjoin perhaps two contrary formal senses. They might indicate the overflow of feeling or thought; but it's also true to say, and this is a boon of the poetic form, that their opposite, constraint, periodicity, could also indicate the same, inversely. In a way, Sampson's thoroughgoing flow in this collection does both: indicates osmotic oneness and the contrarieties of the ambiguities of, and enacted by, the same. In the way in which, consistently, it effects plosive meanings, making-senses well-nigh kaleidoscopic at times, the aesthetic chosen and deployed by Sampson is neither periodic nor is it seamlessly fluid; it effects what Theodor Adorno once called 'continuous discontinuity'.[21]

By now proceeding, if briefly, to read this opening poem in a bit more detail, I hope to begin to open out the thoroughgoing aesthetic of this latest work. It's not just that, as an opening eponymous poem it seems to name the overriding concerns of the book as a whole; but that, also, it does that very same in its own opening formal dynamics. Which is to say, as read here, below, it serves 'two movements', conjoining them. It presages some of the imagery that will predominate, and in its paraphrasable argument, too, highlights some of the thematics of the book; it also serves, quite musically, as a microcosm through which to discern the executive poetic vision that runs, fast-moving and slower, through the movements of the work.

After we read, as per above, of the two movements, 'contrary and conjoined', the poem continues:

[W]here water
rushes against stone
that hands itself
like a passing shadow

---

[21] See Theodor W. Adorno, *History and Freedom: Lectures 1964–1965*, trans. Rodney Livingstone, ed. Rolf Tiedemann (Cambridge: Polity, 2006), 91–2.

> *over the bright*
> *surface of river*
> *racing away*
> *from the shock of self.* (CD 1)

The verb chosen and deployed, 'hands itself', as throughout this collection typifies Sampson's poetry more globally – both a salutary shock and a relief, both striking and bold as well as comforting. Hands of course are also proverbially busy with artwork. Then the *'passing shadow'* goes over the *'bright / surface'*, *'racing away / from the shock of self'*. The two contrary movements, 'bright' against 'shadow', compound, duplicitous, ambivalent but also polymorphous. The river of time races 'away' from the realizations of the self; and, yet, it is the authorial self who is handcrafting these conflations. As later in the collection, the egoism of defence, the ego 'organization', is both eschewed and evinced, inside and outside the frame, like two more (meta-) movements: *'through water cold enough / to drown you'*. Then, again, the *'two movements crossing / over cannot / pass but they do'*. Failure somehow still succeeds, paradoxically, *'as'*, the poem ends, *'sky steps / continually out / of the river'*. And it's not just the paradox of contraries conjoined here, sky out of river, realization, illumination, perhaps, out of the passing shadows of memory; and it's not just the miming of the striking verb choice of 'hands itself' mirrored in the 'steps' of the 'sky'; it's also, most significantly perhaps, that the sky as it were solicited in and to 'come down', goes upwards, onwards. In many ways this poem does its eponymous business via two complementary movements, contraries conjoined; the discourse and its shaping, two, too.

Regulative ideals, or, knowing and unknown

> [A] world turned upside down. ('Wharf')

> between fir trees and roses
> where summer smells of something

> she already knows though she
> hasn't yet caught it up. ('Frame')

The mark of the Saturnine temperament is the self-conscious and unforgiving relation to the self, which can never be taken for granted. The self is a text – it has to be deciphered. (Hence, this is an apt temperament for intellectuals.) The self is a project, something to be built [...] And the process of building a self is always too slow. One is always in arrears to oneself. (Susan Sontag)[22]

As she is an adopted child, *Come Down* is dedicated to Sampson's 'unknown family'. And Sampson's poetic choices reach back, as it were, to the dedication. For here are two movements, contrary and conjoined again. As two prominently paired (but spaced apart in the collection's sequencing) titles have it, the two movements in question being conjoined are like 'Noumenon' ('unknown') and 'Phenomenon' (within the horizon of the knower and the known). Indeed, the opening poem of the main, first partition of the collection, 'Deaf', like many if not the majority of the verse encapsulates, but in radically alternate concrete lyrics or narratives, the same desire at or for the unknown – becoming increasingly familiar, if perhaps never quite 'caught up' with. I will begin by demonstrating how this is the case.

The poet opens with a deep ambivalence about egoism. Sampson, as seen elsewhere, is a highly self-aware poet. But self-awareness need not mean, by any means, egoistic tropes or gestures – quite the contrary of course. She is self-aware to the extent of critiquing her self-awareness and thus, as seen elsewhere in this study of Sampson's oeuvre, is able to allow her selfhood to exist in or with, to partake of what Keats called 'negative capability'. Opening 'Deaf':

Are you listening you are
listening to the world
you think but you hear yourself
over and over the dark tongue

of world.

Self slates it-self here as much as self also conjoins with world. The contrary senses, though conjoined, are not resolved. Sampson is both listening to the world, which is a good thing in the value system of this work, as well as listening to the world she (merely) 'thinks', which might be viewed as a mode to be transcended. And then – in a different way of reading – even if she 'thinks' she's 'listening to the world', she also realizes in this second amphiboly that she only hears herself, 'over and over'. But whether that last option has negative connotations is not clear, because in this poem self becomes a part of world, no longer apart; which means what may seem a

---

[22] Susan Sontag, 'Introduction', in Walter Benjamin, *One-Way Street and Other Writings*, trans. Edmund Jephcott and Kingsley Shorter (London & New York: Verso, 1998), 14.

pejorative self-criticism is becoming something sublimated or indeed 'sublated' into its better half. Indeed, in the next, second, stanza we read of 'darkness falling from your feet / so deep you could fall through it' and the darkness of the poet's 'feet' fall in a negative sense, 'deaf' to the world, but also 'come down' as it were, falling into the world, which is itself in a manner of speaking 'deaf'. Deafness is both a problem and a solution, as contraries join hips. In the next, third, penultimate stanza, 'night in the trees' is 'like a roost of parakeets'; and then, closing, 'the dark tongue of world' rises through the poet as she falls, 'dear self dear / lonely self falling silently / mouthing through sound'. The going down, falling, is both falling into deafness, but also coming down to the truer (more risen) world she entices to come down. Even if the poet in the later 'March Lapwings' can say 'how lost / the senses are / in this disturbance', there remains in 'Deaf', as in most of this opening part of the collection and beyond, a familiarity and intimacy with that nightly absence so often articulated, invoked and enticed to come down. The roost of parakeets makes colourful sounds in all this darkness and silence; which is to say, faced (as we will see more clearly presently) with the now-beseeched noumenal, there is much hopefulness in attitude for what must remain to a certain extent beyond the ken of the poet's awareness, 'falling silently' and yet 'mouthing through sound'. Self and the ultimate reaches of world, though in some deep signifying way necessarily unknown to each other, nonetheless turn and fold across each other, becoming familiar, more familiar.

In the second (mythologically-titled) poem, 'Lady of the Sea', again, the natural world seems to stand in for the sublime reality of the noumenal realm, which is to say that elicited in the verse is that which is somehow both beyond but perhaps also regulative of the ego or imaginary issuing or at issue. Later, in 'The Nature of Gothic' we read of how

> our desires make
> currents stir
> in tall air
> that asks us to see
> something perhaps
> the roof of
> the world
> [...]
> but stone shifts
> endlessly
> into itself
> it disappears

and reappears
like hours that slip
out of mind. (CD 26–27)

Equally, the first part of the four in the sequence 'Lady of the Sea' runs:

[S]he is going
already she is
travelling
past us and away

ancient star
flying so slowly
we do not
see her move. (CD 6)

But there is more to this elusiveness than this. It is not just a regulative ideal that conditions one's searching, groping towards it; it is also, like 'sea' or 'night' or later 'snow', a way of personifying or inhabiting in more intimate images the ultimate reaches of experience. The lady of the sea, still in this first section, 'does not / regard us her / regard is drawn / back from us'; and paradox abounds as ever. The sublime reality (embodied in this verse by nature's mythoi at times) is of course beyond us, drawing us in as much as drawing us out, calling us out. And yet the drawing of our regard is not just a passive and subservient movement, as already suggested; the ambivalence of the verse's shaping may suggest in ways already discerned, that when we are drawn by the ultimate reaches of the world (of experience), what draws us is also drawing-forth itself. This duplicitous movement, between knowing and unknown, is relayed in the second part:

[C]ould she
move among us
then or what

would be broken
and fired again
what understanding
newly perfected. (CD 7)

Though 'She' is (part 'iii') 'high and far / very high / and far like / the disappearing // note of wind', yet (part 'iv')

> we carry you
> in the eye's
> reliquary
> like a mote
>
> or like a beam
> that drowning we
> could hang on –
> Lady stronger
>
> than time stronger
> than light we see you
> invisible
> and everywhere. (CD 9)

For all the progressive flow of this sequence, note how complementary or contrary images are conjoined. Wind and sea and sunbeam; the 'ancient star' and the 'reliquary' of the eye ('I'), 'a mote'; stronger than the light we fail to see by, 'invisible', yes, but also 'everywhere'. The many dual movements multiply and coalesce both within poems, as here, and across the collection, signifying a unitary and unitive poetic vision; and a way of accessing numinous experience in the immediate vicinity of versification.

Or, take the commissioned poem 'Frankenstein's Golem',[23] placed as it is before 'Modern Prometheus'. The poet questions: 'who is this [...] / in a landscape / not yet given / form by daylight'. The landscape, the natural world is not yet a 'given' for the 'golem' as well as not 'given / form'. These two sliding senses differ as much as they coalesce inside and outside at least two frames – Sampson and her poem, and Frankenstein and his outlandish creation who is yet to con-form. The fact that it is, as elsewhere, the nature of the gothic at issue, is clear when we read of how this 'who' in or at question 'was lifted / not by love / by power alone'. Poor creature, as he is

> forced to pass
> again through his own
> dying who
> slips away
> between rocks. (CD 11–12)

---

[23] This poem, commissioned as others are in *Come Down*, was composed at the behest of the Bristol Festival of Ideas.

The monster forced or enticed to come down into existence, to fall, is forced or enticed to fall again. The fall into the knowing or the known elides that latter as well. And, yet, in 'Modern Prometheus', following, this fallenness is seen in a more positive light, if redolent still with ostensible darkness – two (consecutive) contrary accounts conjoined. The 'Modern Prometheus' is 'a live thing / not yet separate from the dark / soothing his nakedness'. The dark doing the 'soothing' here (again a bold and yet comforting verb choice, typical of Sampson) is a lighter burden for one not yet separate from it; one that is to say, not quite fallen. However, the earlier wish for 'companionship', 'someone to see yourself by', is defied by the closing, of how 'he recognizes / the one he turns away from'. The dialectic of Nature, or as it stands in for noumenal reaches, revenges it-self against man for his very unnatural and fallen endeavours and experiments with what remains at the last beyond and 'unknown' still. Whether it's Frankenstein or his outlandish creation, 'he listens without realising / hears rustling / doesn't want to be alone / as night listens back'. This of course recoups some of the duplicitous movements between subject and object worlds that were apparent in 'Deaf' and 'Lady of the Sea'. Here, this quid pro quo is again both a vengeance and a companionship, of the unknown upon the presumptuous knower or known and of the unknown coming down to know the known and the knower. The untoward fallenness of attempts at familiarity with the unknown has its rewards as much as its punishments. The chiaroscuro, the moral occult of the gothic,[24] seem to haunt as well as inhabit this work, close in time to Sampson's major work of biography, *In Search of Mary Shelley*.

Indeed, in 'Noumenon' the (re)sounding (syllabic) presence of the opening falling movement of 'Snow falls and fills a valley', 'falls like something speaking / noiselessly into silence'. The noumenal is empathized with in parts of this poem; the unknown, it is intimated, invited to become familiar, however distant it may still remain. The noumenal ('snow' here) is 'something that's all alone / in silence can't hear / itself'. The dreamer in this poem who is both called to and calling of the snow coming down – the dreamer recognizes in her own dream of snow coming down that 'falling snow cannot feel / the world it longs to touch'. The snow is like the 'golem', monstrous, sublime and alone. And yet, the poet and/or dreamer is able to empathize and personify in a way that makes the resolute coming down welcomed, if not invited.

[I]n the dark the sleeper dreams
snow is falling on her pillow

---

[24] I owe my use of this term, 'moral occult', to Peter Brooks' *The Melodramatic Imagination: Balzac, Henry James, Melodrama, and the Mode of Excess* (New Haven & London: Yale University Press, 1995).

> as wide wet words the night
> speaks about itself snow
> speaking the words for night. (CD 16)

The contrariety of movements conjoined here are vertiginous. Among them – snow, white (light-giving) – is part of the darkness; snow is dark with its own absence (night) as it is dreamed into the presence here of 'wide wet words'; and snow is light again as it speaks, a deployed image, for night. And so on, the poet seems to intimate.

I will close this part by visiting some more overtly intimate pieces. In 'Mother as Eurydice', 'she was beautiful / in ways impossible / to understand'. This retraces in a more intimate way some of the ground already covered. But it is also interesting to perhaps discern (in a collection where Mary Shelley is redolent) identification with that same Mary Shelley, and the monstrosity as it were, of having an absent mother, Mary Wollstonecraft. The impossibilities of grasping, then, are not just to do with metaphysical observations about the grounds of being and/or experience, and what Strawson calls in his work on Kant, 'the bounds of sense'[25] – but also about the ground of one particular (part of) being or experience. Indeed, in the long sequential poem, 'Boat Lane', a poem dedicated 'for my adoptive father', a series of recollected scenes and gestures make up the long sequence, but the narrative design is not quite serial or chronological. Near the opening (and reprised close to the close) we read of how, 'once again / and for the first time // I am following / my father'. Like the contrariety in or of 'Cold War: Afternoon', where we see a similar metaphysical gesture of 'once again / and long ago' – temporal as much as spatial bearings are both condensed and displaced in this intimate and touching poem, 'Boat Lane'. The 'sea' (again) the poet's persona, following, is led down to 'remembers how / all of this // belonged to it / once before', as much as further along the poet knows 'my grandparents // live here time / without end'. Again, that is to say, the world's most sublime natural reaches are mirrored and conjoined with far more intimate ones, whether in time or place. Indeed, the poet follows 'the lane / leading towards / them and away' – contraries conjoined here across two short flowing lines. And much as the sea 'murmurs *loss*', earlier the 'owls flutter / like rags trapped // above the tideline / calling me / out of sleep / *wild child / wild child*'. The wilds and the wilderness of 'out there' are married onto the self-awareness of the poet, unknown, wild and yet still errantly familiar as such to herself. '[B]ut still

---

[25] See P. F. Strawson, *The Bounds of Sense: An Essay on Kant's Critique of Pure Reason* (London & New York: Routledge, 1999); see in particular, p. 16, where Strawson dubs this basic aspect of the Kantian framework, tellingly, as 'the principle of significance'.

the waves / lie and lie / the sea is never / satisfied'. That choice of line-ending is more than just a musical choice: 'the sea is never' means just that, as much as it overflows onto 'satisfied'. Which is to say, as much as the poet calls down her adoptive father via the reaches of memory, the recollection is tarred with loss, the known somehow still unknown; or perhaps, better, the known returning to the unknown. The poem closes with the poet following again:

> I am following
> my father
> who belongs
> to marsh water
> and to the sea

Marsh water and the sea make here and there, the vast unknown and the more familiar vicinity, neighbours, as much as contraries conjoined.

Some searching mythoi

> [B]ecause film judders
> in the yellow doorway
> of early memory
> before the words come in
>
> her gaze was
> a blue
> burning gasp
> terrifying perfect gone. ('Mother as Eurydice')

As already indicated, *Come Down* makes deft use of many known and unknown mythoi. Such skilled use of known patterns to tease out unknown (as yet) personal territories is not a foreign or new move for Sampson. Much of her previous work does so as well. But it remains the case, as will be demonstrated by some present readings in this part, that in this latest collection Sampson's use of mythological references and patterns is made far more idiosyncratic and searching. There is less overt conclusiveness and more enquiry, as though in this work, which comes down to us only a couple of years past Sampson's 'search' for 'Mary Shelley', she is now readied, emotionally and intellectually, to do bouts of more intimate searching of herself, her past, known and unknown. All that said, however, even in the poems discussed below, which make overt allusions to mythoi, the same metaphysical gestures continue as in other less overtly mythological tales, such as: dreaming, waking, turning and folding, the moral occult of light and darkness, coming down, falling and going up, ascending and the resolute play between the animate and inanimate worlds, interpenetrating each other with life, the life of the poet's searching feet, her wandering, wondering footfalls.

In 'Line, Manticore', an invoked, invited mythological creature equivalent to the more well-known Sphinx, there is a Socratic dialectic between what, in her honorary lectures, *Music Lessons*, delivered in 2010, Sampson dubs 'approach' and 'standstill'.[26] A poem made up of a sequence of six parts, six parts which dovetail and echo with contrapuntal effects, such as variations on and about cognate imagery – part 'i' opens with the same melding of self and world we have come to know in this collection so far:

> The line that is a creature
> scratched in stone is
> also a line of light
> lipping along the mineral
> edge of itself.

The inanimate record, animated here in a way also illustrated in the section of this study on Sampson's *Limestone Country*, is lit up and illuminated; and note how it is not just the intention to tease out of the inanimate record the human and humane truths buried and scratched-in therein, but that this play between the 'edge' of two worlds, past and present as much as anything else, is lived out in that canny verb choice of 'lipping'. Such small poetic decisions seem to be microcosms of the whole poetic conception and execution. As elsewhere in this collection, the past, gone, 'speaks' or 'mouths' through the poetic vision of the poet's searching gaze, searching ear, searching tongue.

In this 'holy stone', 'man shines and burns', and the cut of line in stone is 'like tears / that absorb and spread / brightness its mineral / grain comes to light'. The cut of line in stone is lit with the fertile ('grain' may be seen as a pun) animation of the past as much as the same of the poet's reading of the 'line that is a creature'. The cut in stone, thus, belongs both to the line out there and the lines in here. Indeed, part 'ii' invites the reader to 'Come touch the cut and feel / it open pale lips / that were spread already'. Invocation

---

[26] See Fiona Sampson, *Music Lessons: Newcastle/Bloodaxe Poetry Lectures* (Newcastle: Bloodaxe Books, 2011), 20.

again, the drawing-out of what has already been drawn out, in, again – but also the trope, much redolent in the collection, of speech, or of speaking out. The section ends:

> [C]ome
> hold my hand so we
> can fall hand in hand
> together through the air
> as we breathe it.

Falling, coming down into breath, in a poem that starts with a line buried in, if speaking out from stone, is the kind of magical paradox we have come to recognize in some of the dynamics of Sampson's use of imagery. But the dialectic goes on. Even if, starting part 'iii', 'Nothing much except / intention remains / of whoever scratched / a human beast into the wall', part 'iv' redeems with, 'Wet stone smells / of lost meaning smells / of mysterious / wise intention / the unlived-in stonework / drawing back from us'. And, again, that drawing-back is both a distancing and an enticement; because the stone in question (part 'v') is also 'blood-warm' when it draws from human touch 'a trace of oil'. Edges (turning points) between worlds are everything, as much as they are so for Sampson's short, flowing lines. Indeed, ending in part 'vi', 'The line that is a creature / meets itself coming / the other way' in this 'marriage between / man and beast / who are one flesh holy / and fallen'. The man and beast here are both a literal demarcation of the nature of the 'Manticore' in question, half man, half lion, but also put to use in the evident, more symbolic, sense of the poet breathing life into both what she sees and feels and/or what she is made to see and feel – the line in stone mirroring her own lineation.

'Juno's Dream' is also busy with conversions and inversions, moving, movements, which are both contrary and conjoined. It's not just that Juno is presently in the underworld of 'dream', but that this matronly goddess 'lies / under the earth' 'as her bones make / a white sickle / as her skull / fills with the roots / [...]as she / *barks* her mouth / full of the good / earth'. It seems thus that she who has come down is now going up again. But the way Sampson tells this magical tale is full of tensions, dramatic and lyrical. A 'white sickle' may well till and turn the earth, but it echoes with the pursuant 'skull'. Her mouth, not just mouthing, but 'barking', full of goodness and of the good earth, is both in a literal sense stoppered of course, but also expressed in the flourishing she enables above her. She is 'changed' in this poem as 'the dream turns' and the poem ends with her 'running / towards us / running through / the turning earth / towards us she / is almost home'. One can't help but feel the identification via the dreaming mythological goddess with Sampson's own searching after and for home. The turning earth turns like, well, the turning earth of reality as we know it, but is also an image of that kind of transformation that verse such as this, employing known mythological patterns, makes use of to search at and for that which is just beyond, unknown as yet, 'almost home'.

The last poem I wish to sample and read in this section, 'The Last Man' is 'after Mary Shelley', referring as it does to a Shelley novel different from *Frankenstein*. But the poem, tallying with many, starts with the same tell-tale verb, as this 'last man' 'Comes barefoot' this 'first morning'. The feet again are bare, which speaks to the (now-inverted) mythos of a creature as yet unfallen in the human sense – but also represents the nakedness of the poet's own searching vulnerability. Indeed, see what Sampson writes, tellingly, around and about her mentioning of Mary Shelley's *The Last Man*, as much as many of Shelley's other novels, in her major work of soul-searching biography two years prior to *Come Down*:

> She uses orphanhood to create degrees of isolation for her characters. Of course, for her this *is* a freighted concept. All the more fascinating, then, that she seems less interested in writing family sagas than in exploring what it's like to feel unsheltered in the world at large. Such unshelteredness is a real piece of *zeitgeist*, the dark *tain*, or back of the mirror, which creates the image, the Romantic idea of the individual human who is at the centre of her own universe. To be at the centre means to be no longer sheltered by a notion of God, or even by legal or familial authority. The cost of existential freedom is an equal loneliness.[27]

And yet, in the poem at hand, the last man

> comes walking
> barefoot on grass
> that bends and bends
> under his feet
> this is the rhythm
> of prayer this
> is how we always
> knew it would be.

---

[27] Fiona Sampson, *In Search of Mary Shelley: The Girl Who Wrote Frankenstein* (London: Profile Books, 2018), 88.

'Rhythm' and 'feet', as well as the persisting trope of knowing, falling, seem to make the working identification between the poet and her chosen mythos clear, but there are other fruits as well: the poetic exploration out there permits insight to 'come down'. Fallenness is transmogrified into prayer here, after all; orphanhood, that kind of aloneness Sampson knows or has known, seems to become more familiar by way of the verse, 'how we always / knew it would be'. And the last man, at first morning, seems to capture the ancient Sphinx-like question (a well-known paradox) – new and old as it always will be. Sampson is in a manner of speaking answering a riddle, her own, in this poem.

Falling into hope

[C]lamber out
of yourself

little bare
creature from your
sleeping self? ('*Surfacing*')

These lines close the collection. Sampson surfaces at the end of *Come Down* as she 'climbs' '*out of the dream / as if from / a dark valley / into light / letting all that was / uncertain come / clear*'. Much like the structure of her previous collection, *The Catch*, which was also split between two parts, the first longer than the second – the second, shorter, section of this collection at hand is titled, eponymously, 'Come Down', and is comprised of a long versatile poem, dedicated however to Sampson's 'immigrant ancestors'. Indeed, as we open this poem, invited to 'Come down where it / narrows down / over the last field / where the valley squeezes / almost shut', this conclusive, or closing, movement also, in the next stanza, 'opens', as we are, equally, invited to 'come down / into light and dark / systole and diastole'. As at the start, whose title was a mirror, these are two movements, contrary and conjoined. It's startling and remarkable how all this unificatory visioning across the collection can still remain radically concrete through each page. Which is to say, one of the most salient accomplishments of this collection, where Sampson seems to be 'coming into her own' and, in more than one sense (towards her 'unknown family', her 'immigrant ancestors'), is precisely the way it can be seen to be one long poetic meditation in search of her selves as they come down, into a matrix, earthed by now more exponential insight.

Sampson in search of herself, she reads 'traces of the ones who left / just this morning / centuries ago'. She is falling in this section into the knowledge of a truer more berthed selfhood, and the movement redounds with hope, grace, rather than the other, more staple mythos of 'falling' or 'fallenness':

> [I]n one stone where the red
> stain spreads like something
> entering a wound
> to turn the blood that gallops
> into your ears.

Yes, there is the wound, but the wound seems also to redress itself. Even if the addressees of this powerful poem 'stand just / out of frame', they've 'always / known the light lying // along the top field / and the pear tree's / hieroglyph'. While Sampson travels, out there and in here, 'amid the ragged light / and bird-screams / of memory before / words', she sees 'the fast distant ship' which 'dreams of a child / who floats her face pale / her hair spread and tangled / like the dream'. There is a constant movement between knowing and unknowing, dream and waking, that at times makes the poem as visceral as it is magical. This is so because the girl detailed in this poem conflates with Sampson herself, the past, unknown, distant, coming down to meet the poet, like her destiny, like the fiat of the gods, for 'she is you'. As 'time folds / into another century / where you come walking / down with them // into the future / they won't arrive at', while 'three lost children' take 'the measure / of their strangeness'. The acts of counterfactual recollection, retrieval, in this poem are filled with light, hope: 'heat and juice / in the smile / of a stranger / who will never / speak your name'. '[S]mells as old / as another country / this too is belonging', as, closing the poem, 'narrowing' now,

> breathing seems
> to fill the leaves and look
>
> the old ones
> keep passing through us
> saying world is wide
> we must come down
> together into its valley.

The mutual, reflexive play between the inanimate and the animate, now interanimated, is like an image deployed for the relationships between pasts and presents and futures, which keep on passing as well as keep on being passages, breathing as much as narrowing, systole and diastole. And it's poignant that that last invocation to 'come down' is no longer as riven by self-searching and self-questioning, but is a resolute invitation to come down 'together'. Ending this poem, a poem both magical and real, this trope of community – so persistent in Sampson's oeuvre – speaks not only between Sampson and her ancestors, Sampson and the different movements of her selves, but of course is also a welcoming gesture towards her readers, who will have felt their way through the perambulations and permutations of what is one sustained poetic searching, made up of many contrary but conjoined movements. As per the epigraph of this concluding part, both Sampson and we, her readers, 'surface' at the last, going upwards like skies stepping out of the rivers of time. We are enjoined to clamber out by what has, or will have, come down to us.

Indeed, towards the end of 'Come Down' and towards the end of the book, *Come Down* – before the surfacing, that is to say – we read of 'night' again being illuminated:

and all night long
digs in sand believing she

can reach Australia
down and down she digs
and suddenly here
is wide scrubland
red rock the colour of home.

This searching-out of the 'red rock' of 'Australia', the outback from which Sampson's ancestors emigrated, ends up being both earth but also: an earthing. And perhaps by alluding to Seamus Heaney's early, iconic poem, 'Digging',[28] Sampson – going down and down here, into the good earth – is also going and coming; coming down into hope. *Come Down* can be seen to mark the ending of what since *The Catch* is a new departure.

---

[28] See Seamus Heaney, *Death of a Naturalist* (London: Faber & Faber, 1966).

Chapter 3

PROSE ANIMATIONS

Animating Places: Reading Fiona Sampson's *Limestone Country* beneath a Durrellian lens

Introductions

Fiona Sampson's *Limestone Country* (Little Toller Books, 2017) proves to be a riveting *tour de force*. While being, ostensibly, a work that speaks to and of and through the 'spirit of place', it manages in a manner to reinvent a genre or genres. Part memoir, part travel guide, part intimate diary, part dramatic novelistic narrative, part extended meditation and part exuberant celebration of different 'limestone countries' – the writing here eludes hammer-like naming. It is as various and as variegated as experience itself, without ever losing coherence and the unities that make any work of configuration poignant, redolent and susceptible to being a kind of education for the reader. And that tutelage as it turns out in this work is factual, sensual, technical and philosophical, among other kinds of teacherliness. Sampson herself calls it a kind of 'attention' that 'is patient and detailed. It's a kind of "slow knowledge" that is the opposite of generalization'.[1]

Equally, in his 'Introduction' to his (very late) book on Provence, Lawrence Durrell writes, as elsewhere, that 'thanks to them' – the dramatis personae who happened to precipitate then came to inhabit his narrative:

> I can honestly say I have experienced the country with my feet as well as my tongue: long walks and longer potations have characterized my innocent researches, the ideal way to gain access to a landscape so full of ambiguities and secrets.[2]

Or: if *'Provence is not really a place!'* for Durrell, and if it is 'paradoxical', it is 'because of the overlay of different cultures which are slowly conforming to the genius of the place, but at different speeds'.[3] Just so, life in Sampson's

---

[1] Fiona Sampson, *Limestone Country* (Dorset: Little Toller Books, 2017), 10.
[2] Lawrence Durrell, *Caesar's Vast Ghost: Aspects of Provence* (London: Faber & Faber, 1990), 6.
[3] Ibid., 32.

'limestone countries', is 'messy with overlaps and repetitions: which' she 'has simplified'.⁴ Indeed, it was 'a shock, and an epiphany, to realise that they were all made from – and in and on – limestone. Surely, I thought, this has to be more than mere coincidence. Limestone', she continues, 'has a special relationship with water, by which it's shaped at every stage of existence'.⁵ Hence, we must suppose the supple fluency of 'overlaps' but not repetitions, of dovetailings and analogies between her four 'limestone countries'. *But to return to Durrell's Provence. [...]*

This late work of Durrell's was to be, in fact, a 'compendium of poetic inklings',⁶ comprised of 'some history, some myth, some insights and striking metaphors appropriate to the glorious landscape, the whole fitted out with the appropriate tourist information'.⁷ Indeed, prefacing his earlier travel book, *Bitter Lemons of Cyprus*, an 'impressionistic study', Durrell writes how he had 'tried to illustrate' the 'Cyprus tragedy' of the early fifties 'through my characters and evaluate it in terms of individuals rather than policies' – it not being 'a political book'.⁸ Or, similarly, opening his book on Rhodes, *Reflections on a Marine Venus*, Durrell outlines and precipitates his characterological method of illuminating place like this:

> I have attempted to illumine a single man by a single phrase, and to leave him where he sits embedded in the slow flux of Grecian days [...] a good host should [...] Gideon with his monocle screwed in sitting soberly before a bottle of *mastika*; Hoyle winding his enormous watch; Mills talking; Sand sucking his pipe; Egon Huber walking the deserted beaches hunting for scraps of wood to carve, and the dark-eyed E [...] putting on a flowered frock in the studio mirror with her black hair ruffled. I have tried not to disturb them in the little eternities of their island life, where somehow their spirits mingle and join that of the Marine Venus standing in her little stone cell at the Museum like a challenge from a life infinitely remote.⁹

Durrell's aim is or was (or both, perhaps) to allow the 'common reader the feeling of living in a historic present'.¹⁰ Indeed, this particular kind of 'mythic

---

⁴ Sampson, *Limestone Country*, 10.
⁵ Ibid., 8.
⁶ Durrell, *Caesar's*, 3.
⁷ Ibid., 4.
⁸ Lawrence Durrell, *Bitter Lemons of Cyprus* (London: Faber & Faber, 2000), ix.
⁹ Lawrence Durrell, *Reflections on a Marine Venus* (London: Faber & Faber, 2000), 2–3.
¹⁰ Ibid., 4.

method', in direct continuum with his novels – where the choice work of the imagination takes the barer (previously lived, but now quite literally recollected) reality into the more poignant zone of what Durrell called 'reality prime' – is shared in many ways with Sampson's recent Little Toller monograph.

Limestone Country is comprised of a quartet, as it were, of four parts, all representations and reflections of limestone countries: Autumn in 'Le Chambon'; then Summer in 'Škocjan'; Spring, then, in 'Coleshill'; and finally Winter in 'Jerusalem'. The unruly seasonal chronology is perhaps a wink and a nod to the exigencies of what is eminently *creative* writing, a way to emphasize both: the inherently artistic and selective nature of this kind of life writing, whereby choice configuration, skewing with bold intent the more numb or staple order of things, is highlighted – and a hint at the near-mythic stilling of time, indeed the near-mythic replacement of chronology via a more ecstatic (or paratactic) representation of experience, unified by an inner clock rather than an outer one.[11]

This last observation is a small part of the reasons I have chosen to discuss here Sampson's work beneath the lens of one of her modernist forebears, a known influence on her, who excelled and in part himself reinvented writing of and about and through the 'spirit of place': Lawrence Durrell. The first paragraph of the first chapter of his Cyprus book reads:

> Journeys, like artists, are born not made [...] They flower spontaneously out of the demands of our natures – and the best of them lead us not only outwards in space, but inwards as well. Travel can be one of the most rewarding forms of introspection.[12]

It should be noted from the start that the few travel books of Durrell's I make use of in this chapter are in many ways very different, longer on the whole and more copious than the single Sampson work which is my main purport here. However, for all the differences, I aim to show how both authors animate places in very comparable and quite (literally) brilliant ways. Among other things by the wayside, I aim to discuss and to compare and contrast, as it were, different aspects of the two sensibilities at work: namely, elements of style and voice that may serve to light up each other; aspects of narrative technique and genre; as well as the role of character and dramatis personae as a well-nigh novelistic technique and conduit for illuminating the nature

---

[11] All this said, it should be noted that Sampson's stated reason for the anachronisms is to allow them to be read, if chosen to, 'separately,' rather than as a continuous chronological narrative. Sampson, *Limestone Country*, 11.

[12] Durrell, *Bitter Lemons*, 1.

of a place or places. Character after all, is shared by both authors and those they meet and by the synergy of the two, when welded with expert skill, they quite literally 'animate' place; *that*, as much as for both authors, as we will see, place it-self is (already) animate – but waiting for what Sampson would call, musically, the right 'attention'. Thus, there would seem to be a similar dialectic between place and personhood in both authors' experiences and in the (twinning) work of their recollecting of impressions and the configuring of their representations. In her own 'Introduction', Sampson writes,

> After all, how can we separate what a place *is* from what it is *for us*? Places are meanings as well as conditions. They act upon us and we act upon them, in the dialectic we call *living*. This is a book about trying on different ways of living – or dying – in limestone country.[13]

Synesthesias

The opening section (*Santat!*), opens, much as in Durrell, with a litany or display of dramatis personae being recollected in their (and Sampson's own) 'historic present':

> The Savignacs are in the kitchen when we arrive for *un petit apéro*. The stove is lit and, with all five of them already crowded round the table, there's hardly space for us. Heat; noise. Here's Jeannot, the paterfamilias, hitching up his trousers below his belly [...] Here's Madame Savignac, monumental and frowning with friendship [...] And here is Clarette, with little Josette on her knee. Clarette is the one who got away, the educated daughter who works at the *Mairie*.[14]

So, we enter dramatically in medias res. However, the one glaring feature of the opening section 'One Day', where all these personae figure in ambulant and vibrant ways, is that the writing is not only filmic, but also that there is the sense that the writing grows or grew out of the experiences, much as the limestone detailed in the 'Introduction', waxes and wanes slowly, with 'a particular plasticity'.[15] Indeed, the most striking feature of the writing in and of and through 'Le Chambon', is that it is literally *sensational*. All the senses are triggered and spurred, with at times synesthetic effect. Here are some examples of sensual style, where character elicits place as much as vice versa:

---

[13] Sampson, *Limestone Country*, 11.
[14] Ibid., 15.
[15] Ibid., 8.

> In fact it's barely dawn. When P opens the bedroom's shutters he reveals a velvety blue sky. In the west, over the river, it's still night. Only to the east, between the Savignacs' barns, can we see a smudge of purplish pink. It seems impossible that this could become heat and light. The night-freeze hangs in the air, missing the yard romantically. A white frost stands on every surface, delineating the lumpy stones of our garden wall, the corrugated lines of the tiled roof.[16]
>
> As we stroll and poke, searching for the dark green of this local pottery among the dark-green waterweeds, the thawing earthen bank beside us gives off a clean clay smell. The paddling dogs kick up a faint, greenish aroma from the riverbed.[17]

Note how the provenances of different senses are solicited and twined in the writing. The writing veers between, welds and synergizes, what are normally construed as different, or separate, aspects of visceral experience. Smell, touch, sight, taste, hearing, as throughout this opening chapter, *dictate* to the reader a synesthetic world, where the overall effect becomes somehow more than a list of sensations. As in Durrell, to be seen presently, the woken litany is more than its addled parts. So, Sampson again:

> It's quieter on this side of the house, away from the birdcage tangle of our neighbours' trees; in any case the dawn chorus is beginning to dissolve as the morning warms up. Instead we hear the isolated, almost tentative clinks and raps that reveal how the hamlet starts its day. A door opens somewhere. A car drones along the lane from the bridge. A dog bowl is dropped with a bright metallic *twang!* A snatch of children's voices from the schoolteacher's house: abruptly cut off as a window or a door is slammed shut. Someone knocking out the ashes riddled from the overnight stove. Someone, Michel or Marie, coughing down by the river. The distant snarl of a chainsaw at work somewhere in the woods.[18]

Note, but not trivially, how this list of sounds (eliciting as it were both sight and insight) reveals how it is 'the hamlet' that starts (its day.) Just as Sampson can speak directly of the possibility of 'seeing' 'a taste',[19] so at chapter's end

---

[16] Ibid., 20.
[17] Ibid., 29.
[18] Ibid., 26.
[19] Ibid., 41.

a noise outside is undecipherable by narrator, partner or pets, as all freeze at the window.

> The noise seems not to come from any one direction but instead to surround the house. Even to call it 'noise' seems not quite right: it doesn't have, so to speak, discrete edges. It is, rather, *a state of* noise; something like air pressure. Still it's getting louder and closer. The air vibrates. And now this airy teeming begins to make sense, resolving itself into a carpet of cries, into the creaking, swiping sound of wing beats. It's clearly the sound of birds.[20]

Though both writers use verbs, participles in particular, in filmic and painterly ways, perhaps it's no accident that some of Sampson's most poignant passages (and/or as with Durrell: *tableaux vivants*) are to do with sounds, if nearly always parsed by other tactile reservoirs. For Sampson has a long history of engagement with the musical, in different modes since the start of her professional life. Durrell by turns, though equally labile across the sensual array and arenas, is more emphatically painterly. To sample here is a dilemma, not because of lack of instances, but because of how prolific Durrell's synesthetic passages are. A few examples here, then; describing the trip by sea to Rhodes:

> The snarling of the great engines wrapped us all in a deaf silence – a marvelous brutal music of vibrating steel and wood. Behind us we left great stains of oily heat upon the waters and a white cicatrice which slowly healed again.[21]

In that final 'healing' image, Durrell, like Sampson conjoins sight with insight, sensation with its value. In Cyprus, later, while on his way to meet a government official, Durrell speaks of the 'ugliness of the plain', as 'so to speak, at the height of its beauty – a range of tones vibrating with the colours of damson, cigar-leaf, putty and gold-leaf'.[22] Even ugly sights, thus, are rounded as beautiful – but not beautified. Which is to say, the holism of synaesthesia, whether present or merely implicit, is a kind of osmotic gambit, not only for sensual facets to overlap and charge each other almost electrically – but also a space of sensibility, where place and its effects *are effected* in a sweetly overdetermining way. Indeed, synesthetic description might be both the sensual equivalent of and an apt modal metaphor for sight (always) becoming insight.

---

[20] Ibid., 56.
[21] Durrell, *Marine Venus*, 5.
[22] Durrell, *Bitter Lemons*, 148.

> One day we woke to a sky covered in ugly festoons of black cloud and saw drift upon drift of silver needles like arrows falling upon the ramparts of Kyrenia castle. Thunder clamoured and rolled, and the grape-blue semi-darkness of the sea was bitten out in magnesium flashes as the lighting clawed at us from Turkey like a family of dragons.[23]
>
> In the fragile membranes of light which separate like yolks upon the cold meniscus of the sea when the first rays of the sun come through, the bay looked haunted by the desolate and meaningless centuries which had passed over it since first the foam-born miracle occurred. With the same obsessive rhythms it beat and beat again on that soft eroded point with its charred-looking sand: it had gone on from the beginning, never losing momentum, ever hurrying, reaching out and subsiding with a sigh.[24]

And perhaps this give-and-take, loss-and-gain, is an apt image for the rhythms in Sampson just as much as in Durrell between immanent visceral impressions and the more transcending reflective bite such impressions trigger in us as realizations – when we pay the right 'attention'. For, in the passage preceding the last-cited, Durrell pivots between the temporal and the mythically still(ed):

> It was a good idea to surprise the dawn at this forgotten point in history – the hollow curved beach with its great finger of rock raised in patient admonition – and to listen for a while to the oldest sound in European history, the sighing of the waves as they thickened into roundels of foam and hissed upon that carpet of discolored sand.[25]

Typical Durrellian features shared by Sampson in her little monograph are adverted to by the animating tropes of persons 'surprising the dawn' and the use of soul-fuelled words for the sea like 'sighing' and 'hissing'.

Indeed, opening her second chapter, in '*Na Zdravje!*' Sampson shows herself an avid avatar and epigone of Durrell, here describing the impression of a cheering drink local to the place – *become, becoming, thus, local to us, too*:

> What we're sampling now [...] sends a glowing, pleasurable ribbon along the tongue and down the throat. Plum, quince, grape; thyme and

---

[23] Ibid., 46.
[24] Ibid., 178–79.
[25] Ibid., 178.

apple; hot earth, sunlight and a mountain wind. What would you get if you concentrated and attenuated all these ingredients – distilled them in fact?

If whisky should be cut with water, slivovitz should be cut with air.[26]

Connoisseur-ships and conserv-atives

Another motif redolent in the texture of Sampson and Durrell's prose, a motif that speaks both to the tales about and 'about' (animating) place and to the authorial intentions and methods are the gestures of connoisseurship. Durrell calls himself a 'conservative', but the political tales he tells in his fiction or in his (creative) nonfiction are never trenchantly political. His mythic and mythopoeic sensibility would deem a direct temporal take on politics, one not steeped in the more lasting and self-forged verities of character and place, as in bad and truncated taste. No; it seems clear that one of the most overt ways in which Durrell is a conservative, both formally (narrative framing) and in content, is that he is always like an avid collector of curios, a recollector in fact, whether it is as I say aspects of characteristic presences, personae, of national ethos or identity, of food and wine, of types and timbres of crucial experience, like love or death and so on. In short, Durrell's is not only a 'style' impregnating his prose, but that the latter is merely the stigma or symptom of a more global search for, and conservation of, 'style' in sucking the marrow out of a life. When Durrell writes of his friend Austen Harrison that he 'represented that forgotten world where style was not only a literary imperative but an inherent method of approaching the world of books, roses, statues and landscapes',[27] he is, like a true impressionist, speaking of himself as well. Durrell abounds in types and typologies; he makes, as Eliot would say, nice distinctions. So, here, speaking of the British failures in that troublesome time for Cyprus, he speaks of the failure in the British 'angle of vision' (painterly even here!):

> Colonial officials, trained to direct rule, will always find this difficulty in dealing with problems outside the rule of order [...] Those who work in sovereign territory have to cultivate a suppleness and dissimulation, a tactical mind and a reserve because no issues can be forced: they must be engineered. The difference is between the craft of a fly-fisherman and someone who dynamites from a rowing boat.[28]

---

[26] Sampson, *Limestone Country*, 64.
[27] Durrell, *Bitter Lemons*, 97.
[28] Ibid., 151.

This is a reflection on politics. But it is also a way, intimate to an aestheticist sensibility, of classifying types: and even if it has political provenance, it is a very apt illustration of how Durrell goes about feeding from his experience and impressions. Similarly, discriminating between the Cypriots and the Greeks of the mainland, Durrell adjures,

> [a] *feeling* of foreignness, of alienation from themselves, persisted: somewhere, dimly, they felt that this weird, padded, essentially suburban life was not theirs. Somewhere the values they sought would be found to depend on the spare, frugal Mediterranean pattern of things – the light-intoxicated anarchy of Greece always leaped at them like a panther.[29]

A situation is animated by distinctions of national ethos. Persons are (soon to be) determined by the skyscape and sea of the Mediterranean. It is a 'feeling' that is being gauged. And in that dim and repeated 'somewhere' the hallmark of a rabid impressionist makes itself felt. The 'panther' is not only a brilliant touch, but is, again, an overt stigma of how different areas of animation may (come to) 'light' each other up. Indeed, if Durrell's style is bold, muscular while remaining highly sensitive, his voice always incurs a sad touch of irony, a light(er) touch. There is always the sense that for all the strumming of the deep-bellied cello-like notes, laughter is not far away.

In parts of *Limestone Country*, the same could be said of Sampson. However, look to the title and the opening of the second Chapter: 'Elegies and Ballads'. Romance and loss are evinced in this section of the book, a section very different in narrative technique to the first. If in the first there is a sense (actually less like Durrell's commanding recollecting mode) of the writing being wholly immanent to itself, reflecting and reflected moment to moment as it were, here in line with the romance notions of the title, there is closure so to speak from the beginning. In other words, there is an overtly worded story arc of a beginning, middle and end. I will cite here the opening and closing of the chapter:

> This is the story about the former Yugoslavia, and about how sometimes it becomes necessary to visit a place only after you've fallen in love with it. Or maybe it's about how narrow the gap is between the people we love and the places where we love them. Or else this story is about how ideas and dreams, stories and proverbs, create the places that mean something to us. It's certainly the story of how a particular

---

[29] Ibid., 139.

place is highlighted and shadowed by death […] the high, half-forgotten limestone country that the tragic Slovenian poet Srečko Kosovel made his own a hundred years ago.

We have jumped back in time with this chapter. But we are overtly told so: the writing is valedictory not only in content but in temporal mood. She starts the next paragraph: 'To begin with[,] though, it was just a dream of the good life. My lover S was Macedonian but I worked in London, and we used to fantasize about ways to stay together'.[30] And the last passage of the chapter runs:

As we lie in the late sunlight that warms the pebbles of the riverbank, what we feel is a kind of fullness; as if the things we need in life might all, for once, have come together here.[31]

At a purely formal level, note how the beginning opens on a tragic note, the ending on one close to that of plenitude. Both modes and both conjoined at either end of a more controlled or controlling narrative (than the first chapter) are romantic. And in this chapter, with the very executive conceit of telling a finished or already-made story, Sampson shares with the Durrell of the travel-books made-use of here, a kind of meta-fictional conceit, where the author is both inside and outside the frame of then, as now. Indeed, in *Caesar's Vast Ghost*, *Reflections on a Marine Venus* and *Bitter Lemons*, Durrell's narrative persona (unlike in his novels, to a certain extent at least) is very much himself, and he often prefaces those narratives with metafictional talk, *metafictional planning*, about and 'about' the very work underway beneath the wave-strokes of his pen. In this sense, *both* Durrell and the Sampson of the Summer in 'Škocjan', are conservatives.

Like Durrell, Sampson makes use, here as elsewhere of historical contexts like wars and the experience of wars, within a more global piece of (personal) memoir. Larger contexts are compounded with even larger near-mythical contexts; the blurring of boundaries (already detailed in part) of persons and place, persons and their intra-personal spaces over time, persons and others and these with or against historical and political contexts, all unified and resumed in the authorial take of things by the repeatedly mentioned 'bowl-shaped' topographies endemic, we gather across the work, to 'limestone countries'. Indeed, all the above dramatic and dramatized tensions typify the lessons one might give about how to write 'creatively'. One might almost say

---

[30] Sampson, *Limestone Country*, 65.
[31] Ibid., 113.

that there is thus a more than trivial sense in which creative writing and non-fictional writing bend and swerve into each other in Sampson, as in Durrell.

That said, Sampson is also interested in facts; indeed, one instance made use of as a unifying literary device, one of a won or newly won connoisseurship, is the way Sampson peppers her mix of memoir, diary, meditation, storytelling and her eliciting throughout the genii of places – with Latinate names for all the flora and fauna she comes across. These discoveries, as it were, *in Latin*: a romance, then, of finding romance there, waiting, for or with the right 'attention'.

> I like the way the Coleshill snowdrops don't know whether they're wild or cultivated. *Galanthus nivalis* is regarded as naturalized in Britain now; but it's not *native* here as it is on the European mainland. The drifts of bulbs we're here to see, spreading for yards between the trees of this elongated little copse, were originally planted by gardeners for the Coleshill Estate – how many centuries ago? One? Two? Even three? I touch down on the driest slope I can find to try and catch their perfume. The dogs wonder what's going on. They push their muzzles in my face, giving me quick interrogatory licks. But what interests them more are the innumerable, much stronger odours that the February damp has loosened. Rabbit, fox, rat? We guess – and they know.[32]

It's not the interested, interrogating dogs that tell here, so much as the snowdrops which beg to know if what they are themselves are wild or cultivated. Indeed, we might infer from this and all noted so far, that just as both authors use dramatis personae as conduits to illuminate place, the very continual gesture of ventriloquism, vicarious staging, is as it were a writer's way of eliciting for him and/or herself insights and expressions of insights that take wing and are somehow more to the person than the erstwhile person. It is magical, alchemical, or, as Durrell would say: 'heraldic'.

Indeed, echoing (layering, 'overlaps' again) with apt tension the already-cited opening of the second Summer section – opening the third, in 'Spring' again, at 'Coleshill', we find the following passage; it echoes, as I say, but in a different way, the mutual play of two kinds of romance – between the gasp of shock and the gasp of relief. Opening 'Parish Map', then:

> Being a tourist is easy enough. But how do we map the localities we know really well, the ones we don't choose to explore but where we find

---

[32] Ibid., 135.

ourselves – often with a slight sense of surprise, as if waking up from some long sleep – spending our actual lives?[33]

Sampson is, overtly, a connoisseur of the place here. And yet: Spring here follows Summer; *and yet*, the opening passage is phrased as *a question* – perhaps for a reason? *And yet*, that is, there is more to be said […]

Conclusions: from 'Parish Map' to 'Jerusalem' or, closure and exile

I force myself to concentrate. You're saying how much you'd love to go to Jerusalem. The place itself, you're saying: all those layers of settlement like sedimentary rock formation. You think it's the sort of city photos tell us almost nothing about. It's not the facades that matter, you insist, it's what's underfoot.[34]

This is an exemplary passage, starting as it does the third, 'Coleshill', section – and for many reasons. The note of the culture and of cultivation meeting, place and personhood, again; the return, chequered, to the temporal mood of the first chapter, skipping over the head of the second, which was more emphatically a story related from a distance; and, perhaps most importantly, if we're scenting out a modernist animus against chronology in favour of a historic consciousness that involves parataxis and dovetailing, analogies and juxtapositions – this nod to Jerusalem comes a section before the section so-named, as though all the four 'limestone countries', being of the same rock, interpenetrated each other in the personal experience as much as any global sedimentary community. Also, by thematically jumping between this third chapter, a 'Parish Map', and the fourth-to-come, at 'Jerusalem', we would seem to have a comprehensive gesture; just as much as the first section, 'One Day', is by titular trope here and execution, proto-Joycean, so the titular move from a 'Parish' to a world-pivotal place like 'Jerusalem', would seem to be a gesture of totalization and resumption – if with a light touch […]

Three early notes on Sampson's 'Parish Map', then. First, she reflects, again, between the gasp of shock and the gasp of relief; flexes between the romance of what we, questing, may find, and the more conserv-ative romance of knowing where we stand, mapped as we are, by and with quiddity.

---

[33] Ibid., 119.
[34] Ibid., 117.

We can locate ourselves: on the weather map, in the train timetable, by the echo chamber of local accents and familiar voices. Some of this is yawningly familiar; some of it we don't even recognize we know.[35]

And again: the breeding liminal ground where person and place inform each other. Then, here are two passages in the tradition of the Durrell elicited so far. First, and like Durrell, Sampson names the complementary sedimentation, complementary to that of juxtaposed limestone countries, of culture in a place, its burdens of animus or anima; second, the motif of 'map' and 'mapping' becomes, as in Durrell, a metaphor for self-discovery, a trajectory of self-realization(s) [...]

> What I really think is that this village I know so well is less a vital, living ecosystem than a map of its own history and geography – of how it was made.[36]

> Ownership imposes limits, something English hedges ('vegetable walls', as a Romanian friend calls them) have long marked out on the landscape. In a way maps limit us too. To be 'off the map' is not to count: to be mysterious, unknown, forgotten. The edge of the map is the limit of the known. And yet. To map is to unify, to draw together the disparate pieces of knowledge that make up a place. That delightful arcana of Ordnance Survey symbols – windmills, cuttings, and contour lines – says, in part, there are *all these things* making up a landscape. And browsing a map is one of the most pleasurable forms of reading; a way to take an imaginary journey through a place you don't yet know.[37]

To recoup, the discernment and the pleasure here are ones of (incumbent) connoisseurship. As with Durrell, there is the sense of discovering, realizing new senses; but senses that, for all their brilliance and quested-significance, were perhaps always there – waiting for the right 'attention'.

> The fossils I have always picked up and discarded when we walk our local fields in spring are like nothing so much as rumours, hints of a radical past in which countries rose from the water and fell back into it.[38]

---

[35] Ibid., 119.
[36] Ibid., 120.
[37] Ibid., 121.
[38] Ibid., 164.

As with Durrell, the wax and wane, the wavy transpiration of geography and topography, are metaphors, dialectical images, almost, for the self: engaged with and about and through them. It is as I say a kind of mythic or at least mythopoetic method. Closing the Coleshill section, 'the only barn owl from Middle Leaze [...] maps her hunting ground methodically, up and down over the dark acres [...] It's not so bad, after all, to know that she'll still be here when we are gone'.[39]

And it goes without saying that Durrell's list, cited earlier, his almost shopping-list of what was to be included in his Provence book, myth, history, metaphor, insight, travel-guide and so on – is both named and spent through Sampson's own descrying of the genii of place. Indeed, this mapping chapter is the most overtly, as it were, factually informative – as though to offer a long and enduring lesson in geography (and history) were a way, like Durrell's own 'travel', cited earlier, of 'introspection'. Even the sensations of the weather are maps of personal experience and personal realization: 'In the brisk early-spring air, everything ought to feel as though it's starting. But today even the dampish, earthen twang to the wind no longer smells of possibility, but loss'.[40]

And speaking of possibility, of loss: now, at the close of the final chapter, 'Winter' in 'Jerusalem' – winter before spring, as it were – we read of hope and of its dire slippage:

> The light makes everything dreamlike. There's haze: a dustiness settling at the bottom of the sky. In this version of limestone country, it's impossible to see anything clearly. Still, the light says: hope. What can we do but hope? From far away, it is what Jerusalem represents. For those who live at close quarters, that hope is mixed.[41]

The liminal mix, the back-and-forth, the give-and-take, the dialectic of how things – this thing (called) 'living' – transpire, is lived out by sights and by their entailed, incumbent in-sights. As with Durrell, both in general, but also peppering his books of place – Sampson, a prolific and distinguished poet in her own right, ends with the quotation of a poem by Mahmoud Darwish, translated by Fady Joudah. The last line reads: 'I said: You killed me [...] and I forgot, like you, to die'.[42] To paraphrase part of the opening cadence of Durrell's major fiction, *The Alexandria Quartet*: in the midst of winter we can feel the inventions of spring. [...]

---

[39] Ibid., 169.
[40] Ibid., 121.
[41] Ibid., 228.
[42] Ibid., 229.

At the conclusion, then: an image of closure; and yet, an image of prolific exile, as well.

In the second section of this chapter I go on to discuss a second inspired prose transpiration of Sampson's, her acclaimed biography of Mary Shelley. In the section that follows, while I certainly do not make any thoroughgoing comparison with another author (as with Durrell, in the case just past), it does still remain the case that Sampson's soul-searching work is just as redolent with play between self and other. Whether it's the auto/biographical parallels between her subject and herself, or between the various instruments of life that enliven her working-through of the life in question, Sampson's inquisitive mode and manner shows and tells again in ways that are replete with crossovers and cross-currents. As ever, many of the truths in Sampson's work reside at the liminal space of the frame, where being outside and in oftentimes merge and multiply fruitfully. And the frames, borderlines, that in part at least form many of Sampson's works are where her self-awareness as a writer are or become, turning as it were, most self-aware. The distances between on the surface different limestone countries commune in a paralleling manner under Sampson's (shifting) vision, and in her work on Mary Shelley, other 'distances between' home, too, while remaining as distant as they are (now more) real.

Animating Instruments, Or, the Creative Artist as Biographer: On Fiona Sampson's *In Search of Mary Shelley*

> We must always take the novelist's and the playwright's and the poet's' word, just as we are almost always free to doubt the biographer's or the autobiographer's or the historian's or the journalist's. In imaginative literature we are constrained from considering alternative scenarios – there are none. This is the way it *is*. Only in nonfiction does the question of what happened and of how people thought and felt remain open. (Janet Malcolm, *The Silent Woman*)[43]

---

[43] Janet Malcolm, *The Silent Woman: Sylvia Plath & Ted Hughes* (New York: Alfred A. Knopf, 1994), 154–55.

Introduction: Method and intention, or, a new biography

In many evident ways Fiona Sampson's *In Search of Mary Shelley* does what one expects from a modern-day literary biography. But to suggest that hers is also very much a new kind of biography is the main purpose of this introductory section. While Sampson writes the biography in ways which are deeply creative and ways which fold onto the kind of creative flair discussed in other parts of this study, it behoves us first to clear the ground for these discernments by first listing the ways in which she does staple biographical business. To my mind, this frees us readers to then explore the newness of the biography at hand and the way in which it animates (by) what the first, longer section of the book dubs 'the instruments of life'. You cannot leap into forms of biographical apprehension and representation which are palpably idiosyncratic and original unless the older paraphernalia of biographical writing is first taken care of. Thus, I will briefly give some illustrations of Sampson's due diligence before working out from such, to inspect what differentiates, individualizes, her biography from what we might have come to expect of most rigorous, skilled works of contemporary literary biography.

Whether it's Mary Shelley's life and experience and how it fed into her iconic work, *Frankenstein*, or perhaps other staple biographical moves, such as the teasing out of influential oedipal patterns, Sampson is as duty-bound as we expect her to be. For instance, Mary Shelley's childhood reading patterns are enlisted as part of Sampson's early weaving of Mary's early, prefatory life. Mary, like many children of her time literate enough, was often directed to read books, Sampson relates, intended quite purposively to 'reflect' the child in question and his or her behaviour; reading mirrors as it were that led to deeper reflection (in the other sense) on the part of the child who, thus, 'observes and learns'. And then, Sampson extrapolates, tying different moments of the life into a now-moving arc, by saying that this is 'just the strategy Mary will use to implicate her readers in *Frankenstein*, where our loyalties change as we learn more of the story, but not because the narrator tells us they should' (MS 34). At the other extreme of nineteenth-century biographical experience, the hazardous nature of childbirth in Mary's life, as in that of her epoch, is enlisted into insights about *Frankenstein* (116–17); or, as a cognate instance, the relationship between the higher mortality rates in early nineteenth-century Britain and in Mary's own life as well, are also signally connected to *Frankenstein* (153). Title and subtitle of this work seem to marry then in an evident and fruitful sense. And Mary's at times exilic psychology can be seen, too, to feed into her seminal novel (223), the tropes of orphanhood and their specific kinds of loneliness (88), or, perhaps direct evidence for overt details in the novel derived from Mary's contemporary experience and surroundings at the time of its composition (92). Sampson's animating of or by 'the instruments of life', those in Mary's individual life and those in that equally individual life of her iconic work, also stretches to landscapes experienced and anthropomorphized by Mary Shelley in her (later) novel (69 & 130). And then, as another staple biographical move, Sampson can write passages like the following:

> Wollstonecraft, who has symbolised so many things successively over the years to her growing daughter – maternal love and its unattainability, the feminine ideal, the active and intellectual woman, the Romantic, unconventional heroine and lover – is the perfect touchstone for Mary's relationship with Percy. (94)
>
> Mary's relationship with Margaret 'Mason' is part of a pattern. All three of her key friendships in the Pisa years – with Margaret, Maria Gisborne and Marianne Hunt – are with older women who, as well as being mothers *like* herself, could be mother figures *to* her. (191)

These psychological insights are insightful, evidently. However, for all their pressing interest they remain, when compared to some of the other 'instrumentations' animating the past in question which are discussed below, the kind of thing many other skilled literary biographers are wont to do as well. They move us, mentally and emotionally, but don't quite yet capture what makes Sampson's technical orchestration in this work the kind of music that is fully individualized. Because Sampson's *is* an original endeavour, not only a new biography of her subject, but one which evinces the kind of creativity one might or should expect from an experienced and distinguished creative writer in her own right. Below, I hope to show how Sampson does biography in a radically idiosyncratic way that mirrors the radical idiosyncrasies of her subject – title and subtitle bridging, folding across each other, again. But first, I want to outline some of Sampson's meta-biographical remarks as they on the whole open her work of animations and lively instrumentations.

In her seminal, famous essay, 'The New Biography', Virginia Woolf starts by saying that the modern biographical endeavour is in effect a kind of dialectic between truth or facts and the other kind of truth: of 'personality'. She writes,

> For in order that the light of personality may shine through, facts must be manipulated; some must be brightened; others shaded; yet, in the process, they must never lose their integrity.[44]

---

[44] Virginia Woolf, 'The New Biography', in *Selected Essays*, ed. David Bradshaw (Oxford: Oxford University Press, 2008), 95.

The modern biographer for Woolf 'chooses', 'synthesizes' and, having 'ceased to be a chronicler', 'has become an artist'.[45] And yet, for all this Jamesian modernism, Woolf near-closes by saying however that the truth of fact and the truth of fiction are 'incompatible'.[46] This early twentieth-century comment, laying the battlefield and the stakes of modern biography (as opposed to outdated Victorian moralism, rigorism), we will see is a challenge which Sampson answers in some very compelling ways. Sampson marries, in very particular ways to be enlisted below, the two models of life-writing which James Olney in his classic work dubs the 'archaeological' – where the past is a fixed given to be dug up as a given – and the other kind, textual, which is captured by the verb or trope of 'weaving'; where, in short, representing the past can also discover it, like a weaving which takes given materials but creates what become solid patterns which hadn't in some important way existed before.[47] So let's start by noting Sampson's own prefatory remarks about her method and intentions in this work. Sampson writes early on in her 'Introduction':

> Mary Shelley was a literary star. But too often she appears as little more than a bright spot being tracked as she moves from one location to another. This is no replacement for encountering the person herself. We know *where* Mary Shelley was, yet I still find myself looking for her. (5)

As much as Sampson records here how she noticed in her own youthful reading of *Frankenstein* 'the book's shifting, ambivalent sympathies' (4), she also and perhaps consequently wishes for us, with her, 'to see the actual texture of her existence, caught in freeze-frame. I want to ask', she continues, 'what we do in act know about who and how and why she is – who she is – and about *how it is for her*' (7). That said, Sampson's is *not* a 'fictional reconstruction' (6), nothing so postmodern as that; rather, via rigorous access to and use of journals, letters and publications, she will discern in her own narrative what Shelley (might have) truly 'felt and thought' (6). In particular, Sampson's work sets itself up as an attempt to redress implausible and short-sighted assumptions about Mary Shelley (2, 3, 6, 100). In a way that typifies the documentary-like nature of Sampson's writing here, a feature to be discussed in more detail below, this rectifying animus behind her tale will involve detective work of a kind (147 is a good example), trying to solve what she calls, tellingly, at one point, 'puzzles'

---

[45] Ibid., 97.
[46] Ibid., 100.
[47] See James Olney, *Memory and Narrative: The Weave of Life-Writing* (Chicago & London: University of Chicago Press, 1998), 20–21.

(65). These puzzles, to repeat, are not about the documented record so much as they are about what such *might mean*, for Mary Shelley, for Sampson, and now: for us.

Indeed, just as Sampson notes the seminal concern with psychology and motives, a romantic turn to the subject, in *Frankenstein* (140), so she can note the same romanticism is Mary's own more biographical itinerary:

> So when Mary's *Journal* for July 1814 records her own and Percy's responses to the countries she finds herself travelling through, she believes such responses are part of the observable nature of things. She's undertaking the Romantic project of self-examination: putting herself under the lens along with the places she sees. (85)

However, for all Sampson's acuity in and for psychological observation and reflection, whether to do with Mary or Percy Shelley (see, for instance, 128, 143), she is in a manner of speaking out-romanticizing Romanticism in this biography. Rather than over-visit the staple and much-documented system of relationships and histories of the Romantic movement, Sampson's 'search' details the lives and works of a young woman, creative artist and intellectual in the early nineteenth century, as she 'develops' her (individual) 'identity' (98). And that verb chosen by Sampson, 'develop', is again quite telling. Apart from the pictorial significance, her search is for *the (infinitesimal,* as it will turn out) *process* of Shelley's coming-into her own; which is why, as Sampson herself notes, *the build-up* of or to Shelley's (later) life and works is longer and more copiously searched in this biography. The past, after all, affects the future in a life in a simple chronological sense, which the future can't the past (7). And, furthering her meta-biographical commentary, even if access to intimate life in childhood and youth may be restricted, Sampson rises to this challenge as follows:

> [P]icturing Mary's childhood and adolescence means piecing together often circumstantial evidence. What we can guess is back-projected from what we know: enlarged and unclear, like nothing so much as those creatures generations of grown-ups have made out of the shadows of their hands against candle- and lamplight. (33)

Apart from the empathy here (note the common habit made use of as a simile above) – another feature discussed in more detail below – it's significant for a work subtitled, *The Girl Who Wrote Frankenstein*, that the occult of light and darkness in Mary's life as much as in her works proves a key instrument in Sampson's animating activities. This dialectical chiaroscuro, which opens and closes in a striking manner the first chapter, is also and again typified by how she opens chapter 6, 'At Villa Diodati':

> The first scenes of Mary's life are brightly illuminated. She spends her childhood in a house lit by huge, modern windows. But by the time she's eighteen a chiaroscuro seems to enclose her. Things have dimmed: her certainty about what she's doing, and ours with it. We get this impression if shadow partly because the loss of *Journal* volumes make it harder to visualise what she's doing. But this is also a time in Mary's life that is murky with cross-currents: a period of personal and domestic upheaval and repeated house moves, but also of wide reading, continued self-education, further pregnancy and the birth of her second child, William. (118)

Evident here is a back and forth, a loss-and-gain, a dialectic between frames or focalizations, between Mary's moves and Sampson's own, which mirrors some of the framework(s) of *Frankenstein*. In a *Cyclopaedia* entry from 1835 cited by Sampson, Mary speaks of her own later biographical practice as aiming to discern from sources such as letters, 'the peculiar character' of her subject, 'his difference from others' 'and the mechanism of being that rendered him the individual he was' (234). By turns, Sampson's instrumentations and lively mechanisms set out to do something very similar and, perhaps, something even more ambitious than her subject, Mary Shelley. And it can't be an insignificant detail that Mary Shelley, woman intellectual, creative writer, was also a biographer. Though Sampson spends far less time discussing these later works (Shelley's biographies) towards the end of her 'search', it does remain the case, as picked up in the concluding remarks of this section, that Shelley is in many ways an avatar of her biographer; and that such 'cross-currents' prove illuminative.

Portraiture of the real

Sampson envisions and effects her biography of Mary Shelley, we will see, as a 'series of portraits' (98). Indeed, each chapter starts with a visualized and visualizable tableau, caught in freeze-frame, only to be ratified and enlivened by backstory and narrative fleshing-out of different sorts over the course of whatever the chapter may be in question. Moreover, as already noticed, 'light' and its effects on seeing, looking (and looking-away) are central to how Sampson understands Shelley's 'plea for understanding' (6). Opening the first chapter at Shelley's nativity, her parents hovering above: 'Light from the household's oil lamps [...] concentrates in all three faces, finding them the way it does in one of those studies of the Holy Family by Rembrandt' (11). But the reference is animated with more purpose than a mere (ornamental) observation: 'Rembrandt's paintings tell us to trust the light because it finds where the action is, and is always on the side of the protagonists' (11). Sampson as we will see titles the next chapter, 'Learning to Look'. But more pressingly, this opening with Rembrandt is mirrored, after all the elicited biographical texture in between, by Sampson's peripatetic use of a famous 1839 Richard Rothwell painting of Mary Shelley near the close of her search (213–14, 224, 234–35). And again, here towards that close of her search, the skill of the Rothwell painting is matched by Sampson's skill at reading it and making illuminating use of it – a play between frames or focalizations again, which typifies some of Sampson's moving portraiture in this work. It leads into a filmic logic and/or a filmic grammar at times. And the way in which the 'series of portraits' or tableaux opening demarcated parts of (searching) narration are enlivened, animated, by the weaving of subsequent backstories into a more moving portraiture can be seen to ally with certain modernist fictional techniques. In this case, with what Ian Watt, discussing Joseph Conrad, famously dubbed 'delayed decoding',[48] whereby, speaking globally, chronological time frames are disrupted precisely to enliven and dramatize the makings of sense – such untimeliness, as we are to see, quite timely.

However, at the cusp of the shift from chapter 1, 'The Instruments of Life', to chapter 2, 'Learning to Look', Sampson returns to Rembrandt, but introduces now a newer variable, making her text as much textured as systematically structured in its depths:

> Rembrandt's paintings use the portrayal of light to affirm their protagonists, to create a sense of something shared, and invite us in. Mary's chiaroscuro works the opposite way. It seems to ask us to look, yet also to look away. (28)

Sampson in effect enacts both these push-and-pull movements in this work: she looks for, searches out the way life was, and felt for Mary in all her individuality, but does so as well with more relish and gusto precisely because Mary and/or the record seem at times enigmatic. Indeed, discussing the Rothwell painting mentioned above, Sampson seems to approve of the fact that Rothwell has captured in his portrait both Mary's self-assuredness as well as a more elvish playfulness, where she seems either on the verge of saying something, breaking into a smile, or perhaps on the verge of having just stopped herself

---

[48] See Ian Watt, *Conrad in the Nineteenth Century* (Berkeley & Los Angeles: University of California Press, 1981), 269–86.

from saying something (213–14). Which is to say, Sampson enlists Rothwell in particular, it would seem, because he matches her own filmic endeavours to effect a portraiture of the real. And again, enigmas are of central concern to this kind of fine-grained representation. Painting a real picture and a moving one, seems in both senses to involve pressuring the dregs, as it were, looking at the interstices, bringing them into the light. It's in this sense that Sampson's aim is targeted at making continuous the evident discontinuities in the record at hand. But before elaborating on this, it is interesting as well to note how throughout this eminently concrete and textured narrative, which is literally soul-searching, Sampson is also able, as in much of her poetry, to belie or complement, simultaneously, these individual(ized) notes with a more abstractive unificatory visioning. Later in the biography, the already-cited antagonism between light and dark, looking to be looked at and looking away, is mirrored when Sampson notes, discussing Percy Shelley's poetry together with his wife's creation,

> [t]his portrayal of the push-me-pull-you of awe by Percy's poems is very close to Mary's portrait, in *Frankenstein*, of a wildness that seems to look back at us uncannily through the eyes of her creature: both when he's half-hidden, part of the pattern of the wild landscape, and when we encounter him directly. Awe creates transcendent understanding through its lurch into the exceptional, and the occult produces insight in similar way. (135)

Notes, motifs, are picked up and in-gathered periodically, Sampson's instrumentation quite musical in this sense. However, by titling this partition 'Portraiture of the real' I have in mind how Sampson's narrative is quite different to what Max Saunders, in a recent major scholarly work on 'Life-Writing', has called 'imaginary portraiture'. This latter, significant in Saunders's account of the 'forms of modern literature', involved inverting the older method of taking an individual (life) and turning it into a 'type', by rather taking a 'type' and giving it biographical shape, life, animation.[49] Sampson does neither of these; she is, after all, as we saw above, searching-out and searching for the 'actual texture'. Her implicit materialism seems to mean she composes her biography from the ground up rather than the top down. And part of her capacity for real portraiture comes from a feature of her sensibility noted copiously in other parts of this study, which is to say, her empathy. The speculative, but still deeply informed, nature of her well-nigh documentary-like narrative, works both by

---

[49] See Max Saunders, *Self Impression: Life-Writing, Autobiografiction, and the Forms of Modern Literature* (Oxford: Oxford University Press, 2010), 462.

a grammar of the 'historic present' also made use of in her *Limestone Country* (close by in the chronology of Sampson's oeuvre) and other more emphatically empathic modes of sharing with her subject, and thus sharing the same with us, her readers.

From the opening of the 'Introduction' of Sampson's searching soul-searching, where she starts in a personal, anecdotal way – a manner of communing with her reader which is shared in many different ways and in many different genres across her oeuvre – through to the biography's close, the verb tense, speaking globally, of the narration allows the reader to walk-with Sampson's searching tale as though contemporaneous in time with her subject. Note the verb tenses, which set up the grammar of the opening of chapter 4, 'Elopement':

> Mary is only sixteen, and she is running away with Percy Bysshe Shelley, a man five years her senior who is not only already married but the father of a young child. It's 28 July 1814, and they're in the middle of the English Channel, and of a summer storm that has come on with night. (75)

Then, equally, closing the same chapter, an operative empathy at both the levels of content and form goes,

> She's a young woman who has spent almost all her life living in the same household as her closest friend: when it isn't Jane in London, it's Isabella in Dundee. The idea of setting out not only for another country but to *elope* with no such a companion or witness might be vertiginous. [...]
>
> If she burns her bridges by leaving, she can expect a more exciting life, but it's also one whose shape is very unclear. It's a weighty decision for a sixteen-year-old. And, ultimately, she must make it alone. (96)

Strangely, this aloneness is (now) shared. A similar move of looking at how Mary looks-away, that push-me-pull-you dialectic, closes the chapter titled 'Learning to Look': 'Most children pass through phases of self-consciousness and outgrow them. But there's something ineradicable about the experience of resembling no one as you grow up' (53). And yet, Mary Shelley's motherless-ness, via the incumbent insight, comes under Sampson's tutelage and ours.

A final way in which Sampson's narrative is as it were a kind of 'common prayer' is indicated by how she not only inhabits Mary's mind, speculatively and empathically, but also pans out to share such with her readership. A typical gesture, for example, comes in the chapter at the 'Villa Diodati', where Percy and Mary Shelley (and others) visit with Lord Byron and where, more pressingly, the famous challenge of a ghost story competition will come to fruition with such a seminal work as Mary's *Frankenstein*. Sampson zooms out to the readers' own present, contextualizing conversely: 'Today a similarly gifted and highly educated house party would read these stories to howls of laughter, and set themselves writing pastiches; these young Romantics do not' (125). Or take the following passage from later on in the book: Sampson speaks in her own person in her (and our) own reflective present, as well as bridging that tense onto the past in question, making, it needs to be said, the arc of event and action in the past a part of the present:

> The trouble with (emotional) infidelity, even when excused by ideals of free love, is that it throws everything around it into doubt. It must be difficult for Mary, as Percy unignorably flirts – at the very least – with Sophia, Emilia and those who follow them, to escape the retrospective conclusion that whatever 'connection' with other women she may earlier have suspected did take place after all. And what does this mean for the times she thought her relationship was happy? Things are shifting. And she can't be quite sure how. Infidelity is particularly abusive in the mixed message it sends; a kind of stop-start *He loves me, he love me not* that makes it hard for the cheatee either to know where she stands or to move on to better things – whatever those might be for a married woman in the 1820s. As with Harriet, so with Mary: it turns out that, though Percy may want her, he doesn't want to be 'chained' to her. And, also like Harriet, Mary is becoming exhausted by the life he leads her. (188)

What makes this portraiture of Mary (in her times) so realistic in its grain is not just the play between contemporary, at-hand reflection and retrospective empathy, but that it seems to also name in its discourse a liminal moment in Mary's life. And it seems that Sampson's success, indeed her originality, lies very much in this realism aimed to search out the interstices of the past, bringing them into life, light. History in this book is in the making, in more than one sense, as we will see, presently.

History in the making

There are two predominant ways in which Sampson's biography shows history in the making. As with other parts of this study, discussing what is very much an inquisitive, Socratic literary temperament, Sampson's narrative in this work, filmic in so many ways, is able to create a conversation between objective historical details or contexts and their closer subjective correlates. And this applies, both to global history and the more personal ones of her dramatis personae:

and to (as with Woolf, above) the play between the documented record and the searching for the soulful insights that, and often counterfactually, animate the former, giving them meaning and purchase for the reader.

To start with the first of the above. They can be tentatively broken down into two complementary halves. Times when the times 'out there' feed into the experience of time 'in here', and the times when a more local or personal historical context informs personages in this narrative. Times, also, where a mixture of these ensue. The book makes use of this background–foreground movement and technique continuously and often seamlessly; but I will only give a few telling examples here.

> Children like Mary Godwin, who grow up on estates that are still being built out of the surrounding countryside, have a special sense of how precarious that habitation is. They see how society is a matter of invention. Often it's only one house deep, sometimes a matter of weeks old. The finished streets on which their friends live resemble suburbs yet seem little more than stage sets when they give way to farms and fields. But at the pre-dawn of the nineteenth century – as in the twenty-first – children of respectable but not wealthy middle-class families cannot play outside, however seductive the environment. (14)

From this more generic observation, which still works to set up a historical context for individuals, we move close by into a more real and riveting historical present:

> [O]utdoor activity of any kind is difficult in the rain, and it's been a wet summer. We can imagine what a combination of rain, clay soil and the perpetual building site of the surrounding developments have done to domestic order. (15)

Equally, later in Mary's life, we read of how

> [t]he Godwin girls have been conditioned to associate both elopement and a European destination with revolution and freedom. With the double solipsism of privilege and youth, Percy can encourage them to conflate free love with social liberty, possibly even supplying egregious financial detail to the young woman he hopes will run away with him. That he's leaving a pregnant wife penniless and socially in the lurch – that once love wears off a woman can simply be abandoned and, if she is, will have no way to support herself – must seem to the teenagers like the tedious small print of a shining new social contract. (82–83)

The informing and transforming movements between the past's global contexts and persons in that past, and between both and us, now, grammatically at the least, walking with them, is a striking feature of Sampson's poetic skill. History is in the making here, in patently more senses than one. Early on, discussing Mary's mother, soon to die near childbirth (the intellectual and writer Mary Wollstonecraft), Sampson writes, seaming different frames of signification:

> She has managed to secure the future of both her first daughter and this new baby through marriage. Above all, she has seen and survived the Reign of Terror that grew out of the French Revolution in 1793–4. Indeed, she gave birth the first time, in Le Havre on 14 May 1794, during the Terror and while her own country was at war with France. She must be feeling pretty invincible. (18)

Or, continuing this mode of historiography, a kind of speculative psychologism in both a grand and intimate style, economic contexts or climactic ones, are also good examples of Sampson's history in the making:

> Mary and Percy are short of money, and prices are high. In March 1815 the Importation Act protects landowners' profits by preventing imports of cheap grain. In doing so it makes bread, the staple diet of the poor, disproportionately – even ruinously – expensive. Among the eventual results of this and the subsequent sequence of Corn Laws will be civil unrest, starvation and an atmosphere of near-revolution that, as we will see, is going to alter the lives of the radical circle in which the couple move. (116)

> Across the world, average temperatures are one degree centigrade lower than usual; and the anomaly is significantly greater here in Western Europe, a region that is coincidentally suffering food shortages caused by man-made catastrophe in the shape of the Napoleonic Wars and the British Corn Laws. (119)

But the other predominant way in which Sampson's history is in the making is via the way she parses the documented factual record in a radically searching and counterfactual manner. Which is to say, the givens of fact are given life, animated by the questioning search for what they might mean to the more meaningful components of the past that are persons, like us. Two examples should suffice. Early on in this history in the making, at Mary's birth scene, the 'weird nativity' (3) as it turns out, Mary's father, the renowned political philosopher, William Godwin, is entertained as follows:

What does William feel at this point? Does he think he's retrieved the situation, placing it in the hands of a man of science? Is he in any case too buoyed up by the safe arrival of his child to believe that things will go badly wrong – now, at this late stage? No: I think he is hovering. He knows things are bad. The house must be filled with hurried activity, anxious expressions; perhaps there are screams. (22–23)

However, perhaps the most searching and epitomizing way in which Sampson's biography is a history in (her or the) making, comes in the chapter titled, 'Becoming a Couple'. Percy Shelley it seems has encouraged Mary to sleep with his close friend, Thomas Jefferson Hogg. Our unquestioning assumption, presumption as it turns out, might be that this is merely an effect of Percy's notorious views about 'free love'; but Sampson animates this documented piece of the past like a piece of a puzzle, and the effect, typifying her counter-factual mode in this biography, is salutary. Sampson writes:

> Several motives suggest themselves. One is truly principled: Percy believes in free love and wants to make sure the pattern of an unconventional relationship is set straight away. Second, principled but less generous, he wants to make sure Mary 'lives up to' these ideals. Less principled, third, he's panicked: here he is once again with a pregnant partner who dreams of monogamy, and who is probably not terribly happy at the moment. Whether or not he can acknowledge it to himself, he finds this tedious and feels trapped. Fourth, and more murkily, he's turned on by the idea of Mary having sex with other men. Fifth, and more depressingly, he has made a mistake. Mary represents all sorts of possibilities – for him she symbolises both her parents, after all – including her own tremendous strength of character; but he isn't actually in love with her [...] Sixth, and more reprehensibly, he does love Mary but is easily led, or at least easily distracted [...] Seventh, more reprehensibly still and somewhat on the elopement principle, if Mary once sleeps with someone else, she will be indissolubly committed to free love, and she will lose the right to ask for any other, more settled kind of emotional life. Eighth, and rather fascinatingly, he is bisexual and [...] so Hogg has something Percy wants and which he will achieve if Mary sleeps with both of them. Or else, of course, both men are bisexual, and this is a way for them to sleep (or almost sleep) together. (112)

The truth might well be any one of these, many of them combined, none of them perhaps (though unlikely), but most pressingly I want to suggest that the creativity evinced in unknitting the seam of the historical record like this, searchingly, is actually a kind of instrumentation in Sampson's biographical toolkit that animates history, poeticizing it, as it is, in the making.

Conclusion: A writing-cure?

What is clear from this reading is that Sampson's capacity to see into persons, into history, and into how they interact and reflexively play out – never quite conclusively, but still highly illuminative – is a vital part of her writerly career and her poetic métier more generally. She writes of Shelley: 'We already know how much writing means to Mary; it was her father's work that brought the protagonists of this very literary romance together. And it's the figure of her mother that presides over their elopement' (94). And then the mirroring of the makings of both biographer and her subject is almost named later in the work where Sampson seems (only) ostensibly to discuss Mary's prose. Is it too much, one can't help but ask, miming Sampson's inquisitive manner, to suggest some identification here? The sentiment speaks directly to Sampson's own prose in this work of biography.

> Mary's prose turns out not to be naïve, as Percy's corrections have implied, but fresh and vigorous. It allows her to tell the story of *Frankenstein* with nuance but also vividly, rather than getting snarled up in anxious formality. (165)

I will close by returning to Woolf and her (very innovative) period. In a copious study of modern auto/biographical discourse, Laura Marcus notes how, at the incipience of that modern discourse, the relationship between biographer and biographical subject turns into a well-nigh 'transferential relationship'.[50] And 'transference' of course is the Freudian term for the drama enacted between analysand and analyst, a peripatetic space where tensions can be worked out and worked-through. Telling is not enough; in good modernist spirit one needs to 'show' as well. Perhaps something similar is going on in Sampson's searching for Mary Shelley? Both are or were women writers and women intellectuals; both were left motherless close to the time of their births. And both seem in their works to represent and, in a manner, atone for the resultant liminality and the (so to speak) monstrosity of being and/ or feeling abandoned. Indeed, ironically, serendipitously, Marcus's chapter on this period of and about the 'new biography' is titled, 'Bringing the corpse to

---

[50] See Laura Marcus, *Auto/biographical Discourses: Criticism, Theory, Practice* (Manchester & New York: Manchester University Press, 1994), 90.

life'. If Frankenstein and his monster are animated to come alive – to 'come down' into existence (as Sampson's latest, 2020 poetry collection eponymously has it) – by Shelley and the variegated hoard of her experience(s) and imaginary, then perhaps Shelley is Sampson's own untimely creation? The good thing is Sampson's discerning, poetic constructions of a life have a happier fate than Shelley's. Thus, 'transference', if parsed this way, indeed; or, perhaps, what Heaney has called 'redress'.[51] Except the redeeming poetics, as per the Malcolm epigraph to this section, are the more poetic for being deployed (developed) in nonfiction; the silence of the woman in question, and the eventual silence of her sublime creations cosseted in their frames, are given voice, much as they have given it.[52]

Coming full circle: Simon Schama writes early on in his study of the same Rembrandt – whom Sampson, we have seen, enlists in her biography of Mary Shelley – something of the seventeenth century that may seem to play out in (and light up) both Sampson's writing and that of her nineteenth-century avatar: 'Though artists were notorious for falling into the dark humour, the discipline of drawing was thought to set this to rights'.[53] As in Elizabeth Bishop's famous pun, both the women writers at question here seem to write it like disaster, righting it, too.[54]

---

[51] See Seamus Heaney, *The Redress of Poetry; Oxford Lectures* (London: Faber & Faber, 2002).
[52] Indeed, note how Mary Shelley's *Frankenstein* was originally published 'anonymously', many at the time, thus, taking Percy Bysshe Shelley as the real author. This is a concern dealt with as well in Sampson's biography (MS 233).
[53] Simon Schama, *Rembrandt's Eyes* (London: Penguin Books, 2014), 9.
[54] See Elizabeth Bishop, 'One Art', in *Complete Poems* (London: Chatto & Windus, 1983), 178.

Chapter 4

FOR THE LOVE OF MUSIC

Literary Friendship(s), Or, 'trying, to get closer […]': On Fiona Sampson's *Beyond the Lyric*

Introduction: Content of the form

> In other words, intention is the link between idiosyncratic view and the communal concern. (Edward W. Said)[1]

> The two directions of sensibility are complementary; and as sensibility is rare, unpopular, and desirable, it is to be expected that the critic and the creative artist should frequently be the same person. (T. S. Eliot)[2]

Let me start with a literary–critical riff on some of the titles, which are borrowed phrases from Fiona Sampson's marvellous education, *Beyond the Lyric*. Friendship, community, we will get to, hook onto, presently. Let me start, however, with the idea of – as Sampson introduces her map of contemporary British verse – 'trying to get closer' to that verse; and, also: 'trying, to get closer […]'

Sampson writes, opening this major work of critical mapping, that she doesn't want to read the gamut of contemporary British verse in a partisan or, as she puts it tartly, glass 'half-empty' manner, but rather, with cup-to-lip, glass half-full; with a brief, that is, not of demarcating the good from the bad to the ugly, but 'seeing' rather 'what's actually going on, in all its pleasurable variety', and concentrating on 'what a poem *does*' (BTL 8). Opening with this welcoming gesture, she is adverting to her critical role as one of 'critique' in its traditional sense. According to the distinction I'm adverting to, 'critique' is different to 'criticism' in the more colloquial sense; 'critique' is more an

---

[1] The two opening phrases used in this section's title close and open, roughly speaking and respectively, Fiona Sampson's *Beyond the Lyric: A Map of Contemporary British Poetry* (London: Chatto & Windus, 2012), 1 & 279. See Edward W. Said, *Beginnings: Intention & Method* (London: Granta Books, 1997 (originally, 1985)), 13.

[2] T. S. Eliot, 'The Perfect Critic' in *The Sacred Wood: Essays on Poetry and Criticism* (London & New York: Methuen, 1983), 16.

effort to comprehend the ground and base of a sensibility, according to its own terms and/or context.

Like John Burnside (a poet whose fiercely intelligent poetics ally somewhat with Sampson's) noted in a later chapter of *Beyond the Lyric* (significantly titled, 'The Expanded Lyric' – expansiveness: tell-tale) for his radically inquisitive rather than teleologically closed and/or assertive verse (252), Sampson's map is made in an inquisitive mode. Not only is it the case, like Edward Said beginning *Beginnings*, that she often makes use of the very arms-opened pedagogical or peripatetic gesture of the question followed by teased-out answer, but also that her judgements, which from another perspective are conclusive (not to mention, instantiated), are always as much complimentary as complementary.

Friendship in what is perhaps the inevitably narcissistic space of the poetry world is rare. Forgetting her immensely creative and facilitating role as editor, here, as critic, she makes bonds between poets and between poets and herself, poet, too. And as Eliot suggests (epigraph above) this double-binding of bonds is itself a poetic gesture – and that, whether we read Eliot to mean that only poets are good critics or, reading him a tad more generously, that the best critics are themselves doing poetry, by other means, in or by their criticism. Indeed, Sampson ends her previous, 2011 Newcastle/Bloodaxe Lectures, *Music Lessons*, with a citation of a citation, in translation. Baudelaire there is seen to say that in the heart of all the best or truest poets there needs must lie a critic (whether, as above, full-blown or implicit) (ML 62).[3]

So, trying to get closer, and trying, to get closer. While the word 'aesthetic' may date to 1750,[4] Sampson's *contemporary* map is a mapping of very different, polymorphous, hydra-headed *aesthetics*. Not the obsolete position of the aesthete, then, more the girding of companionship. Each of the thirteen chapters dovetails in the writerly organization – not only from one to the next – but also in a neat, often tripartite manner within the structure feeling-out each individual chapter. And all the figures, from Prynne to Cope, are treated with a fairness and a friendship; read, lit up, according to their own lights. Indeed, in the pursuant part I try to illustrate how – both a critical contemporary poet and, at the same time, a poetic critic – Sampson is able to be both horizontal

---

[3] As one small illustration of Sampson doing poetry in a critical setting, see how poetically she explains the repetitive headiness of the villanelle form to the neophyte, in her *Poetry Writing: The Expert Guide* (London: Robert Hale, 2009), 130: 'Think of the claustrophobia you feel in a room with patterned carpets, wallpaper, curtains *and* upholstery. But now visualize something just as ornate, but that is perfectly judged'.

[4] I believe the term 'aesthetic' is first introduced by Baumgarten, one of Kant's predecessors – before, that is, Hume awoke Kant from his 'dogmatic slumber'. See, in this respect, Ermanno Bencivenga's *Kant's Copernican Revolution* (Oxford: Oxford University Press, 1987).

and vertical in her critical endeavours; she grounds the different sensibilities, but she does so, in an important sense, according to the specific resonance of her own individual sensibility. Poet: critic, critic: poet, she seems to be both self-effacing and, simultaneously, self-expressive.

Sampson opens each poised chapter of *Beyond the Lyric* with a fleshing, a bodying-forth of that chapter's eponymous theme, often enough with historicist and biographical contextualization – be it on or for 'The Oxford Elegists', 'The Touchstone Lyricists' or those grouped beneath the title, 'The Expanded Lyric', and so on. This first move is followed by a quick and more concrete reconnaissance of the to-be-peopled terrain – finishing, with the body (or real presence) of each chapter, by addressing, individually, and with much formal-critical incisiveness, the clutch of particular poets grouped for that foray (and essay). As elsewhere, it's a 'revelation of scale / as it moves through the local' (from her eponymous poem, 'Common Prayer'). The main key to Sampson's analyses is tied up, quite intimately, with her love of music – her major inclusive gambit in the book due, self-professedly, to her 'training as a performing musician' (BTL 7).

However, before I enter (from) the inside of this latter work, I want to alert the reader here to Sampson's dialectical or indeed dialogic mode and manner. In *Beyond the Lyric* Sampson makes use of both incisive historical and biographical knowledge to help spur along and feed her readings, as well as, of course, impersonal and formal analysis (and synthesis). Between these two critical modes Sampson enacts a Socratic to-and-fro. Indeed, to illustrate this point, I want to suggest how even when doing formalist analysis, that analysis is still very much, in its grain and texture, *intentional*. Put otherwise, Sampson is both inside *and* 'beyond' the lyric as she charters spaces in and through this map. Like an archaeologist, what she finds ready to critique is already there, solid, waiting to be elicited; but like a (textual) weaver, too, she weaves up her readings from stuff ready there, but not as yet in the variegated patterns, the texture, she goes on to descry.[5] Thus, though when she does 'critique', in the sense explained above, she is teasing out and trying to 'get' the vast array and panoply of different sensibilities, in their own right and light – none the less, like her critical take on the musical groundwork of poetry, all that self-effacing is *still* not wholly 'impersonal'. Sampson's distinctive critical voice is both resolute, but also quite humane. In parallel, 'form' for Sampson, equally, is definitely *not* 'inhuman' (ML 43); for '[t]he poem must *articulate* such forms *along with* the poet's intent'. (40).

---

[5] This way of showing a doubled relationship to her material, empirical *and at the same time* constructively creative, is derived from an insight in James Olney's *Memory and Narrative: The Weave of Life-Writing* (Chicago: University of Chicago Press, 2001), 19–21.

Form-and-content, when uttered into mutually reflexive existence, immanently posit: 'someone beyond the author' (59). In her critical thinking at this time, Sampson wants to and does invoke 'a community'. And this, years after her Carcanet collection, *Common Prayer* (2007). She reads others, then, who've written to be read (by others). For Sampson poems are both just themselves as well as embodiments of the poet's intentions; so that inside and outside the frame of the poetic artefact are both (spontaneously) *essential* facets of Sampson's take on poetic meaning making. These two takes on the poetic artefact don't exclude each other, however, but are rather like two complementary angles of vision on or about the same thing. To illustrate this point, here is Ermanno Bencivenga speaking (in an analogical manner, for my purposes here) of these two different but complementary angles of vision:

> A good example of retrodictive Hegelian narratives: the careful analyses conducted as the end of a game of basketball or soccer, to show how rational and necessary it was for the winner to win. If you were actually watching the game, you often got the feeling that it could have gone either way up until the very end – that it all came down to a few fortuitous episodes. And if it had gone a different way, a different tale of necessity would have been told.[6]

Poems are like the sports' games here. Under the lens of Sampson's poetic 'critiques' they breathe with poetry as finished artefacts still, in a signifying sense, in the making.

And yet, the dialectic rushes on. Even in her third and closing lecture in *Music Lessons* (a work very close-by *Beyond the Lyric*), talking of 'chromaticism' as that (musical) feature of poetry which is radically *affective* (as *against* 'form and logic') – *even there*, her reading elicits a certain healthy 'impersonality'. And the latter is another of her nodal terms in what are in attitude and tone (and genre) very *personable and engaging* lectures (50).

The intention here to elucidate in brief, in an as yet broad-brushstroke manner the content of the form of Sampson's critical poetics at this stage in her career (c. 2012) might be seen to be just as 'substantive' as Sampson's own reflections on a 'self-generating' form in poetry, as musically lit-up (ML 37–38). Which is to say, I have tried to begin to descry in these opening remarks some of the 'musical' formation(s) of her critical work at this time. For musicality is not just Sampson's theme or critical method and toolkit, but her mode as well. Like music, poetry (*and its critical reception*) for and through Sampson's

---

[6] Ermanno Bencivenga, *A Theory of Language and Mind*, Berkeley (Los Angeles & London: University of California Press, 1997), 3.

sensibility is both constituted *and* constitutive. In the primary analogy of this reading, poems and poets are there to be read and, equally, ready to become what they are under the lens of Sampson's poetic critiques. Indeed, these two terms, constituted and constitutive, are used here as part (discussed in the pursuant section in more detail) of a proto-Kantian take on Sampson's 'critical' practice. Here is modernist philosopher Theodor Adorno discussing this Kantian co-incidence of the constituted and the constituting, the given and the 'simultaneous' *construction of that very given*:

> Conversely, however, the conclusion of our analysis today is that the *constituens* stands in need of an individual subject as the precondition of its existence, and thus of a *constitutum*. Thus the very thing that is secondary according to the Kantian critique turns out to be the precondition of what was primary, just as the primary was *its* precondition [...]
>
> This means that we have shown that what are alleged to be the most abstract and universal factors governing knowledge, the factors that must be present for knowledge to be conceived of in the first place, presuppose the element of factuality, of actual existence, that they are supposed to explain.[7]

I explain this doubled movement in more detail in the pursuant. But to close this introduction with yet another dialectical move, or paradox, I'll cite one of Sampson's very concrete commentaries; and one that comes, not in her far meatier and broader book of concrete readings, *Beyond the Lyric*, but in her book concerned more exclusively with musical *forms*. She writes, with real penetration and freshness of how with Emily Dickinson, the 'virtuoso play with metrical conservatism' suggests what Sampson calls a '*rule of poetic density*':

> [A] principle according to which, the more complex a poem's ideas are, the less baroque its versification may be [...] If combined with expansive versification, highly ambitious thought places poetry under strain. (ML 36)

Something of this kind of paradox, in shape and in intention, lives into and through her next major work of criticism, *Beyond the Lyric* – now discussed, further, and from the inside.

---

[7] Theodor W. Adorno, *Kant's Critique of Pure Reason*, ed. Rolf Tiedemann, trans. Rodney Livingstone (Stanford: Stanford University Press, 2001), 158, 167.

Inside Beyond the Lyric: Fiona Sampson's poetics on poetic form

> And this marriage is rhythmic as well as intellectual. What creates clarity and ventilation is O'Brien's use of *measure* [...] An O'Brien poem is never overcrowded: one image, whether concrete or metaphorical, leads to another in due course, in a *rhythmic deployment* that resists both over- and under- writing. (*BTL* 173)

Fiona Sampson's *Beyond the Lyric* is dedicated to the same Sean O'Brien about whom the above epigraph speaks; but speaks, I want to argue in a self-reflexive manner. It's not just that O'Brien is a close personal and professional colleague for Sampson, but that beyond that, the comment cited above might fruitfully act as a dialectical image for the critical writing in this work. The connection I'm alluding to therefore is not about any contingent biographical friendship; no; rather, as throughout this present discussion, I want to argue that many of the modes and manners *within Beyond the Lyric* actually embody (in synecdoche) what's going on when judged from outside the frame of its discourse.

Indeed, to both develop and immanently illustrate this point, in an earlier chapter, regarding the 'Oxford Elegists', Sampson writes, 'Friendship, after all, arises from like-mindedness'. Subjective or biographical features of contemporary British poetry are or at least can be married, intimately, with objective and formal tallying. Writing then of O'Brien, but also of herself as it plays out in both the conception and execution of this work, is not some loose reflection of a 'repeated professional interaction', but 'a kind of quiet intellectual passion at work' (63). And again, to both develop this present commentary and also to illustrate its present thesis, Sampson is not only talking, say, of Pascale Petit's 'deep imaginative consistency' in her late chapter on 'Post-Surrealism and Deep Play' (218), but simultaneously, I want to argue, of her own critical poetics from her position outside of the frame. If (writing in her chapter on 'The New Formalists') 'Distillation produces a poem that feels not cosy but inevitable: as if it had already been written' (231) – this *insider* comment speaks, and in a way which I hope to show is emphatic in this critical work, to Sampson's own critical mapping. Because her distilling work is, importantly, that *of* an insider, contemporary to her contemporary map. Sampson finds universality thus in all the distinct presences in the universe of contemporary British poetry.

In short, the beeline through this discussion aims, *via immanent critique*, making use of citations as dialectical images (which are critical theory's equivalent of romantic 'spots of time'),[8] to argue that when Sampson writes about

---

[8] On the nature of 'dialectical images', see Susan Buck-Morss, *The Origin of Negative Dialectics: Theodor W. Adorno, Walter Benjamin, and the Frankfurt Institute* (New York: Free Press, 1979), 101–10.

the music of her grouped schools on the contemporary British scene, such discussion is a salutary epiphenomenon to her own poetics, and thus her own poetry. What this means, and what I aim to emulate and mirror in my own discussion, is that though there is much about (in the logical sense) different, grouped lyrical aesthetics in this work, nonetheless, the penetrating analysis is also 'about' in the topographical sense. While in one sense, clearly, Sampson as critic here is 'beyond', there is an equal measure of working through and working up her critiques that is, like music – and as part of the same family as her strictly speaking poetic works (and music) – built upwards into the whole, and not willed in some overdetermining gambit to judge from a distance. She is beyond by being within and through.

Sampson discusses a plethora of contemporary poets, but does so *as a poet*, where this latter is meant as an empirical fact and/or as a constructive principle as to how she effects the critiques in this contemporary map. By thus showing that her critical poetics are not willed from above, top-down; by showing how they are in a philosophical sense 'spontaneous', I am not (to illustrate, but in negative, again) equating her work to the kind of 'automatic writing' (260) Sampson indicates typifies exponents of 'The Exploded Lyric' such as J. H. Prynne (who, despite this, is yet dealt with, with as much care and literary friendship in this work as is of the essence of her creative, musical attentiveness). The 'spontaneity' I mean here is the way Sampson's critical adventures are forms of apperception, those of a contemporary poet.

And what I mean by the philosophical term 'apperception', is the idea that when making a judgement, I want to argue that what is happening implicitly is that – *as a contemporary poet* in some essential rather than happenstance sense – Sampson is perceiving her-self at the same time as the 'other' poet under the lens of her critique. That, in other words, her poetic critiques are like poems, triggered by or embodying empirical experience (in this case, the poems of other poets) but not reducible to that 'other' work. Insofar as Sampson is doing poetry by other means here, her critiques involve 'her' in an important sense, beyond 'what' she happens to have to say about the artefact under analysis. And, to repeat: that 'beyond' is not strictly speaking 'transcendent', but rather 'transcendental'.[9] She is not 'beyond' like some top-down willing God, in an absolute and determinant sense; the 'beyond' in question is indeed the (logically separate) foundation or ground of her literal readings as they play out, but is also a reading space that would never (have) come into any meaningful existence *without* the empirical circumstance (poems under analysis) at hand.

---

[9] For a lucid explanation of this distinction, between the 'transcendent' and the 'transcendental', see Adorno, *Kant's Critique of Pure Reason*, 21.

This proto-Kantian take on things becomes specifically and overtly relevant to Sampson's critical poetics when we get to her later work, *Lyric Cousins* (2017).

So, below are three comments on three separate (now-joined) contemporary poets, three judgements that, as per my expressed intention, reflect back on the very mode by which Sampson effects the unity of this work. It is a unity forged from and by and with differences, a thoroughgoing logic of analogy across the work, which is actually much like the Wittgensteinian notion of 'family resemblances'. Indeed, the contemporary philosopher, Ermanno Bencivenga, elucidates and makes use of this notion of Wittgenstein's as very much a dialectical trope:

> A more promising course is to consider someone A in the picture and point out that A obviously belongs to the same family as someone else B because of how closely they resemble each other; and then that B obviously belongs to the same family as C because of how closely *they* resemble each other; and so on. By the end, you may have reached someone Z who doesn't look at all like A but still belongs to the Brown family because of how closely he resembles the person who immediately precedes him in this trajectory. And then you can say that it is the trajectory itself, the path leading you from A to Z that constitutes the meaning of 'the Brown family,' *not* any definite collection of traits.[10]

Or, alternately, here is the modernist philosopher, Theodor Adorno, outlining his epistemology of 'constellations', which is cognate:

> The unifying moment survives without a negation of negation, but also without delivering itself to abstraction as a supreme principle. It survives because there is no step-by-step progression from the concepts to a more general cover concept. Instead, the concepts enter into a constellation […] By themselves, constellations represent from without what the concept has cut away within: the 'more' which the concept is equally desirous and incapable of being.[11]

Sampson ties all her analytical flair into one whole, moving dialectical endeavour, thus. The others she combines are, under the lens of this present reading, apperceptions of her own place and status as a critical contemporary

---

[10] Ermanno Bencivenga, *Hegel's Dialectical Logic* (Oxford & New York: Oxford University Press, 2000), 24.
[11] Theodor W. Adorno, *Negative Dialectics*, trans. E. B. Ashton (London: Routledge, 1996), 162.

poet. She, or the 'I think' she embodies, that accompanies all her acts of thought, is in effect that 'more', that 'trajectory'. On John Kinsella, then:

> He combines profound intelligence, political conscience and a sort of Shelleyan rapture in a fast moving hyper-lyric which prickles with detail and idea. (247)

Or speaking of John Burnside and the influence of his poetics:

> Perhaps, it has taken so long for a group of poets directly influenced by Burnside's work to appear because the project of joining multiple impulses to each other, rather than focusing on a single principle as lyric has largely done, is profoundly thorough-going. (254)

Or, later in this same late-coming chapter, Sampson adds a third comment I'll use here that is both specific to the 'other' under analysis (Lavinia Greenlaw here), but that is also a dialectical image from inside Sampson's 'beyond' that speaks to its very working-texture:

> A poet's themes don't necessarily form part of a poetics, but here the preponderance of ideas about ungraspability, mutability and absence does amount to a project. (256)

The list on Kinsella – which as we will see further below typifies Sampson too, or the idea of 'joining multiple impulses', which is in a manner of speaking what Sampson is doing in this work – are as (paradoxically perhaps) revelatory about the text in which they are stated as (doubling the dialectic) the paradox illuminating Greenlaw – whose thematic of absence and its cognates turn out to be the real presence of her erstwhile project. Self-effacement and self-expression kiss, inside and outside this text. And that melee of inside and outside elucidated so far and in what follows, follows from Sampson's love of music:

> Music is, after all, rarely representational. What it represents is *itself*. Understood as a term for abstract form, 'musicality' pushes its way into poetics somewhere between aesthetics and the legacy of particular poetry movements. (243)

Similarly, Sampson inside *Beyond the Lyric*.
In the introduction, Sampson writes:

> Perhaps it's my training as a performing musician – an interpreter, whose own professional failing it is if I can't 'get' a particular piece – that makes

me return repeatedly to the importance of understanding that there's more than one kind of poetry in the world. (7)

Sampson refuses to conflate or confuse 'questions of taste and merit' (277). She wants to 'concentrate on what a poem *does*, rather than what it *doesn't* do, reading and enjoying it on its own terms' (8). In what she calls a 'quasi-Linnaean' classification of poets in this work, this work 'about reading' and about 'pleasures taken' aims to 'identify, demystify and share' (10). But the important point to keep in mind at this stage is that the classificatory tree (as with Linnaeus, I gather) Sampson enacts in this work is not some willed agenda but grows from won and winning pleasures in reading; but, that is to say – more typically said of music or indeed poetry – it achieves its unity and wholeness from the ground up, rather than otherwise. As Sampson writes 'unity' is not the same thing as 'stasis' (249). Like the 'Plain Dealers' of her first chapter, producing 'clarity from the chaos of experience', Sampson 'lays the best possible foundation for the diversity and eclecticism that has followed' (35). This ends her first chapter, setting up both the inside and the outside of her tale: which is to say, as now-parsed, the 'Plain Dealers' set up both what follows inside *Beyond the Lyric and* what, according to that same critical conscience beyond the lyric, has in fact followed in the inside of the recent history of British poetics. The positioning is like that of an apposite word or phrase in a poem – necessitated in more than one sense.

And the dialectical paradox can be elucidated further. Her work of sharing, which classifies, as we have seen, 'identifies' in order to 'demystify', is both (again, to use dialectical images inside *Beyond the Lyric*) a 'form of appropriation' (49) and 'charged with the given' (89). The first phrase refers to Glyn Maxwell's jaunty use of staple pentameter and the second discusses how 'touchstones' are used by 'The Touchstone Lyricists'. But note how the 'inflexibility' of the use of touchstone-symbols by the latter group, as flexed in Sampson's constructive reading here, is 'charged'. That verb, with its associations of deep enervation, captures the paradox at hand. The 'given' is 'given', but also electrified by the reading it is given. Sampson *is* 'appropriating' many different 'others', unifying them in classified groups, but this unitive effort is not purely determinant, and instead arises from the specificity of her poetic 'pleasures'. She is reading, in an emphatic sense, as much as a poet, a parallel practitioner, as a critic from some 'beyond'. Indeed, in that same chapter, what Sampson says of or about Michael Longley applies, perhaps, to herself, in this part as elsewhere: 'Unity of voice and content make Longley a truly lyric poet. Song doesn't trump his message: it takes ownership of it' (92). Just so, Sampson's classificatory appropriation sings, too.

While Sampson is rigorously lucid inside this work, the light she shines comes, as we have seen, from personal pleasures aimed at the same time in and for her readers. Of the post-surrealists, she writes that such 'affect-led writing [...] carries the reader along by assent and feel' (215). And in a minor way, for all Sampson's evident analytical skill here, she too carries the reader away with her, marrying imagination with reason. Another way to put this is to say that when Sampson discusses the career of Anne Stevenson, distinguishing between the latter's 'critical work' (such as her biographies of Plath and Bishop, which gave Stevenson heightened 'intellectual standing') and Stevenson's 'literary' activity (183), Sampson is, *in an exceptional case for this present discussion, not* truly naming her own activity at the same time. Because Sampson is indeed thoroughly 'literary' or creatively poetic in this work, a work thus, not to be distinguished in its intentions and methods from her poetry, except superficially:

> While poetry avoids what's too casually generic in favour of the resonant specific, it nevertheless aims to echo as universally as possible. The paradox is that a poet must rely on his or her own sensibility to test that resonance. (173)

Sampson enacts this paradox in a fertile manner. She writes, again *inside/ beyond*, that formal 'connection works throughout a poem, in every direction at once. A Sonnet can only *be* a sonnet when every line behaves in a particular relation to every other' (37). This comment on musical convention, again, images Sampson's critical work – *about musical convention*. The 'balancing variety' Sampson elicits (8) is like her reasoning about the relationship between particular poetry and its historical and/or biographical context. Like the poet aiming at universal reach via the resonant specific, Sampson gets a structuring principle of the work 'in' here, a work whose substance unifies the different aesthetic groupings. *But does so by suggesting* here in her introductory that 'that context is more nuanced, even fragmented' (6), than the fantasy, inherited from the avant-garde, of different chronological 'movements'. By fragmenting the old progressive line, she begins to form her multifarious beeline. As we will see, Sampson adds verticality to horizontality, using both at the same time in the weaves of her readings.

Insofar as (to continue inside/beyond) the 'plain dealers' 'are engaged *in*, rather than simply *by*, what they write' (14), Sampson by turns does or is both, *precisely by so naming* (having apperceived) the distinction here. Her work is about and 'about'. She is both mapping contemporary verse in order to 'identify', 'demystify' and 'share' – those seemingly self-effacing gestures; she is refusing to 'perform' in this sense, like her 'plain-dealing' friend, Elaine

Feinstein (29), or like Jo Shapcott as Sampson sees her (54) – but is *also* virtuoso insofar as this very facilitating work of sharing is and could only have been put to the test by Sampson's own 'sensibility', her own very poetic and musical attention. A modernist, she uses as it were the 'local' of her readings to suggest the universality of all localisms, as per her discussion of Basil Bunting (188), say, or Geoffrey Hill (193–94). Sampson's analogies are in effect 'elective affinities'. In the Afterword, so subtitled, she writes, 'Poetry is no more composed independently of context than are volumes of philosophy, or recipes' (277). Indeed, that very pairing is tell-tale: insofar as this twinning poignantly indicates abstract critique married to, well, quite concrete 'tastes'.

Unlike the 'poems' of John Burnside, or indeed her own – which 'rarely state beliefs or arrive at conclusions, either narrative or intellectual' (252), and for all her classificatory thinking in this work – Sampson, I want to continue to argue, is *still* doing a kind of poetry in this work, nonetheless. Still with Burnside, she seems to offer a kind 'surrender' (248) as much as any 'form of appropriation'. '[S]eparate and joined' (250), hers is what she calls close by (again, regarding a different poet than herself, Burnside) a 'longitudinal unity' (249). Indeed, to tie up this point, about and 'about' text and context, universal and specific, see how she discusses some women poets, herself one as well, early on inside/beyond the lyric:

> For women poets, gender is part of where we live; the familiar home of the self. It is a legitimate and indeed unavoidable subject matter. However, women's *poetic* identity has been under-explored. (19)

It's not just that Sampson will go on to explore this; it's that in exploring it, she remains herself context-bound as the very woman poet doing this strictly 'poetic' identification. And so on. Another way of putting this, to use two of her groups, is to say that Sampson evinces baroque virtuosity and is also plain-dealing. Opening the book, on 'plain dealers':

> Beware any poetics that protests its innocence too vigorously. No poem is ever entirely an Honest Joe, doing what it says it does without reflection. By definition, it is the result of artifice. (12)

The irony here is quite serious. And another instance is when Sampson descries the 'vertical' logic (rather than the narratological ('and then [...] and then') 'horizontal' logic) that works in her group of 'Mythopoesis' (139). By making this judgement she is at the same time dialecticizing it; which is to say, *precisely because*, as shown throughout this discussion, she is both inside and beyond the various lyric principles at play. Because she is predominantly or, better put, essentially a poet, and a contemporary of contemporary poetry in Britain, she can be both horizontal and vertical at the same time. She can't include herself in the contemporary map, of course; but of course, she has.

Conclusion

> Conscientious in the modernist sense, he frequently uses the first person plural of shared experience in poems addressing the state of the contemporary world or the human condition. (BTL 190–91)

To conclude, note how Sampson analyses the 'free verse' of the 'Free and Easy?' group – if, tellingly, as part of a segue into a second, separate (joined) school of free versifiers, in the following chapter on the 'Anecdotalists'. *A part* of this *formal* mapping, then, Sampson writes, with light and praise as ever, of the free and easy gestures in question as 'capacious, various and revolutionary'. By contrast, and at the same time by complement, at 'the second stage', of 'Anecdotalists' now, 'free verse acknowledges *itself* as form, and starts to develop techniques and conventions of its own' (121). By distinguishing *and* yoking the two, she is being both as free and easy as her poetic readerly attention allows her, as well as of course 'forming' a now-won pattern.

The work I have discussed is a work about groups and grouping, *which are both on and off the page*. The groups she groups are at times biographical colleagues or mentors and protégées, but at others merely share a certain poetics as descried by Sampson's acts of attention. Throughout, whether the links are biographical or made by Sampson in a more purely aesthetic classification, both forms and formations are of the essence, both historical individuals and poetic ways of going on. And of course, ideas 'of craft and apprenticeship suggest that there *is* something to learn' (75). Without being in any way elitist, this book educates about Sampson's own education. She is neither pre-modernist nor postmodernist.

Unlike the postmodern ethos, also named by Sampson, modernism still believes in progress and is conscientious in its searching poetics in search of such. And both these features (of modernism) apply to Sampson as a poet and as poet-at-work in and by critique.

> This link with the principle of progress not tied to any particular time or place means that modernism is still available as a cultural strategy today. (187)

But Sampson's modernism is certainly not exclusive. In her 'Afterword' she writes that 'the best way to make sense of what an individual poem is doing is to read it for degrees not of separation, but of connection' (278). To repeat, Sampson's analytical prowess goes dialectical thus. Hers is a 'palette of variation rather than absolute differences' (283) – and note how the synesthetic trope uniting time and space via music and painting helps her to help us to understand what she sees, rigorously, as a 'shared culture' (280). As she writes at the start of the work, poetry 'it sometimes seems, is everybody's secret vice'. What Sampson offers, by turns is 'a rarer bird altogether', namely, 'poetry that serves its readers' and, '*as* readers we're able and entitled to find out what we want to read more of' (4).

The last line inside/beyond the lyric reads, 'To be welcomed in, all you need do is open the door' (284). The play and parley between the passive and the active verbs here are redolent with Sampson's inclusiveness; an inclusiveness that never wishes to reduce or dumb down. The work is a portal, thus, but as we have seen, is not an overdetermining or indeed overdeterminant one. Sampson's unities in this work, work and work-up from an individual's acts of (musical) attention. Indeed, opening this work's door, we are reminded that any 'critical reading which doesn't proceed from close reading muffles, rather than clarifies; it damages the very thing it claims to promote' (4). And in my own immanent tour inside/beyond *Beyond the Lyric*, I hope to have learnt some kind of music lesson.

Expanding the Formal Project: On Fiona Sampson's *Lyric Cousins*

Introduction: Beginnings and ends

In the 1984 'Preface' to Edward W. Said's *Beginnings*, written that is to say nine years after its original publication (1975), Said makes two remarks about both the content of that major work and about, tellingly for that work, its intentions. He writes, summing up in retrodiction:

> To a considerable extent then one of the central points made by *Beginnings* is that modernism was an aesthetic and ideological phenomenon that was a response to the crisis that could be called *liation* – linear, biologically grounded processes, that which ties children to their parents – which produced the counter-crisis within modernism of affiliation, that is, those creeds, philosophies, and visions re-assembling the world in new non-familial ways.[12]

And then, closing that same Preface, he continues, less now in summation of the thesis of the work in question and more now of its spirit:

---

[12] Edward W. Said, *Beginnings: Intention & Method* (London: Granta Books, 1997), xix.

But if there is some especially urgent claim to be made for criticism, which is one of the major claims advanced by this book, it is in this constant re-experiencing of beginning and beginning-again whose force is neither to give rise to authority nor to promote orthodoxy but to stimulate self-conscious and situated activity, activity with aims non-coercive and communal.[13]

One of the reasons starting with these citations of Edward Said seems quite apt and pertinent here is that, from the start of the 'Introduction', titled, 'A Little Conversation', Fiona Sampson's *Lyric Cousins* opens with an active engagement with that same cultural critic (LC 1–2). For the particular nature, themes and contents of *Lyric Cousins* – a work that aims to see as it were and, as will be detailed below with more specificity, offer an 'affiliation' (*rather than* an overdeterminant application of one *upon* the other) *between* musical form(s) and poetry – Sampson's opening discussion has recourse to Said's 1991, *Musical Elaborations,* lectures he had given at the University of California. However, eliding that actual discussion of Said for the moment, I want to begin my reading of *Lyric Cousins* by adverting, equally, in complement, to its ending, or near-ending. My hope is that by synchronizing in this way the sense, or implicit sense, of the beginning and the same of the ending, I will be able to tease out something essential about *Lyric Cousins*. And that, quite apart from the evident common ground between Said and Sampson in their quite 'situated' *and* self-aware, or 'self-conscious' critical activities.

Towards the close of the twelfth and final chapter, Sampson cites and makes use of two different translations from Mahmoud Darwish's *Mural* (2000). The first from Palestinian-American poet, Fady Joudah; the second, quite different but of the same passage of verse, from Rema Hammami, 'a (female) Professor of Anthropology in Ramallah', and John Berger, the 'possible relevance' of whom, as we read in pursuant parentheses, 'is that Berger is British, of Jewish descent, and living in France' (219). The specific poignance for Sampson of using these translations towards the end of her work, I will address below. But the significance I want to draw out for the present is that these two poised openings and endings of the work can't be fortuitous in the way they cousin each other. I would say for a work so adamantly questioning about form, that this kind of apposition has or might be seen to have some kind of important significance for or speaking-to the work in which they find themselves counterpointed. While, notoriously, Edward Said is writing from a position of quite resolute exile, Darwish in the c. 2000 we are concerned with here, is, Sampson writes, 'a poet [...] created through a dialectic with a

---

[13] Ibid., xx.

community who wait for, memorize and quote the poems "their" poet writes *for* them: that's to say, in the knowledge that they do so' (218). And what I want to suggest here, by placing and affiliating these opening and closing gestures like this, is that this dialectic between being situated and grounded and being exiled or estranged is, in a manner, at the heart of some of the paradoxes (and parallelisms) of Sampson's analogizing of 'poetry and musical form'.

She says in that same 'Introduction' of 'A Little Conversation' that she's 'trying to write [...] from a maker's standpoint' (2) – having been a trained performing musician and being a contemporary poet. Her 'process' in the working-up of this work 'has been as "makerly" as was its starting point' (2). 'Though', she writes, 'my thinking has been painstaking, and I've read widely in my search for answers or at least answering ideas, its origins are in little more than a maker's hunch' (2). Thus, she starts in a sense as a biographical individual. But then, close by, a rival insight begins to make itself felt.

> I simply noticed that when I'm giving a poetry reading the experience is similar to that of giving a concert. There's a kind of estrangement from the material I'm performing which is not present in speech or other forms of *telling*. It almost feels as though this material goes at its own pace; as if it goes through its own process, into which I merely fit my actions as a reader. (3)
>
> And one way to describe my original hunch about a relationship between music and poetry would be to say that I noticed myself making interpretative gestures – inflecting my voice upward, or observing the end of a breath as marked by a comma or line-break – with the same detachment as that with which I had been able to observe myself playing in concerts. I did not feel like I was *talking with* the audience, but that I was *delivering a text* to them. (4)

For all this feeling of self-estrangement, though, notice how it is very muchSampson's feeling, in all her biographical specificity. And then, from the above suggestion of 'makerly ness' as the root of her 'hunch', we see emerging a more 'technical' sense of 'makerly concerns', 'more concerned with something intrinsic to how music and poetry are structured' than 'the giving and receiving of a particular experience' (5). What seems to be happening over the course of a few (introductory) pages in this 'little conversation' is that the senses of 'experience' are modulated differently. Earlier it was very much 'her' experience; a bit further on it is more like the principle of experience (in general). Indeed, as with the (heuristic, here) pairing of Said's exilic mode and Darwish's more communal grounding, at least as read there, there is a very pertinent asymmetry in Sampson's overall thesis (if there is one overall thesis) in this book. In a manner of speaking, poetic meaning for Sampson cannot exist except as 'experienced', whether read or written or listened to. Its immanence depends upon its being experienced. However, it is *at the same time* never *reducible to* any particular or any added sum of particular experiences. Like Kant's somewhat uncanny 'synthetic a priori' truths, 'poetry' would never be without individual poems and individual experiences of them, but it is also Sampson's view that those poems would never be without having been grounded in or by something about 'poetry' that *precedes* in a logical sense any particular set or sets of words.

> Despite the self-protectiveness of the discourse of poetry as a whole, in other words, it appeared that an individual poem might be something that could go on even without the particular, original words in which it had been written. (7)

'But here metaphor came to my aid, resolving paradox into parallelism' (7). After learning through her own practice of 'translation', Sampson realized that 'the work of the poem that was carried across by translation' was the 'movement of thought', '*connection*' (7). And this movement of thought between words and what transpires through them is later observed of music as well, showing just how much Sampson uses music '*on behalf of* poetry' (1); not poetry as music, but poetry 'as if it were' music (6):

> [M]usic is in some ways dependent upon those who make it happen, not only in performances but, on other occasions, simply by reading a score or remembering a tune. Yet that dependence only has to do with each *particular* occurrence. Existentially – in the nature of its existence – music has to satisfy not tastes but formal criteria. (155)

So poetic form like musical form is in an emphatic sense grounding for any poetic or musical artefact – which is not to say that such 'formal criteria' are transcendent, existing in some autonomous realm of 'forms'. Rather, what they seem to be for Sampson are 'transcendental' in the Kantian sense – Kant famously arguing that there was no concept without an 'intuition', which amounts for our purposes here to saying there is no 'form' in the metaphysical realist sense, as much as there is none in a purely nominalist sense. 'Poetry' doesn't exist except as 'poems', but there is something 'more' to poetry for Sampson than the addled, listed content(s) of all particular poems, past, present and/or to-come.

To close these introductory remarks, I will return to the near-close of *Lyric Cousins*. Here the 'movement of thought' alighted on in the 'Introduction' seems to be recouped by Sampson's discussion (then citation) of a Romantic poet who is very closely 'affiliated' with some of her other published work as an editor and biographer, namely, Percy Bysshe Shelley.

> Percy Bysshe Shelley was fascinated by movement and change and wanted to generate them himself, not only as a schoolboy chemist or adult revolutionary but in his verse. So his long lines rush onward, speeded along by extended sentences, piled-up adjectives, and toppling lists. (217)

Shelley's 'helter-skelter forces the reader to participate' in his versification, 'to become literally breathless' (217). What this indicates for my purposes is that Sampson's 'topographical map: the kind we use for railways rather than roads', mapping 'a web rather than a terrain' of 'connections and intersections between the two artforms' (10), is also a criss-cross between her two roles, amorous cousins, as an engaged practitioner and one in a certain sense and through that very practice in salutary exile from the same.

Grace notes, or, music lessons and beyond

I want to substantiate what I've descried so far, further; however, I will do so at this intermediate stage of my reconstructive argument by addressing some of Sampson's hunch-like insights as they find themselves in her earlier Newcastle/Bloodaxe lectures, upon which the later, more copious *Lyric Cousins* is built. I want to talk about 'grace' in fact, the 'more' as it were beyond language and entailed by music; even if that more, as we start with Sampson's opening lecture in *Music Lessons*, is also a 'before'. Indeed, as Sampson writes, and to preempt: 'This would mean that musical form could entail the textual, rather than necessarily the other way around'. (ML 25)

I should say that in making, and in sustaining below, a mild exploration of and between Sampson's 'music lessons', whether here, eponymously, or there, I restrict myself to a basic literary-theoretical and conceptual grasp of musical-critical terms, domains.[14] Just as at the end of Lecture One, 'Point Counterpoint', Sampson calls her lessons 'speculations' (28) – so: my own endeavours; objectivist, as far as I can be, like Sampson, often enough, *but*

---

[14] I leave it to the reader, or in any case, someone more competent to make more substantive links between Said and Sampson, specifically musical–critical ones, given, as is well-known, that both started their literary careers after rigorous bouts of musical education. Indeed, (ML 8) Sampson mentions at the beginning of her lecturing renditions, that her intuition of and about breath-beginnings, was gained in those very beginnings: her early musical training.

certainly not always, herself (9). Sampson's notion of music as a heuristic tool to tease-out, and to go beyond the linguistic utterance in all its positivity, is precisely that, a going-beyond; as she herself dubs it at the end of Lecture Two, '*Here is my space*', she is speaking (of a kind of) 'grace' (45).

Sampson's Newcastle lectures are introduced as played, as it were, between subject and object, or, much like much of her poetry, in a 'liminal' space between, as she puts it clearly, readerly and writerly worlds (7). Speculative, we are asked in these lectures – which are overtly rendered and named by Sampson as heurisms, 'useful', 'suggestive' – to 'listen differently' (7 & 9). In this, her lyrical defence, a foundation-work for poetry, what she means is – by way of parallel with what Shelley called 'imagination' (10)[15] – again, the will not to be partisan, constricted to the empirically or close-minded; the will, rather, to 'see' the way things work, or at least, playing, how they *may* work. She wants us to 'listen' with a new 'attention'.

Sampson's main gambit in the first lecture, in which she elaborates on the musical notion of 'breath', is to show that there is thought, therefore semantic meaning, before and (as I've indicated) 'beyond' the textual or uttered datum. For Sampson the breath, the inspiration (14), so to speak (as it transpires) is, or may be, both the limit and the groundwork or precondition of 'the spoken unit'. She suggests that that ineffable breath is not an empirical or literal precondition, conditioning the first phoneme; rather, that it is constitutively structural to the whole of the poetic artefact (18, 23–24 & 16). The 'and then [...] and then' of 'melody' is more than diachronic in Sampson's gaming gambit; it is radically and constitutionally synchronic, to boot (13–14). This seems to mean at least two things.

First, is the as it were 'secular' insight that Sampson elicits, quoting Pierre Boulez quoting Henry Miller, about how the process of meaning-formation is a messy and endlessly palimpsestic one (13) – much like some of the opening reflections of Edward Said's *Beginnings*.[16]

> By *intention* I mean an appetite at the beginning intellectually to do something in a characteristic way – either consciously or unconsciously, but at any rate in a language that always (or nearly always) shows signs of the beginning intention in some form and is always engaged purposefully in the production of meaning. With regard to a given work or body of

---

[15] Two things here: Coleridge, after German Idealism, uses the (constructive) term, 'imagination' (as opposed to 'fancy') in a similar way. Secondly, it should be noted that Sampson has edited a small selected edition of Shelley's verse, published by Faber in 2011.

[16] See Said, *Beginnings*, 3–26.

work, a beginning intention is nothing more than the created *inclusiveness* within which the work develops.[17]

The semantic, thus, is not just the pinioning of the denotative or finished datum.

Then, pulling against this is the more transcendental idea that there is, after music, thought *before* language. And this 'before' of grace, which is also a 'more' or beyond, is both empirical and logical. It entails, or suggests, both the idea that musicality, in this case melodic line, is the immediate ground of the literal forthcoming poetry, as well as its ultimate (or foundational) purport.

Now that I have introduced some of the insights Sampson began to develop in her Newcastle/Bloodaxe honorary lectures, I hope to continue their elaboration in the pursuant section; but I also wish to tie that latter with more understanding of how Sampson's critical method, mode and manner are very much, not only self-aware, but that they immanently gesture to the communal, to the common ground. There is not only a community between the progressive efforts of her intellectual and poetic itinerary, but very much one with her readers and the reader in general.

A newer community: On *Lyric Cousins*

At the start of *Lyric Cousins,* Sampson subtitles the introduction, as we have seen, calling it 'A Little Conversation'. As in some of the other parts of this book-length essay on Sampson, we've friendship, community, again. And in continuity with her previous major critical works, Sampson remains resolutely inquisitive, rather than teleologically assertive.

Like Said whom, as we have seen, she invokes in the introduction, Sampson is not claiming in this work to be executing a thoroughgoing musicological endeavour; she merely invokes and pressures forms of music 'on behalf of poetry'; which is to say, her dominant insight to be followed up is that abstract form itself is content; that, in a felicitous pun, the pure connectedness of poetic artefacts, like musical ones, is 'a form of going on' – out there in poetry, music, and right here in exploring their formal webbings.

There are four aspects of this latest work I want now to explore in more detail, furthering my own formal mapping of Sampson's predominant mode of critique. First, the existential or humane purport of *Lyric Cousins*; second, the ways in which – very pertinent to explorations about form – a dominant tenor of her probing understanding involves reflexivity, the coming of a certain consciousness of things into self-consciousness; third, to expand on earlier comments, the way in which her views on abstract form involve a coterminous

---

[17] Ibid., 12.

synchronicity and diachronicity; and finally, the ways in which she teases out abstraction and abstract form as their own, and our own, content.

As this work, we have seen, follows up on 'a maker's hunch', let me start with the way in which Sampson often preludes her explorations, based on common experiential features of reading and listening. Often, quite personably, Sampson will invoke a common or trivial idiom and elicit, in conjunction with such intuitive phrasings, the depth they hold. She writes how 'it is the contention of this book that, in music and poetry, abstraction *is* what can be counted' (LC 103). And yet, she links this elicited argument to commonsense phrases, like a 'balanced account' or 'keeping it in proportion'. In other words, part of her reflective or meditative mode in this book is conservative. Not only is she developing discourse of a highly sophisticated nature based on her own practices and experiences, but she shows the reader how much of the developed thinking at work here is rooted in everyday experiences, ones we all have – even those of us far less cultured, or familiar with high-art forms.

More depth-charged, there are also instances where she discusses features of the writerly world which also make, as it were, common sense. The idea, say, that not only linguistic connectedness in poetry (as with notes in music) is semantically full, but that disconnectedness also signifies, is a note many readers of poetry can understand implicitly, however unbeknownst till then. Invoking high-brow thinkers like Lacan and Kristeva, Sampson explores the idea that the pure-sound element of poetry is linked to traumatic preverbal (pre-denotative) infantile experiences. For Lacan and Kristeva, it is the evident *dis*ruptions in adult therapeutic transference that indicate where the real infantile wounds are to be found. The truth is in the interstices, musically (37–50). And yet, many of us, intelligent poetry readers, may have noticed how a tendency to radical musicality in this sense, is associated with identity-diffusion or even psychosis – whether it's Gerard Manley Hopkins, Dylan Thomas or Sylvia Plath.

For Sampson, human meaning and abstract form are 'not inimical'. Indeed, abstraction 'pulls on denotation' and 'transforms representation' into 'pure pleasurable sensation' (109). But another repeated trope, if implicit, in Sampson's exploration of the analogy of musical forms and poetic, is the coming into self-consciousness of a more basic consciousness. In the first chapter, titled with a pun, linking embodied topography with a logical sense, 'About Time', it is suggested that time is not only a narratological feature, but also an 'existential' one. Indeed, much of that opening chapter explores how time becomes self-aware in poetry and music, making the latter the most eminently humane forms; time timing itself, so to speak. 'Poetic language can gesture to itself' via its formal connections, or recursions, or what have you (115). Or, in a later chapter, speaking of 'chromaticism', Sampson writes that 'it's arguable that chromaticism reveals and celebrates the *experiential* nature or art forms in which it makes an appearance: in *what goes on* in the viewer, listener or reader that art produces;' which is to say, forms of affect make the reader more self-aware (as a reader, or listener). And in that chapter, as throughout, she offers thumbnail instantiations from literary history to give flesh to her ruminations. Here, Symbolists like Rimbaud and Verlaine are discussed as poets with poetics that draw attention to the very verbal texture of their verse. For Sampson, chromatic effects are not just 'formal disobedience', purple passages, say, the poem drawing attention to its own viscera – 'but more broadly whatever's put in the poem for sensory', rather than denotative or grammatical, reasons (84–86). And what I want to suggest here is that this combination of theoretical wandering with poignant instantiations, is itself Sampson's own methodical micro-logical representation of a truth becoming a reflexive truth. Which is to say, Sampson lives out, bodies forth her manner of theorizing in the very forms and make-up of her book. She is as ever about, and 'about'.

As with her earlier *Music Lessons,* a key feature (and perhaps the most notably seminal one) of Sampson's thinking about poetic form is the coterminous-ness of diachronic and synchronic intents in poetic artefacts, as much as musical ones. Key to this notion is how intentional/expressive aspects of poetic telling are also carried out by abstract form.

> In that strange experience of understanding without understanding, we glimpse the shape of the phrase *itself*: a set of speech forms or relationships prior to any particular vocabulary […]
>
> Breath, it transpires, is not only the human measure within language, but its animator – giving musical sense to semantic content, and creating a grammar for sound. (67–70)

The melodic unit, thus, is also a 'semantic unit' (67–70). As another example of Sampson's thoroughgoing instantiations, here's a thumbnail reflection of and about John Burnside, from much later in the work:

> A Burnside line sets out from the left-hand margin in the usual way; then, as if to create a caesura, both full of tension and opening up a pause, it may 'step' down to the next, not returning to the margin but continuing where the line above left off. Some of these 'steps' have a feel of qualifying clause or parenthetical comment; not quite asides, since they move the narrative main line of thought along, they work like 'gear-changes' into another pitch or tone which, as gear-changes will, can create momentum rather than put a brake on it […] (180)

> John Burnside's stepped lines set up a [...] process of mental superimposition. That stepped-down alignment between the first phrase and second *shows* (both ear and eye) that they belong together, and this belonging together makes them at the same time, and respectively, nostalgic and prospective. (182)

And this conjunction in time, of anticipation and recollection is paralleled by the final lesson in the book, whereby 'here' and 'there' are also paralleled, if with mild paradox. Sampson argues that 'what happens' in or by a poem, and 'what happens *to me*', are 'uniquely coterminous' (209). 'One way to say this might be that experience is something that cannot exist without us, but is built into verse and music *so as to be released by us*' (220).

Put in a cognate manner (from earlier in this work), while abstraction (and its paid dues) releases us from the 'obligations of the realist contract', it 'offers the challenges and scope of engagement with apparent limitless possibility', and yet, 'making is always limited by intention' (199). All of which is to say, that when music is thought 'about', as here, on behalf of poetry, not only is there a content of form, but there is a signal asymmetry, though tangential, between the objective content of a poetic artefact and the subjective ignition of such. As already suggested, Sampson's overall argument seems to be close to Kantian. Just as abstract form is itself semantic, thoughtful, but also, and at the same time, dependent on a subjective engagement, so: Kant, famously, spoke of phenomenal and noumenal worlds. Yes, poetry and music only exist, meaningfully, when experienced; however, the subjective experience is also delimited by the weight of the object. It's not a slippery slope into radical subjectivism. The fact that there is a meaning, semantic or otherwise, is not dependent on me or you and our concrete, specific, spatio-temporal contexts.

To conclude by returning to Sampson's engagement with Said, where I started – partially critiquing the latter's materialism, Sampson offers her own more ineffable materialism.

> While I can convey *what I know* as a result of having an experience, my experience *itself* is by definition mine alone, since *having* it is part of the boundaries of *me*. While Said is partly right about the meanings of music's social context, then, music is also 'about' the actual sounds it makes. (113)

What I believe Sampson is saying, at least partly here, is that meaning, musical, poetic, is *infinitesimally* real; which is to say, to use Lacan's terms, it 'ex-sists', rather than 'exists'. It is like the prone larynx, constitutionally, constitutively before, as opposed to, the uttered phoneme, or word.[18] Poetic meaning, after musical ana-logy, is what *conditions* the poem, not the poem, *necessarily*, itself; or, perhaps, a (liminal) conjunction of both. Like Heidegger in his *Introduction to Metaphysics* – another philosopher Sampson references in this latest work – we can indicate the positivity of all extant things, sure; but to show the being of Being *itself*, is an ineffable gambit (which is not to say there is no Being!).[19] For, at the last, only 'the poem itself does being the poem' (92).

---

[18] See, for instance, Bruce Fink, *Lacan to the Letter: Reading* Écrits *Closely* (Minneapolis & London: University of Minnesota Press, 2004), 141–66.

[19] See Martin Heidegger, *Introduction to Metaphysics*, trans. Gregory Fried & Richard Polt (New York & London: Yale University Press, 2000).

CONCLUSION

Democracy and Excellence

> The truth is that there is good and bad paradox, just as there is good and bad art, just as there are shut and open eyes. Chesterton used paradox safely because he was first a contemplative and second an artist; first he saw, and then he made. Those who have made bad paradoxes, and dragged paradox into such disrepute thereby as to deprive Chesterton of half his proper audience, have spoken first, and not seen at all. (Hugh Kenner, *Paradox in Chesterton* 17)

As I understand it, among Chesterton scholars, Kenner's short book quoted above is deemed perhaps the most penetrating and incisive of critical takes on said 'jolly journalist'. I have made use of this citation as an epigraph here, at the opening of these concluding remarks, not because the work of Fiona Sampson is somehow close in style or ethos to Chesterton's, but because it seems to me, after all of the above, that Sampson is in her own, far more complex way, a contemplative.

Another caveat to make, though, regarding this, is that the movement between seeing and configuring alluded to above – which is in a manner of speaking a movement between seeing (understanding) and seeing (embodying that vision), or vice versa – is certainly not, or at least not necessarily, some chronologically discrete movement. It has been seen that at the heart of Sampson's most developed thinking on poetry and the poetic is a notion of organicity – if perhaps such a notion in a more complex form than the purest of romanticisms or romanticisations. So that, if I may be right in speaking of Sampson as a contemplative, the distinction or separation she enacts or embodies as a poet and writer between 'seeing' and seeing, is only a logical or conceptual one and not an empirical one. The collated, unified and unitive vision whose description has been one of the main aims of this book-length essay happens as it were in the *kairos*. Epiphanies redound in her work, a good later modernist, and the very notion of epiphany indicates that there is some progressive truth to be had, incrementally, as a result of the development of an aesthetic or poetic, or at a more local level, as a result of the deep process of sensitization that goes to form a sensibility. And as seen, while I have *not* been engaged with the more biographical brief of tracing influences on Sampson – that would have been a different kind of book – I *have* tried, essayed here, to locate the seam and flow of her *sensibility*. The content of her form(s).

There is a reason, I'd venture, in line with Kenner among others, why truth-seekers and truth-tellers end up speaking in tongues: even if such an end is that kind of generic tongue that is poetry. Poetry, via many of its most native facets, including the way it is embodied on the page, allows us to access truths which don't fit neat ('clear and distinct') categories. Truth is liminal, perhaps, and that is why, perhaps again, a sensibility as fine-tuned as Sampson's must also play spectral and shadowy games with meaning and meaning making. As per a citation earlier in this study, the late modernist philosopher (among other, simultaneous roles) Theodor W. Adorno argued in one of his later essays on Hegel that the submerged, serendipitous truth in the latter's positive dialectics, where the whole is totalized, achieved, finds its place in the twentieth century as a negative dialectics, as, that is to say, a whole that completes itself in or as radical 'antagonism', as a holism of conflict and elision, not closure. What later theorists I believe dubbed 'the absent whole'. And even though I have tried in this study to offer *some* kind of closure, some kind of unity to the now-read oeuvre (such is my own ineluctable tendency) – perhaps it might be true to say that the thoroughgoing 'common prayer' that Sampson's oeuvre to date exemplifies is close to a communitarian one, a far haler version of the structure of antagonism. As with Chesterton (as descried, illuminated by Kenner in his seminal work), Sampson's 'dialectics', her dialogue with herself, her readers, and all the other possessives the generic range of her oeuvre permits, *analogize differences*. The 'distances between us'. What I suppose this may amount to is the idea that her oneness of vision is a oneness of many-ness, where the many commune, while still being allowed to be quintessentially individual. Again, it is the Wordsworthian paradox – a paradox Sampson directly speaks of and also one she happens in this critic's view to enliven and embody – of the communing of the exception and the rule. Her work in poetry is beautiful, but also, sublime.

And like Chesterton, too, (this is what Hilaire Belloc averred) she is a teacher. Not only empirically (myself, her one-time mentee, a goodly example), but in the way she goes about her literary business – never dumbing *anything* down, but rather eliciting and evincing a rhythm in nearly all her writing which balances democracy and excellence; high intelligence with empathy; a rigorous and long-borne engagement with form(s) and a common prayer. This is perhaps what we might most wish for from a literary artist. That she should, not only affect us emotionally and intellectually, but that this effect should also take us in some important sense *forward*. Just as a good editor will insist that to 'cut, cut, cut' is the first, most foundational rule for editing (a bit like 'butter' for French cooking), so, I like to think I have shown many ways in which Sampson's writing across many genres has moved me, because it *has* that necessity that makes great work, work. And I hope it will (increasingly now) also move any and/or many of the readers who go (back) to her work(s) with more appetite. Sampson writes that the 'literary' is not just an 'occasion' for language to be made use of; it is that occasion with its own 'sense of occasion'. And the book that now closes will, I hope, have displayed at least some of those senses.

Appendix

INAUGURAL WELLCOME TRUST ANNUAL PUBLIC MIKE WHITE MEMORIAL LECTURE, JUNE 14, 2016

Seminal Publication of Professor Fiona Sampson's 'A Speaking Likeness: Poetry Within Health and Social Care'

Here is a poem:

> Love bade me welcome. Yet my soul drew back
>   Guilty of dust and sin.
> But quick-eyed Love, observing me grow slack
>   From my first entrance in,
> Drew nearer to me, sweetly questioning,
>   If I lacked any thing.
>
> A guest, I answered, worthy to be here:
>   Love said, You shall be he.
> I the unkind, ungrateful? Ah my dear,
>   I cannot look on thee.
> Love took my hand, and smiling did reply,
>   Who made the eyes but I?
>
> Truth Lord, but I have marred them: let my shame
>   Go where it doth deserve.
> And know you not, says Love, who bore the blame?
>   My dear, then I will serve.
> You must sit down, says Love, and taste my meat:
>   So I did sit and eat.

The Anglican metaphysician George Herbert wrote 'Love'. He had survived the religious politics of the court of King James to become the priest of a small country parish, Bemerton, which lies among rolling Wiltshire hills and shallow chalk streams.

Something of the hospitality of this landscape seems to have got into his famous poem, which speaks to us regardless of our religious beliefs.

'Love' is a poem of longing for a hospitable acceptance of our very selves. This longing is among the most profound human needs. We can imagine it as halfway between 'Consider yourself / at home', as the boys of Fagin's kitchen sing in *Oliver* and the 'Somewhere over the rainbow', that Dorothy longs for in *The Wizard of Oz*. It's the object of redemption songs and revolutionary rhetoric; of liberation theology and utopian communities; of migration and enfranchisement. It's also, as it happens, the object of talking cures and of person-centred healthcare. Gerard Manley Hopkins, in 'Heaven-Haven', called it 'Where springs not fail / [...] where flies no sharp and sided hail / [...] Where no storms come / Where the green swell is in the havens dumb / And out of the swing of the sea'. The German philosopher Martin Heidegger called this notion of perfect adaptation to an ideal home 'dwelling'.

Some of these models are tendentious, some positively dangerous and a high road to extremism of various kinds. The need to be 'bade welcome' is always imperfectly realised in our actual lives. Yet it's constantly manifesting itself. And it does so in two, not quite matching, ways. The first is that, when we feel *ourselves* to be far from the laden table, or the unfailing springs, of comfort, we struggle with meaning making. We need to make sense of bad experiences in a way we don't of good ones, which speak for themselves. The second is that when we see *other* people struggling we feel an impulse, somewhat akin to hospitality, to do what we can to put them at ease. Thus the Californian poet Robert Hass starts his poem 'Faint Music':

Maybe you need to write a poem about grace.

And he ends it, heart stoppingly:

I had the idea that the world's so full of pain
it must sometimes make a kind of singing.
And that the sequence helps, as much as order helps—
First an ego, and then pain, and then the singing.

Two different human efforts, then: to cope with what, employing a slightly dramatic-sounding shorthand, we could call suffering - and to alleviate it. And nowhere do they meet more intimately than in care settings. In health and social care, societies construct their *best* attempts at managing the suffering of individuals within their community.

Today, almost everywhere in our unequally resourced yet globally aware world, healthcare is still built on the *approximate* principles of the Hippocratic

Oath. The doctor cannot promise to cure; but he or she can - and often still does - vow to 'help the sick according to my ability and judgement, but never with a view to injury and wrong-doing'. 'According to my ability and judgement': this means that I (simply) need to do the best I can. In other words, there's 'fuzziness', a reliance on *best intentions*, in place of absolutes at the heart of care.

This *has* to be the case because - as we know from our own experiences - healthcare needs are individual. Yet healthcare is an absolute: a human right. It's enshrined in the Universal Declaration of Human Rights under Article 3 - 'the right to life, liberty and security of person' - and Article 25 (1), which states:

> Everyone has the right to a standard of living adequate for the health and well- being of himself and of his family, including food, clothing, housing and medical care and necessary social services, and the right to security in the event of unemployment, sickness, disability, widowhood, old age or other lack of livelihood in circumstances beyond his control.

The *European* Charter of Fundamental Rights puts healthcare itself, and a more proactive model of that care, centre-stage. In its revised Article 35:

> Everyone has the right of access to preventive health care and the right to benefit from medical treatment under the conditions established by national laws and practices. A high level of human health protection shall be ensured in the definition and implementation of all Union policies and activities.

The European Charter also has a more intimate starting point than the Universal Declaration. The latter, written in 1948 in the immediate aftermath of the Second World War, opens with the Article:

> All human beings are born free and equal in dignity and rights. They are endowed with reason and conscience and should act towards one another in a spirit of brotherhood.

This is a model of a just, egalitarian *society* of rational equal citizens, rather than of individual human experience.

By contrast, the first Article of the European Charter, originally promulgated in 2000, and made legally binding by the Lisbon Treaty in 2009 (though not here in the UK), states:

> Human dignity is inviolable. It must be respected and protected.

And this notion of *dignity* is key to everything I want to say today. It's an elastic concept, capable of slipperiness in judicial contexts. Nevertheless, 'dignity' appeals to a notion of human-ness as more than the sum of its parts. True, it carries with it the risk of evasiveness, pride and a dozen other human failings. But importantly it also allows us to leave what a person *is* as something underdetermined; as a *principle* rather than a *definition*.

After all, we're still finding out the limits of human attainment (not to mention other human qualities). Humans can run faster than we ever thought. They can resolve mathematical conundrums and explore regions of deep space, which previous generations believed were by definition beyond human scope. The era of global communication and travel has allowed each of us, wherever we're situated, to understand that there are more, and more radically varied, ways of speaking about the world than we realized. So the principle that dignity is fundamental to *what we are* is *not* an appeal to good manners. It *is* a capacious (re)definition of being human: one that leaves us growing room and that says, in effect, nothing more or less than that 'humans are intrinsically valuable'.

The actual wording of the European Charter is, 'human dignity is inviolable'. At first sight that seems odd. Of course people's dignity can be violated. I saw a certain amount of such violation in the locked long-stay wards of the old asylums where I first worked. In those 12- and 20-bedder 'Nightingale Wards' where the loos had no doors, where people with dementia were hit when they soiled themselves, where the most severely disabled residents were tied in their wheelchairs, residents were offered no remission in their decades-long punishment for the crime of being ill - or of having learning difficulties. P*risoners* are allowed parole and, largely, the redemptive path of rehabilitation. For these grey ghosts, with their lithium tremors, their rotten teeth and their fingers yellowed by the roll-ups that were their only recreation, there could be no end to the daily round of 'Industrial Therapy' - that cheap labour scheme which had them sorting nails by sizes for hours a day, every weekday for years - occasionally mixed with rug making, raffia and, yes, basket weaving.

What the system that controlled their lives had forgotten was that they were the ghosts of *people* and, like everybody everywhere, had the capacity and need to make meaning in and of their lives. The Romantic poet John Clare, writing in the early years of his own incarceration in Northampton Asylum, speaks for all the inhabitants of what I'd like to borrow from Fyodor Dostoevsky's portrait of arbitrary imprisonment and call *the House of the Dead* in his famous poem 'I am':

I am—yet what I am none cares or knows;
My friends forsake me like a memory lost:

I am the self-consumer of my woes—
They rise and vanish in oblivious host,
Like shadows in love's frenzied stifled throes
And yet I am, and live—like vapours tossed

Into the nothingness of scorn and noise,
Into the living sea of waking dreams,
Where there is neither sense of life or joys,
But the vast shipwreck of my life's esteems;
Even the dearest that I loved the best
Are strange—nay, rather, stranger than the rest.

I long for scenes where man hath never trod
A place where woman never smiled or wept
There to abide with my Creator, God,
And sleep as I in childhood sweetly slept,
Untroubling and untroubled where I lie
The grass below—above the vaulted sky.

Once again, this is a poem that arrives at the longing for peace.

So human dignity is inviolable in the sense that, while it *can* be attacked, it can't be reduced, because it is intrinsic. 'Dignity' names the fact that what we do to support people in health and social care is the outcome of what *they* are: not of what 'nice' people we might be.

So: insofar as human rights are facts - and, even though they're *ideas* discovered in a particular Western culture, I personally think they are - we have a *right* to be cared for. But no legislation alone can produce this care in its ideal form, because that ideal is as individual as the person who has a right to it. After all, care requires astonishing accuracy; the fine-tuning that makes it, paradoxically, into an inexact science. And not only in surgery, though that's the most obvious example. Prompt, accurate diagnosis can require radical *attention* to, and brilliant *interpretive* skills in, what a patient - inexperienced in their body's new forms of misbehaviour - hesitatingly reports. Medications work *differently* upon individual metabolisms and allergens, to say nothing of bodyweights. We can see how clumsy *legislation* is at providing the best care for each individual when we look at the effects, for example, of targets for treatment times: since though promptness is indeed vital, individual needs don't fit exactly into a single template.

So how can we think about this vital fine-tuning at the heart of care? 'Person-centred care' addresses the need to move away from top-down, 'production line' provision, and shape care around the individual needing it. The term was originally psychotherapeutic – it was coined by Carl Rogers in the 1950s - but has been applied to wider clinical provision in the US since the 1990s, with the Chronic Care Model and the Institute of Medicine's inclusion of 'patient-centredness' in its six criteria for quality care. In Britain, steps towards its adoption have included the 2000 NHS Plan, various reports, the 2009 NHS Constitution (in England), the scandals of Mid-Staffs, the 2012 health and Social Care Act (England), the Welsh White Paper, 'The Listening Organisation', and strategies in Scotland and Northern Ireland. In its 2014 report, *Person-Centred Care Made Simple*, The Health Foundation resists defining person-centred care, since that would undermine its very project, but argues that it should include,

1. Affording people dignity, compassion and respect.
2. Offering coordinated care, support or treatment.
3. Offering personalised care, support or treatment.
4. Supporting people to recognise and develop their own strengths and abilities to enable them to live an independent and fulfilling life.

This '*direction* of care' and the good practice that results from it is and has not been always the case. The American Confessional poet Anne Sexton, who killed herself in 1974 at the age of forty-five, excoriates one-size-fits-all Occupational Therapy in 'Ringing the Bells', from her 1960 collection *To Bedlam and Part Way Back*:

> And this is the way they ring
> the bells in Bedlam
> and this is the bell-lady
> who comes each Tuesday morning
> to give us a music lesson
> and because the attendants make you go
> and because we mind by instinct,
> like bees caught in the wrong hive,
> we are the circle of the crazy ladies
> who sit in the lounge of the mental house
> and smile at the smiling woman
> who passes us each a bell,
> who points at my hand
> that holds my bell, E flat,
> [...]
> and this is how the bells really sound,
> as untroubled and clean

as a workable kitchen,
and this is always my bell responding
to my hand that responds to the lady
who points at me, E flat;
and although we are no better for it,
they tell you to go. And you do.

One problem with the scenario she describes is that this bell ringing isn't voluntary. It's a 'treatment'. Music can be an art; it can also be entertainment. The activity in this poem is neither, because it has nothing to do with a person and how they *choose* to spend their time. Instead it reduces each individual to a 'hand', part of a human glockenspiel.

The arts in healthcare are often confused with Occupational Therapy, but they are not OT. Indeed, they are not any kind of therapy. The reason for this is not that healthcare arts practitioners aren't trained clinicians - though we're not, and should never forget that fact - but that *art itself* is not therapy. In the same way, healthcare arts also get confused with art therapy: which views the artwork - indeed, all symbol formation - as pathological, that's to say as a symptom of what is supposedly wrong with an individual. We see clearly how far this important *clinical* approach is from art when psychoanalytic critics take apart a well-known work of art or of literature. Their reading of it as an *involuntary* tracing of the psyche cuts out everything we might conceivably argue that art is - minimally, an intentional act of making, formally structured, related to other similar work - not to mention more detailed and contested notions like order, beauty, or expression.

Of course, every individual, including the artist–maker, has a psychological prehistory. But human-rights legislation - and the practice of care itself - acknowledge that our human-ness *encompasses and is prior* to such prehistories, just as it is to a broken leg or a blocked artery. So art in health and social care, an intentional, human practice, must be art *in the same way* as if it were produced in any other setting in order to *be art*. (As an aside there's an argument that some people wouldn't produce art in any other setting. Many of the people we work with have no prior engagement with the arts. Some have little literacy, too. This is true, and something we're proud of; but it gainsays nothing of the nature of art. All it tells us is that health and social care represent an *opportunity* for art to happen.)

What, then, *are* the arts doing in health and social care? I think the answer lies in a principle which mirrors human dignity: that of hospitality. The American *literary* theorist Gayatri Chakravorty Spivak talks about *translation* as imposing a duty of hospitality on the translator, especially when she or he is translating texts originally published in the developing world into English, this language of global power. Spivak lives and works in the US, but grew up in Kolkata. She's well aware that poor translations disenfranchise texts, ideas, discoveries and authors. We all know this, too: even without being literary translators. When Hollywood gives villains thick Slavic or Arabic accents, we read its signal that these characters are framed as bad, untrustworthy, and different from the *us* it puts centre stage. What I've taken to calling 'meerkat English' is used to indicate characters are at best naïve or unintelligent: anyway, less than that *us* and disposable as 'collateral damage' in an action movie, or an admiring chorus throwing the blond protagonists of a romantic comedy into relief.

Spivak says a good translator must be like Herbert's 'Love': the proactive host who 'drew near me, sweetly questioning if I lacked anything'. They must *go some way to meet* the guest they are welcoming into a new language. It's not for nothing that we call this new language the 'host'. Such going out of the way to *meet* means thinking through the quality of a translation and paying attention to the very nuances that make it clear, authoritative and characterful in the original language: the exact synonym, the appropriate register, the grammatically elegant expression. This process is by definition antimechanical and conscientiously reflexive. (It is not, and never can be, Google Translate.)

For all that Hollywood suggests we'd prefer language to be a flavourless carrier, which simply lets us digest *what it has to say*, language itself *is* what it has to say. Language *ain't what you do, it's the way that you do it*. Language has our fingerprints all over it. We are all native speakers not only of a national or international language called English, or Urdu, or Finnish but (as Jacques Lacan says in a more complicated way) something much more local, and personal: our own way of putting things. This means that to listen, really to pay attention, to what someone else has to say requires us to step outside our own native idiolect and try on another way of thinking and speaking. It means doing something less automatic than seeing the world 'in our own terms'. That cliché says it all.

When I was first theorising writing in healthcare, I wrote extensively about how language is the way we make through the world (since we 'have' the world via our *experience* of it). I don't want to repeat myself here, but just to remind us how hard different ways of knowing about something find it to coexist. Healthcare's an obvious example: domestic common sense (wrap up warm!), alternative therapies, a GP and a research scientist all frame even the common cold differently from each other. And *each* way of going on feels it has a monopoly on accurate knowledge.

'Tomayto, Tomahto, Potayto, Potahto: let's call the whole thing off!' We're like nothing so much as monarchs of our own little walled cities, occasionally emerging from the fortified barbican to parlay. And emerging thus can make us feel vulnerable. So why do it? Well, the *solipsistic* reason is curiosity. It's interesting to know about different worlds of experience. But the *ethical* reason is that the other person is another self. Immanuel Kant's 'ethics of recognition' (my term) are developed in his *Prolegomena to Any Future Metaphysics*. The other person is my mirror image: and matters as much or as little as I do.

Kant founded his ethics on empiricism - on his study, in *Critique of Pure Reason*, of how we know anything - because he wanted to bind them into the world of facts. But there's another version of rights and obligations, one much closer to the personal, individuated and *fuzzy* heart of healthcare. Hospitality isn't a legal obligation, but it *is* a special kind of deep choice, for which we have words such as 'honour', 'duty' and even 'sacred'. Arguably, it's with such deep choices that we assert our own humanity.

In cultures other than the Anglo-Saxon, where hospitality is a more central form of behaviour than it is here in the Anglo-American North, the special character of this kind of choice is both more apparent and more embedded in tradition. In some cultures, hospitality becomes a proof of power, of masculinity (or of femininity). So it's not surprising that lavish demonstrations of hospitality are promised by, for example, the God of the Abrahamic traditions. The Judaic 'land flowing with milk and honey' has the kind of geophysical detail you'd expect of a desert religion. In Deuteronomy 8 it becomes,

> [7] [...] a good land, a land of brooks of water, of fountains and springs, flowing forth in valleys and hills,
>
> [8] a land of wheat and barley, of vines and fig trees and pomegranates, a land of olive trees and honey,
>
> [9] a land in which you will eat bread without scarcity, in which you will lack nothing, a land whose stones are iron, and out of whose hills you can dig copper.
>
> [10] And you shall eat and be full.

Meanwhile the promise to Christians, 'Come unto me all you that labour and are heavy laden, and I will give you rest', appears in Matthew 11:28, while Islamic descriptions of Jannah (Paradise) speak of a soil made of saffron, pearls or fragrant musk, of fruit trees and of a life of perpetual happiness and youth. Hospitality is the proof of God's power; as well as the object of human longing.

Which brings us back to George Herbert. His hospitable principle is an interlocutor, not merely a provider, who approaches, questions and smiles at the narrator, and even takes his hand. Most memorably, it is 'quick-eyed': that's to say, *reactive* and *individual*. And so we have three strands of the same *flexible* principle: dignity, translation and hospitality. The Welsh word *ystwyth* means winding, flexible (I should know: I was brought up in a town named for it) and this indirect-ness, this hospitable refusal to 'cut to the chase' and do away with humanizing niceties, is what allows the most dazzlingly accurate translations, the most acutely attentive welcome, to greet the guest: whether they're visiting a language, or a healthcare unit.

It's mirrored in poetry's equally capacious indirectness, the 'slant' that allows us to 'tell all the truth', as Emily Dickinson said we should,

> Tell all the truth but tell it slant—
> Success in circuit lies
> Too bright for our infirm Delight
> The Truth's superb surprise
> As Lightning to the Children eased
> With explanation kind
> The Truth must dazzle gradually
> Or every man be blind—

Working with the arts in healthcare adds to the gestures of hospitality being performed by clinicians and social carers. Art is many things, but above all it is additional, creative, disobedient and indirect. Poetry, that cheapest and most portable of all its forms, sneaks into the unit, on the bedside table or overheard in a day room. It arrives as a piece of paper folded into a paperback, a poster in the long corridor down to X-ray, something heard on hospital radio, or as a few words jotted down in a notebook or dictated to an arts worker. Half remembered, it stays in the mind like an earworm or a guide: the 'Everyman, I will go with thee and be thy guide/In thy most need to go by thy side' of the old Everyman's Library books (and the eponymous mediaeval play that is its source).

I like to think there's a paradoxical correlation between the unassuming forms poetry takes in the world - its apparent physical fragility and small scale - and the explosive power of all that can be compressed into it: William Blake's 'World in a Grain of Sand', perhaps. The Chilean poet, diplomat and Nobel Laureate Pablo Neruda acknowledges its power to step forward and greet us, even when we don't expect it:

> And it was at that age [...] Poetry arrived
> in search of me. I don't know, I don't know where
> it came from, from winter or a river.
> I don't know how or when,
> no, they were not voices, they were not
> words, nor silence,
> but from a street I was summoned,

from the branches of night,
abruptly from the others,
among violent fires
or returning alone,
there I was without a face
and it touched me.

I did not know what to say, my mouth
had no way
with names
my eyes were blind,
and something started in my soul,
fever or forgotten wings,
and I made my own way,
deciphering
that fire
and I wrote the first faint line,
faint, without substance, pure
nonsense,
pure wisdom
of someone who knows nothing.

Poetry's capacious makes it somewhere within which to make meaning. In translation by the Palestinian American poet Fady Joudah, Mahmoud Darwish's 'Your Night is of Lilac' opens,

The night sits wherever you are. Your night
is of lilac. Every now and then a gesture escapes
from the beam of your dimples, breaks the wineglass
and lights up the starlight. And your night is your shadow—
a fairy-tale piece of land to make our dreams equal.

Like Neruda, Darwish was a 'national' poet, a spokesman for his generation and people. Like Neruda's, his spokesmanship was all the more powerful because it was not literal but 'poetic'. Poetry allows us to go beyond what explanation and denotation allow us to say: in T. S. Eliot's 'raids on the inarticulate'. Poetry allows for evocation and allusion to what is too risky or controversial to make explicit. Famous examples include the playful, magical realist parables of Central European verse under communist censorship. A poem from, say, the controversial Polish poet Zbigniew Herbert's 1974 book *Mr Cogito* blinks its wide-open eyes innocently at the censor. Closer to home, this makes poetry the advocate's tool in health and social care. Whether they compose or simply quote it, someone in a position of institutional weakness can use it to express, for example, anger or other dangerous emotions.

Speaking from such a position has symbolic value no matter what is said. The passive 'patient', enduring care, becomes a speaking Subject of that care. What they say has yet more power when it has a discrete discursive identity, as poetry does. We can see this from the counterexample of not speaking. The leading British Surrealist poet of the interwar years, David Gascoyne, was famously 'discovered' living in a back ward of Whitecroft, the Isle of Wight County Asylum, when a volunteer on the ward read a poem in the dayroom which had been written by him, and which he spoke up to claim. Gascoyne went on to leave the asylum and marry the volunteer. (Of course, though he was rescued by Judy's recognition, Gascoyne wasn't 'discovered' *to himself: he was there all along.*) While Gascoyne was growing up, another fine poet, Ivor Gurney, was being committed in turn, first to Gloucester County Asylum and then to Stone House Hospital at Dartford in Kent, for the last fifteen years of his life, thus ending his poetry writing and musical composition, too.

For a couple of years I worked with Sue who, mute while sectioned, was released to day care after she began to speak again. She writes about this in her poem 'Lost for Words'. Because of the way she uses repetition and rhythmic line-breaks, you can hear the tearing effort involved in pulling herself out of silence into the position of the one who speaks. To read her poem is to be forced to *go through* these language experiences:

> You see I could
> I could speak
> I could speak a few words
> Some strange
> Some strange half felt sentiment
> I could
> I could try
> If only I could make the connection
> The connection
> Connection between thought
> Between thought and sound
> Sound
> That's it
> Sound
> A collection
> A collection of
> Of what? Yes that's it

A collection of vowels
To string
To string
To string a sentence
A sentence together
To connect
To make
To make some sort
Some sort of contact
A statement
A statement to
A statement to the effect
To the effect
To say
To say
I am still alive!

This is explicitly autobiographical stuff. But poetry can also offer a kind of privacy. Its indirectness is a fancy dress that may disguise serious intent; or anyway distance it. What a poem *says* need not be taken as confessional. This privacy extends to the *amount* that's understood by a poem's readers. Maybe Edward Thomas's 'Lights Out', for example, really is just a poem about rest, despite its military title and the context of its composition; or maybe it's about death. We let the possibilities oscillate as we read, according to the way we're feeling:

I have come to the borders of sleep,
The unfathomable deep
Forest where all must lose
Their way, however straight,
Or winding, soon or late;
They cannot choose.

On the other hand, poetry can make a point memorable. Poetic form is a mnemonic device. Its attractive qualities – attract us. 'What is this life if, full of care, / We have no time to stand and stare?' the Welsh poet W. H. Davies asks in his poem, 'Leisure', as so many have before and since; but because *he* asks in rhyme, we remember it.

Most of the poems I've chosen for this lecture are also well-known: they demonstrate how there *is* no separation between what poems do within and beyond health and social care. Poetry in health and social care is not instrumental: it works *as* poetry. But perhaps because it's positioned precisely here, at the nub of what both art and human nature are, the hospital arts movement has sometimes had trouble keeping its identity straight in the minds of decision makers. The tendency is to see it as neither good art nor germane to health and social care, but as only halfway to art and halfway to care. In fact, of course, it offers the very best of what art and care are, since it goes to the heart of each matter.

The Wellcome Trust's acquisition of the healthcare arts movement's national archives is an important milestone, and I hope will encourage all stakeholders to think again about the field. Medical Humanities can sometimes seem the preserve either of medical historians, or of artists' representations of healthcare, or of scientific research. These are fascinating: but research into what happens when the arts are actually at the place and moment of illness, vulnerability and care is surely as urgently important. We need to ask providers to consider this, so that today's practitioners and researchers aren't forced away from the arts in health and social care, as I was, by the absence of a joined-up career 'path' or the opportunity to research these practices. Today, we do have academic research communities, including the Centre for Medical Humanities at Durham University, where Mike White himself was based. We need to resource and reward such examples of good practice. We need a growing body of curatorial, publishing and archival work to continue to make the arts in healthcare audible and visible. We need to stop assuming practitioners are half-and-halfs, incapable of thinking about and articulating their practice; and instead to see them as *doubly* skilled. And we need to remember to integrate their practice in health and social care with the rest of their artistic practice and their working (i.e., earning) lives, so that the very best people continue to work where art is most coherently and urgently itself.

SELECTED BIBLIOGRAPHY

Introduction

Sampson, Fiona. 'World Asleep', in *When Love Speaks*. Edited by Adam O'Riordan, 217. London: Vintage, 2011.

———. 'What the Water Says', in *Kathleen Jamie: Essays and Poems on Her Work*. Edited by Rachel Falconer, 123–25. Edinburgh: Edinburgh University Press, 2015.

———. 'Drowned Man', in *On Shakespeare's Sonnets: A Poets' Celebration*. Edited by Hannah Crawforth and Elizabeth Scott-Baumann. 67–68. London: Bloomsbury, 2016.

———. 'Cuckoo', in *The Long White Thread of Words: Poems for John Berger*. Edited by Amarajīta Candana, Yasmin Gunaratnam, Gareth Evans. 138–39. Grewelthorpe: Smokestack, 2017.

From the Hebrew Side. Translated by Amir Or. 332–35. Bnei Brak: Hakibbutz, 2017.

Hearthsides and Hospices

Hunt, Celia and Fiona Sampson. 'Introduction', in *The Self on the Page: Theory and Practice of Creative Writing in Personal Development*. Edited by Celia Hunt and Fiona Sampson, London: Jessica Kingsley Publishers, 1998. (SP)

Paterson, Don. *The Poem: Lyric, Sign, Metre*. London: Faber & Faber, 2018.

Sampson, Fiona. *The Healing Word*. London: The Poetry Society, 1998. (HW)

———. 'Towards a theoretical framework for creative writing in health-care'. PhD diss., Catholic University of Nijmegen, 2001.

———. 'Afterword', in Amir Or, *Poem*. Translated by Helena Berg, 74–78. Dublin: Dedalus, 2004. (P)

———. 'Foreword', in *Creative Writing in Health and Social Care*. Edited by Fiona Sampson, 9–12. London: Jessica Kingsley Publishers, 2004. (CWHSC)

———. 'Introduction', in *A Fine Line: New Poetry from Eastern and Central Europe*. Edited by Jean Boase-Beier, Alexandra Büchler, Fiona Sampson, 14. Lancashire: Arc Publications, 2004. (AFL)

———. 'Introduction', in *Percy Bysshe Shelley*, selected by Fiona Sampson, 4–14. London: Faber & Faber, 2011. (PBS)

———. 'Practical Measures: Poet as Editor', in *Creativity in Language: The State of the Art*. Edited by Joan Swann, Robert Pope and Ronald Carter, 245–49. London: Palgrave Macmillan, 2011. (PM)

———. 'Sean O'Brien: The Compassionate Moralist'. *European Atlas Prize Jury*, Introductory Essay, Chair, 2015. (SB)

———. 'A Speaking Likeness: Poetry Within Health and Social Care', in Inaugural Wellcome Trust Public Annual Mike White Memorial Lecture, 1–22. London: Creativity and Wellbeing, 2016. (SL)

———. 'Two Traditions: A Century of Women's Writing', in *Times Literary Supplement* 25 May 2018, No. 6008. 32–33. (TT)

———. 'Introduction: The Journey from Word to Day' on Amir Or'. *European Atlas Prize Jury*, Introductory Essay, Chair, 2016: 2. (JWD)

———. 'Introduction: The Journey from Word to Day'. Poem: *International English Language Quarterly*, vol. 6, no. 2, July 2018: 195–201. Taylor & Francis Online.

———. 'Sean O'Brien: The Compassionate Moralist'. Poem: *International English Language Quarterly*, vol. 6, no. 2, July 2018: 177–82. Taylor & Francis Online. (SB)

———. 'Ted Hughes's Literary Legacy', in *Ted Hughes in Context*. Edited by Terry Gifford, 33–42. Cambridge: Cambridge University Press, 2018. (TH)

———. 'Foreword: The Critic as Pandar' in William Empson, trans., Alipio de Franca, *Seven Types of Ambiguity*. Rio de Janeiro: 34 Publishing House, 2020. (CP)

———. Strait and Slant: Tsvetanka Elenkova's *Crookedness*' in Tsvetanka Elenkova, *Crookedness*, trans. Johnathan Dunne. Bristol: Shearsman, 2019. (TSC).

———. 'After Plath: The Legacy of Influence', in *Sylvia Plath in Context*. Edited by Tracy Brain, 350–59. Cambridge: Cambridge University Press, 2019. (SP)

Wiman, Christian. *My Bright Abyss: Meditation of a Modern Believer*. New York: Farrar, Straus & Giroux, 2014.

From the Looking Glass to the Lamp

Adorno, Theodor W. *Hegel: Three Studies*. Translated by Shierry Weber Nicholsen. Cambridge, MA & London: MIT Press, 1993.

———. *Kant's Critique of Pure Reason*. Edited by Rolf Tiedemann, translated by Rodney Livingstone. Stanford: Stanford University Press, 2001.

———. *Minima Moralia*, London: Verso, 2005.

———. *History and Freedom: Lectures 1964–1965*. Edited by Rolf Tiedemann, translated by Rodney Livingstone. Cambridge: Polity, 2006.

Bencivenga, Ermanno. *Kant's Copernican Revolution*. Oxford: Oxford University Press, 1987.

———. *The Discipline of Subjectivity: An Essay on Montaigne*. Princeton: Princeton University Press, 1990. (TDS)

———. *Hegel's Dialectical Logic*. Oxford: Oxford University Press, 2000. (HDL)

———. *Dancing Souls*. Oxford: Lexington Books, 2003. (DS)

———. *A Theory of Language and Mind*. Berkeley, Los Angeles, London: University of California Press, 2007. (TLM)

———. *Theories of the Logos*. Irvine: Springer 2017 (TL)

Bernstein, J.M. *Adorno: Disenchantment and Ethics*. Cambridge: Cambridge University Press, 2001.

Bishop, Elizabeth. 'One Art' in *Poems: The Centenary Edition*. London: Chatto & Windus, 2011.

Boyd, Bryan. *Vladimir Nabokov: The American Years*. Princeton: Princeton University Press, 1991.

Brooks, Peter. *The Melodramatic Imagination: Balzac, Henry James, Melodrama, and the Mode of Excess*. New Haven & London: Yale University Press, 1995.

Chesterton, G.K. *Robert Browning*. London: House of Stratus, 2001.

Clark, T.J. *Farewell to an Idea: Episodes from a History of Modernism*. New Haven & London: Yale University Press, 2001.

SELECTED BIBLIOGRAPHY

Collini, Stefan. *The Nostalgic Imagination: History in English Criticism*. Oxford: Oxford University Press, 2019.

Eliot, T. S. *Selected Essays*. London: Faber & Faber, 1951.

———. 'Tradition and the Individual Talent', in *The Sacred Wood: Essays on Poetry and Criticism*. 47–59. London and New York: Methuen, 1983.

———. 'The Metaphysical Poets', in *Selected Essays*. London: Faber & Faber, 1999.

Ford, Madox Ford. 'On Impressionism', in *Critical Writings of Ford Madox Ford*. Edited by Frank MacShane. Lincoln: University of Nebraska Press, 1964.

Freud, Sigmund. 'Beyond the Pleasure Principle', in *The Essentials of Psycho-Analysis*. Edited by Anna Freud, translated by James Strachey, 218–68. London: Penguin Books, 1991.

Heaney, Seamus. *Death of a Naturalist*. London: Faber & Faber, 1966.

Heidegger, Martin. *Being and Time*. Translated by John Macquarrie and Edward Robinson. New York: HarperCollins, 2008.

Hunt, Celia and Fiona Sampson. *Writing: Self and Reflexivity*. London: Palgrave Macmillan, 2005. (WSR)

Kant, Immanuel. *Critique of the Power of Judgement*. Translated by Paul Guyer and Eric Matthews. Cambridge, New York, Melbourne, Cape Town, Singapore, & Sao Paulo: Cambridge University Press, 2000. (CPJ)

Kenner, Hugh. *Paradox in Chesterton*. Michigan: Sheed & Ward, 1948.

Korsgaard, Christine M., G. A Cohen, Raymond Geuss, Thomas Nagel, and Bernard Williams. *The Sources of Normativity*. Edited by Onora O'Neill. Cambridge: Cambridge University Press, 1996.

Lacan, Jacques. *The Seminar of Jacques Lacan Book XX*. Edited by Jacques-Alain Miller, translated by Bruce Fink. New York: W. W. Norton, 2000.

———. 'The Signification of the Phallus', in *Écrits*. Translated by Bruce Fink. 575–84. New York & London: W. W. Norton, 2007.

Nabokov, Vladimir. *The Real Life of Sebastian Knight*. London: Penguin, 2012.

Ragland-Sullivan, Ellie. *Jacques Lacan and the Philosophy of Psychoanalysis*. Urbana & Chicago: University of Illinois Press, 1986.

Rose, Gillian. *Mourning Becomes the Law: Philosophy and Representation*. Cambridge: Cambridge University Press, 1996.

Sampson, Fiona. *Picasso's Men*. Newbury: Phoenix Press, 1993.

———. *Folding the Real*. Wales: Seren, 2001. (FR)

———. *The Distance Between Us*. Wales: Seren, 2005. (DB)

———. *On Listening: Selected Essays*. Cromer: Salt, 2007. (OL)

———. *Common Prayer*. Manchester: Carcanet, 2007. (CP)

———. *Rough Music*. Manchester: Carcanet, 2010. (RM)

———. *Music Lessons*. Hexham: Bloodaxe Books, 2011. (ML)

———. *Beyond the Lyric*. London: Chatto & Windus, 2012. (BL)

———. *Coleshill*. London: Penguin Random House, 2013. (CH)

———. *The Catch*. London: Penguin Random House, 2016. (TC)

———. *Come Down*. London: Corsair, 2020. (CD)

Shelley, Mary. *Frankenstein*. Edited by D. L. Macdonald and Kathleen Scherf. Ontario: Broadview Press, 1999.

Sontag, Susan. 'Introduction' in Walter Benjamin *One-Way Street and Other Writings*. Translated by Edmund Jephcott and Kingsley Shorter, 7–28. London & New York: Verso, 1998.

Steiner, George. *Real Presences*. Chicago: University of Chicago Press, 1991.

Strawson, P. F. *The Bounds of Sense: An Essay on Kant's Critique of Pure Reason*. London & New York: Routledge, 1999.

Tóibín, Colm. *On Elizabeth Bishop*. Princeton & Oxford: Princeton University Press, 2015.

Worringer, Wilhelm. *Abstraction and Empathy: A Contribution to the Psychology of Style*. Translated by Michael Bullock. Chicago: Elephant Paperbacks, 1997.

Prose Animations

Bishop, Elizabeth. 'One Art', in *Complete Poems*. London: Chatto & Windus, 1983.

Buck-Morss, Susan. *The Origin of Negative Dialectics: Theodor W. Adorno, Walter Benjamin, and the Frankfurt Institute*. New York: Free Press, 1979.

Durrell, Lawrence. *Caesar's Vast Ghost: Aspects of Provence*. London: Faber & Faber, 1990.

———. *Bitter Lemons of Cyprus*. London: Faber & Faber, 2000.

———. *Reflections on a Marine Venus*. London: Faber & Faber, 2000.

———. *The Alexandria Quartet*. London: Faber & Faber, 2012.

Heaney, Seamus. *The Redress of Poetry: Oxford Lectures*. London: Faber & Faber, 2002.

Marcus, Laura. *Auto/biographical Discourses: Criticism, Theory, Practice*. Manchester & New York: Manchester University Press, 1994.

Olney, James. *Memory and Narrative: The Weave of Life-Writing*. Chicago & London: University of Chicago Press, 1998.

Sabbagh, Omar. 'Animating places: Reading Fiona Sampson's *Limestone Country* beneath a Durrellian lens'. *Prose Studies: History, Theory, Criticism*, vol. 39, Issue 2–3, 2017: 120–31. Taylor & Francis Online, April 2018.

Sampson, Fiona. *Limestone Country*. Dorset: Little Toller Books, 2017.

———. *In Search of Mary Shelley: The Girl Who Wrote Frankenstein*. London: Profile Books, 2018. (SMS) (MS)

Saunders, Max. *Self Impression: Life-Writing, Autobiografiction, and the Forms of Modern Literature*. Oxford: Oxford University Press, 2010.

Schama, Simon. *Rembrandt's Eyes*. London: Penguin Books, 2014.

Watt, Ian. *Conrad in the Nineteenth Century*. Berkeley & Los Angeles: University of California Press, 1981.

Woolf, Virginia. 'The New Biography', in *Selected Essays*. Edited by David Bradshaw. Oxford: Oxford University Press, 2008: 95–100.

For the Love of Music

Adorno, Theodor W. *Negative Dialectics*. Translated by E. B. Ashton. London: Routledge, 1996.

Eliot, T. S. 'The Perfect Critic', in *The Sacred Wood: Essays on Poetry and Criticism*, 1–19. London & New York: Methuen, 1983.

Fink, Bruce. *Lacan to the Letter: Reading Écrits Closely*. Minneapolis & London: University of Minnesota Press, 2004.

Heidegger, Martin. *Introduction to Metaphysics*. Translated by Gregory Fried and Richard Polt. New York & London: Yale University Press, 2000.

Said, Edward W. *Beginnings: Intention & Method*. London: Granta Books, 1997.

Sampson, Fiona. *Music Lessons*. Hexham: Bloodaxe Books, 2011. (ML)

———. *Beyond the Lyric*. London: Chatto & Windus, 2012. (BTL)

———. *Lyric Cousins: Poetry and Musical Form*. Edinburgh: Edinburgh University Press, 2016. (LC)

Appendix

Baum, L. Frank. *The Wizard of Oz*. Hertfordshire: Wordsworth Editions, 1993.

Blake, William. *A Grain of Sand: Poems for Young Readers*. Edited by Rosemary Manning. London: Bodley Head, 1968.

Clare, John. *'I Am': The Selected Poetry of John Clare*. New York: Farrar, Straus & Giroux, 2003.

Darwish, Mahmoud. 'Your Night is of Lilac', in *The Butterfly's Burden*. Translated by Fady Joudah. Port Townsend: Copper Canyon Press, 2007.

Davies, W. H. 'Leisure', in *Songs of Joy*. London: A. C. Fifield, 1911.

Dickens, Charles. *The Adventures of Oliver Twist*. London: Chapman & Hall, 1866.

Dickinson, Emily. 'Tell all the truth but tell it slant', in *The Poems of Emily Dickinson*. Edited by Ralph W. Franklin, Cambridge, MA: Harvard University Press, 1998.

Dostoyevsky, Fyodor. *House of the Dead*. Translated by Constance Garnett. New York: Dover Publications, 2004.

Hass, Robert. 'Faint Music', in *Sun Under Wood*. New York: HarperCollins, 1998.

Health Foundation. 'Person-centered care made simple'. *The Health Foundation*, January 2016. www.health.org.uk/sites/default/files/PersonCentredCareMadeSimple.pdf.

Herbert, George. 'Love', in *The English Poems of George Herbert*. Edited by Helen Wilcox. Cambridge: Cambridge University Press, 2007.

Herbert, Zbigniew. *Mr Cogito (1974)*. New York: HarperCollins, 1995.

Hopkins, Gerard Manley. 'Heaven Haven', in *Selected Poems*, Edited by Bob Blaisdell. New York: Dover Thrift, 2011.

Kant, Immanuel. *Critique of Pure Reason*. Translated by J. M. D. Meiklejohn. London: G. Bell, 1887.

Kant, Immanuel. *Prolegomena to any Future Metaphysics*. Edited by Paul Carus. Chicago: Open Court, 1967.

Neruda, Pablo. 'Poetry', in *Pablo Neruda: Selected Poems*. Edited by Nathaniel Tarn, translated by Anthony Kerrigan et al. Boston: Houghton Mifflin/Seymour Lawrence, 1990.

Sexton, Anne. 'Ringing the Bells', in *To Bedlam and Part Way Back*. Boston: Houghton Mifflin Harcourt, 1960.

Thomas, Edward. 'Lights Out'. In *The Poems of Edward Thomas*. Haddington: Handsel Books, 2003.

Williams, Allison, Jan Davies, Mike Spencer and Terence Canning. 'White Paper Series – No. 11: Ensuring care is person-centred in NHS Wales'. *The Listening Organisation*, June 2018, www.1000livesplus.wales.nhs.uk/sitesplus/documents/1011/1000%20Lives%20Plus%20-%20%27The%20Listening%20Organisation%27%20white%20paper%20WEB.pdf.

INDEX

Adorno, Theodor W. 12, 28, 44–45, 90, 138, 142, 160
aesthetic 11–13, 16, 18, 80, 90, 113, 136, 140, 143, 145, 147, 148, 159
  abstract art 85
  ambiguity 18, 27–28, 31, 34, 66, 90, 105
  amphiboly 57, 61, 82, 92
  Borgesian 65
  chiaroscuro 55, 59, 96, 123–24, 125
  chromaticism 138, 155
  creative writing 2, 3, 8, 10, 14, 19–26, 29–30, 107, 112, 114, 120, 121, 124, 145
  cubism 88
  diachronic 153, 154, 156
  dialogic 137
  dramatis personae 105, 107–8, 115, 128
  eros 40, 42, *See* erotic
  erotic 34
  euphony 67
  formalism 137, 140
  gothic 59, 93, 95–96
  impressionism 39, 61, 106, 112–13
  inter-textual 73, 76
  irony 4, 33–34, 57, 75, 113, 132, 146
  Jamesian 122
  literary-critical xiii, 1, 6, 135
  literary-theoretical 1, 152
  magical realist 173
  in medias res 75, 108
  metafictional 114
  metaphysical poets 31, 46, *See also* metaphysics
  meta-textual 36, 73, 76
  mimetic 64
  music 1, 4–6, 15, 20, 26, 27, 35, 36–37, 40, 46, 49–53, 55, 58, 64, 69, 71, 74, 83–85, 89, 90, 97, 107, 110, 121, 126, 137–45, 147–57, 169, 174
    Royal Academy of Music, The 6
  mythopoetic 4, 112, 118, 146, *See* myth
  negative capability 17, 31, 92
  poesis 12, 41
  poetics 1–5, 14–18, 21, 27, 29–32, 36, 37–38, 45–46, 59, 63–64, 67, 71, 73, 83, 132, 136, 138, 140–44, 146–47, 155
  portraiture 124–26, 128, 166
  post-literary 12
  romanticism 15–17, 101, 121, 123, 127, 151, 159, 166, *See also* philsosphy
  showing and telling 15, *See also* creative writing
  sublime 61, 93, 94, 96–97, 132, 160
  surrealism 140, 145, 174
  synecdoche 76, 140
  trope 2, 4, 15, 28, 44, 64, 77, 92, 99, 102, 103, 111, 116, 120, 122, 142, 147, 155
Andrukhovych, Yuri 9

Baudelaire, Charles 136
Belloc, Hilaire 160
Bencivenga, Ermanno 28, 29–30, 43, 44, 79, 138, 142
Benjamin, Walter 12
Berger, John 7, 149
Bettelheim, Bruno 43
Bishop, Elizabeth 79, 84, 133, 145
Blake, William 172
blogosphere 12
Borodale, Sean 10
Boulez, Pierre 153
Bunting, Basil 145

Burnside, John 10, 136, 143, 146, 156, 157
Byron, Lord 61, 127

Chesterton, G. K. 71, 119, 159–60, *See also Paradox in Chesterton*
chiasmus 14, 17, 25, 34
Cixous, Hélène 7, 44
Clare, John 166
community 4, 5, 6, 14, 19, 20–21, 27, 61, 63, 76, 85, 86, 88, 103, 116, 135, 138, 149, 154, 164
confessional 16, 29, 168, 175, *See also* psychology, religion
Conrad, Joseph 36, 124
Cope, Wendy 136
Cornwallis, Sir William 71

Dante, Alighieri 61, 84
Darwish, Mahmoud 118, 149–50, 173
Davies, W. H. 175
Dickinson, Emily 23, 58, 71, 139, 172
Dostoevsky, Fyodor 166
Durrell, Lawrence 4, 35, 105–19

Elenkova, Tsvetanka 18
Eliot, T. S. 7, 29, 37, 43, 112, 135–36, 173
Empson, William 18
European Charter, The 22, 165–66

Fainlight, Ruth 10
Farewell to an Idea (Clark) 88
Feinstein, Elaine 10, 145
Ford, Ford Madox 39, 41
Frankenstein (Shelley) 4, 5, 9, 59, 95–96, 101, 120–24, 126, 128, 132, *See also* gothic, Shelley, Mary
Freud, Sigmund 39–40, 61, 63, 67, 69, 74, 132

Gascoyne, David 174
geography 4, 9, 15, 117, 118, *See also* topography
Godwin, Mary 129
Godwin, William 130
Google Translate 170
Gospodinov, Goergi 9
grammar 17, 32, 35, 38, 85, 88, 124, 126, 127, 156, *See also* creative writing

Greenlaw, Lavinia 143
Gurney, Ivor 174

Hammami, Rema 149
Harrison, Austen 112
haunting 4, 5, 59, 61–62, 64, 66, 71, 96, 111, *See also* gothic
health and social care 3, 15, 19–26, 163–76
  Age Concern 21
  Chronic Care Model 167
  dignity 25, 32, 35, 81, 165–68, 169, 171
  embodiment 3, 5, 11, 14, 15, 33–34, 35, 38, 40, 41, 46, 53, 138, 142, *See also* incarnation
  empathy 4, 5, 26, 33–34, 35, 79–85, 123, 126–27, 128, 160
  Hippocratic Oath 164
  Medical Humanities 176
  NHS 8, 21, 167
  psychology 19, 21, 24, 30, 37, 39, 43, 85, 120, 121, 123, 130, 155, 167, 169
    archetype 62
    identity 17, 28, 32, 36–37, 44, 56, 112, 123, 146, 155, 174, 175
    therapy 22, 23, 30, 35, 166, 168–69
    trauma 19, 47, 60, 64, 155
    uncanny 4, 37, 150, *See also* Freud, Sigmund
    unconscious 33, 36, 61–64, 153, *See also* Freud, Sigmund
Heaney, Seamus 104, 132
Hegel, Georg Wilhelm Friedrich 28, 43, 48, 138, 160
Heidegger, Martin 20, 67, 157, 164
Herbert, George 22, 25, 163, 170, 171
Hill, Geoffrey 145
Hill, Selima 10, 24
history 12, 20, 24, 35, 41, 43, 48, 56, 68, 87, 106, 110, 111, 114, 116, 117–18, 119, 123, 128–32, 137, 144–45, 147, 155, 169, 176
  '1968' 50
  British Corn Laws, The 130
  French Revolution, The 130
  Harlem Renaissance, The 50

INDEX

myth 15, 17, 33, 51–52, 93, 94, 98–99, 100–2, 106–7, 111–12, 114, 118, *See also* mythopoetic
   Napoleonic Wars, The 130
   Reign of Terror, The 130
   Second World War, The 165
   Soviet Union, The 55
   Victorian 122
Hogg, Thomas Jefferson 131
Hollywood 169–70
Hopkins, Gerard Manley 155, 164
hospitality 3, 5, 20, 25, 28, 164, 169, 171–72
Hunt, Celia 3, 19, 23, 29, 37

internationalism 9–10, 18, 41
Isle of Wight, The 21, 174

Jancar, Drago 9
Jerusalem 70, 107, 116, 118
Joudah, Fady 118, 149, 173

Kant, Immanuel 26, 37, 97, 138–39, 141, 150, 151, 157, 170, 171
Kaplinski, Jaan 1, 28, 35
Keats, John 17, 31, 92, *See also* negative capability
Kinsella, John 142–43
Kosovel, Srečko 113
Kristeva, Julia 37, 155

Lacan, Jacques 36, 39–40, 42, 63, 89, 155, 157, 170
Lawrence, D. H. 36
Linnaeus, Carl 144
London 6–7, 114, 127
Longley, Michael 144
Luik, Viivi 9

Maitreyabandhu, Dh 10
Marcus, Laura 132
Maxwell, Glyn 144
Mike White Memorial Lecture, The 20, 176
Miller, Henry 153
mirror xi, 15, 27, 45, 48, 62–63, 80, 85, 91, 97, 100, 101–2, 106, 120, 121, 124, 125, 132, 140, 169, 170
Moore, Kim 10

Nabokov, Vladimir 43, 61
Neruda, Pablo 172–73
Nostalgic Imagination, The (Collini) 87

O'Brien, Sean 10, 15, 28, 140
Olney, James 122
Or, Amir 1, 11, 16–18
orphanhood 101, 102, 120

Paris 6, 7
Paterson, Don 10
patriarchy 46, 51
Patterson, Christina 19, 23
peripatetic 83, 124, 132, 136
Petit, Pascale 140
philosophy 6, 28, 44, 49, 50, 105, 130, 138, 141–42, 145, 148, 157, 160, 164
   alienation 113
   aporetic 39–40, 46, 47
   Cartesian 49
   conservatism 71, 112, 114, 116, 139, 155
   critical theory 140
   disenchantment 46, 58
   egalitarianism 165
   epistemology 26, 142
   essentialism 12, 17, 32, 37, 49, 50
   existentialism 16, 55, 56, 101, 151, 154–55
   fallacy 17, *See* logic
   freedom 11, 30–31, 70, 79, 101, 128, 129, 165
   Heraclitean 13
   heuristic 4, 35, 37, 150, 152, 153
   holism 110, 160
   human condition 22, 24, 147
   lifeworld 5, *See also* phenomenology
   liminal 4, 36, 43, 52, 57, 61, 71, 83, 117, 118, 119, 128, 132, 153, 157, 160
   logic 4–5, 9, 17, 27–31, 34, 35, 37, 43, 44, 52, 63, 85, 87, 124, 138, 140–42, 146, 150, 154, 155, 159, *See also* fallacy
   analytic 28, 30, 31, 50, 142, 145, 147
   dialectic 2, 11, 12, 14, 17, 25, 28–30, 35, 36, 43, 44, 48, 70, 73, 75–76, 85, 96, 99–100, 104, 107, 108, 118, 121, 123–24, 127, 137, 138–43, 144, 146, 147, 149, 160

philosophy (*cont.*)
    fuzzy 31, 63, 69, 76, 171
    horizontal 61, 136, 145–46
    oceanic 27, 29, 31, 35–36, 37–38, 43, 44
    vertical 61, 136, 145–46
  materialism 126, 157
  metaphysics 27, 31, 32, 38, 40, 41, 45, 59–61, 62, 66–67, 71, 75, 79, 83, 86–87, 97–98, 151, 158, 163, 170
  microcosm 11, 63, 87, 90, 99
  modernism 4, 27, 40, 44–45, 66, 107, 116, 122, *See also* postmodern
  noumenal 89, 92–93, 96, 157, *See also* Kant, Immanuel
  paradox 2, 14, 25, 28, 30, 31, 34, 35, 37, 40, 41–42, 44, 45–46, 47, 49, 59, 60, 64–67, 69, 70, 73, 74, 75, 78, 87, 91, 94, 100, 102, 105, 139, 143, 144–45, 149, 151, 157, 159, 160, 167, 172
  phenomenology 16
  Platonic 40, 42, *See also* Socratic
  postmodern 122, 147, *See* modernism
  scepticism 57
  semiotic 34, 37, 42
  Socratic 2, 25, 29, 85, 99, 128, 137, *See also* Platonic
  solipsism 129, 170
  subjectivity 11–12, 17, 30, 33, 96, 119, 128, 140, 153, 157, 174
  teleology 2, 25, 37, 46, 48, 136, 154
Picasso, Pablo 88, 89
Plath, Sylvia 16, 145, 155
Poetry Society, The 19
Popov, Alek 9
Prokopiev, Aleksandar 39
Prokopiev, Alesandr 9
Prynne, J. H. 136, 141

religion 13, 163, 164, 171
  Abrahamic 171
    Christianity 64, 171, *See also* Deuteronomy, incarnation, Matthew
    Islam 171
    Judaism 171
  Apollonic 49, *See also* music

Augustinian 66
Deuteronomy 171, *See also* Christianity
fallenness 42, 45, 89, 92, 96, 100–2
incarnation 33, 34, 43, *See also* Christianity, embodiment
liberation theology 164
logocentrism 46, 51, *See* logos
logos 28, 30, 50, 60, 64, 66, *See also* logocentrism
Matthew 171, *See also* Christianity
occult 59, 96, 98, 123, 126
Orphic 52, 61, 64, 69, *See also* music
Paradox in Chesterton (Kenner) 87, 159, *See also* Chesterton, G. K.
prelapsarian 37
problem of evil 60, *See also* philosophy
redemptive 64, 164, 166
Tractarian 11, *See also* Christianity
transcendental 12, 25, 34, 35, 41, 66, 88, 89, 92, 111, 126, 141, 151, 154
universalism 9, 50, 145
Rembrandt 124–25, 133
Rimbaud, Arthur 155
Rogers, Carl 167
Rose, Gillian 45
Rothwell, Richard 124–25

Said, Edward W. 135–36, 148–50, 153, 154, 157
Salzburg 6
Sampson, Fiona, life of 1–8
  Beyond the Lyric, reading of 135–48
  Catch, The, reading of 71–87
  Coleshill, reading of 59–71
  Come Down, reading of 88–104
  contemplative 159–60
  creative writing in health and social care 19–26, 163–76, *See* health and social care, creative writing
  editing and curation work 9–18
  Limestone Country, reading of 105–19
  Lyric Cousins, reading of 148–57
  Mary Shelley's biographer 120–33, *See also* Shelley, Mary
  near-death 4, 47
  poetic and critical work 27–45
  Rough Music, reading of 46–58
Saunders, Max 126

Schama, Simon 133
science 45, 87, 131, 167
Sexton, Anne 168
Shakespeare, William 7, 36
Shapcott, Jo 145
Shelley, Mary 4, 5, 7, 9, 16–18, 47, 59, 61, 90, 96–97, 98, 101, 119–24, 127, 132–33, *See also Frankenstein*
Shelley, Percey Bysshe 15, 18, 123, 125–27, 131, 143, 151, 152, 153, *See also* Shelley, Mary
Sontag, Susan 91
Spivak, Gayatri Chakravorty 25, 169–70
Stacey, Ruth 10
Stainer, Pauline 13
Steiner, George 45, 66
Stevenson, Anne 145
synaesthesia 108–9, 110, 147

Tar, Sandor 9
Thomas, Dylan 155
Thomas, Edward 175
Thompson, E. P. 58
topography 4, 34, 80, 114, 118, 140, 152, 155, *See also* geography

totalization 12, 17, 28, 34–35, 37, 39–40, 61, 64, 71, 116, 160
transgressive 32, 35, 44, 49

Ugresic, Dubravka 9
Universal Declaration of Human Rights, The 22, 165
utopia 164, 171

Velockovic, Nenad 9
Verlaine, Paul 155

Wales 8, 167, 171, 175
Warner, Ahren 10
Wellcome Trust, The 20, 22, 176
Wiman, Christian 10
Wittgenstein, Ludwig 142
Wizard of Oz, The (Baum) 164
Wollstonecraft, Mary 97, 121, 130
Woolf, Karen McCarthy 10
Woolf, Virginia 23, 36, 40, 121, 122, 128, 132
Wordsworth, William 14–15, 160
Worringer, Wilhelm 85

Zbigniew, George 173
Zilahy, Peter 9

www.ingramcontent.com/pod-product-compliance
Lightning Source LLC
Chambersburg PA
CBHW021829300426
44114CB00009BA/378